Contemporary Orthodox Judaism's Response to Modernity

Contemporary Orthodox Judaism's Response to Modernity

BARRY FREUNDEL

KTAV Publishing House, Inc.
Jersey City, New Jersey

Library of Congress Cataloging-in-Publication Data

Freundel, Barry.
  Contemporary Orthodox Judaism's response to modernity / Barry
Freundel.
      p. cm.
  ISBN 0-88125-777-X Hardcover
  ISBN 0-88125-778-8 Paperback
  1. Judaism--20th century. 2. Orthodox
Judaism--Relations--Nontraditional Jews. 3. Orthodox Judaism. 4.
Secularism. I. Title.
  BM565.F63 2003
  296.8'32--dc21

                                2003011226

                        Published by
            KTAV Publishing House, Inc.
                 930 Newark Avenue
               Jersey City, NJ 07306
              Email: info@ktav.com
                     www.ktav.com
                   (201) 963-9524
                  Fax (201) 963-0102

Contents

Introduction

In April and early May of 1992, I recall being troubled by what I saw as a lack of commitment to Jewish values on the part of individuals and organizations in the Jewish community. It seemed to me that both here and in Israel, decisions had become matters of political expedience and not expressions of principles. Also, many Jews whom I encountered seemed content to "go along to get along" and appeared hesitant to approach even important turning points in their lives from within a framework of Jewish ethical concerns. I resolved to speak to this issue from my pulpit.

In my preparation for the Shabbat of May 9, 1992, I noticed that the Torah portion to be read in synagogue that day was "Kedoshim", a section that contains a significant concentration of verses that deal with Jewish laws and moral principles. Even the name of the portion, which comes from its second verse (Leviticus 19:2), includes a call to be holy—to live a life of meaningfulness in a spiritual sense.

I used the opportunity afforded by that Torah portion to appeal for an individual and communal recommitment to our basic structures of morality. I argued that we, as Jews, had nothing else to offer this world but values, because, despite anti-Semitic canards to the contrary, we are neither richer nor more powerful than anyone else.

We, do not necessarily possess more values than anyone else either. But we do have unique values that are often different than the prescribed ways that others have of doing things. For this reason we can make a unique contribution to society by adding our particular thread to the weaving of civil culture as it unfolds before us. In addition, functioning within the structures of Jewish law and ethics defines an effective and morally satisfying space in which to live and from which to make sense of the world.

In other words, I argued, that for us to find an ethically secure and satisfying existence and to maximize our contributions to the world, we needed to return to our core values and to live them in our professional lives, in our personal lives, at work, at home and especially in our families.

Ten days later on Tuesday, May 19th, 1992, a well-known individual spoke to the Commonwealth Club of California in San Francisco. That speech made headlines everywhere and sparked a national debate and conversation that continues to this day.

On Thursday, May 21st, 1992, Lisa Schiffren, then a member of my synagogue, called to ask what I thought of this already famous speech. I mumbled something to the effect of, "It was nice," to which she responded, "You obviously haven't read it. If it's okay with you, I will fax it to you?" I agreed that she should do so. Before she hung up she added, "Take a look at the paragraphs I have highlighted." Again I agreed.

The most famous passage from the May 19th speech, the line that caused much of the stir reads " . . . If a single mother raising her children in the ghetto has to worry about drive-by shootings, drug deals, or whether her children will join gangs and die violently, an already difficult task becomes impossible. It doesn't help matters when primetime has *Murphy Brown*—a character who supposedly epitomizes today's intelligent, highly-paid, professional woman—mocking the importance of fathers—by bearing a child alone and calling it just another 'Lifestyle Choice'."

This quote was not highlighted by Lisa. Instead three paragraphs were marked—three paragraphs that paraphrased, quite closely, three paragraphs from the May 9th sermon on values that I had given.

I called Lisa at her office where she worked as Vice President Dan Quayle's chief speechwriter and asked her what this all meant. She told me that the vice-president, for several weeks, had been discussing with his staff the idea of taking a strong public stand on an ethical issue that he cared about. After hearing my sermon in shul on Parshat Kedoshim, she had come forward with the suggestion that he might want to advocate something that would be called "family values". The rest, as they say, is history.

One footnote to that history that may be of interest: I had not mentioned *Murphy Brown* in my sermon, and apparently Lisa had not included her in the speech she wrote. It seems that, for better or worse, Mr. Quayle ad-libbed the mention of the TV character himself.

These events have provided me with an infinite series of secret smiles and an unending stream of sub-audible laughs, as well as with one challenge. The smiles and laughter come every time someone mentions the now ubiquitous phrase "family values" and I realize the immense and serendipitous impact of having given a sermon that almost any rabbi might give, under just the right set of circumstances.

The challenge comes from realizing that there is an important audience—or perhaps several important audiences out there—who might benefit from reading a concise, but hopefully somewhat analytic and insightful book about Judaism; its beliefs, its institutions, its approach to contemporary problems, and most importantly, the values that animate these elements of our religion.

This volume is written to meet that need. In 30 chapters, ranging—as the table of contents indicates—from God to sex, I try to meet that challenge for the contemporary reader.

The chapters move from basic elements of Jewish belief such as the Bible and Messiah, to discussions of significant Jewish rituals such as prayer and Shabbat, and finally to an analysis of Jewish approaches to contemporary or sensitive life issues such as abortion and euthanasia. Each of these chapters provides another opportunity to further present some of those Jewish values that started the process of writing this book.

All authors are asked what audience their book was intended to reach. If you write a book such as this one, you hope and pretend that the impact will be universal. When fantasy gives way to reality, while it remains my hope that any reader who takes the time to read these words will find at least one insight to make the effort worthwhile, it seems to me that three audiences will best be served by the words on these pages.

Within the observant or at least Jewishly-well-educated community, those whose training has been limited to the study of Talmud and Halakha (Jewish law) or those who know the practices but not the theory behind the practices, will hopefully find this volume valuable in opening the door to a somewhat broader view of Jewish thought. A part of that group may well be older Jewish High School students, where this text might serve as the basis for a course on Jewish law and ethics. So too a college course on those subjects might benefit from its use.

The second group consists of those trying to draw closer to Jewish heritage. A Jew coming to observance and greater involvement with his or her tradition (the so-called Ba'al [Ba'alat] Teshuva or "master of repentance") may find that process helped along in reading through these chapters. So too, prospective converts (several of whom I have asked to review this volume) may find the material that appears here to be valuable to them in their quest for a place within the Jewish people.

Finally those outside the Jewish community, who are interested, for whatever reason, in acquiring some understanding of how traditional Jews live and think in the contemporary reality will hopefully also find some answers in these pages.

The nature of this book is that it surveys and tries to provide some insight into each of the issues it takes up. The sources in Jewish literature, from which these discussions emerge, are referenced in the endnotes to each chapter, though the endnotes are not as comprehensive as one would find in a more scholarly volume. If one wishes to read further on the subjects found here, a list of other publications on these topics appears as one of the first few endnotes to most of the chapters. These additional references are almost always articles or books written in English, except where no comprehensive source exists other than in Hebrew. Consulting these publications will help broaden and deepen one's understanding of the material found in this volume.

Prior to each chapter one or two relevant Rabbinic sources are cited in full to give the reader a sense of the texts from which Jewish law, thought and values are drawn, and to stimulate individual study and discussion. These additional elements will hopefully make this volume even more valuable to those who choose to make use of it.

We come finally to the acknowledgements and the thank yous. This is a somewhat difficult task, because the list is too long for any reasonable presentation in this introduction. Also, I am sure that if I tried to list everyone to whom I feel a debt of gratitude in connection with this book I would undoubtedly leave some people out. Therefore, other than for a few special individuals who played particularly important roles, I will mention those who had a share in this volume by the contributions they made.

I start with my teachers who opened my mind to exploring the intellectual underpinnings of my faith and my world. Among them I single out Rabbi J. B. Soloveichik (z"tl), perhaps the greatest teacher and Jewish thinker of the past century, and Rabbi Norman Lamm (shlita), who has been both a teacher and second father to me.

Next there are those who typed the chapters and the manuscript. Many of them worked as my administrative assistants and one is on the support staff of Baltimore Hebrew University. Hanan Bashe Himelstein, deserves special mention for excellent service in this regard, reviewing the manuscript and indices with absolute diligence. Their contribution was far more than the mechanical act of typing. Their comments, questions, suggestions and editorial input was invaluable in making this a better book than it would have been otherwise.

We move to the members of that special community, Kesher Israel Congregation in the Georgetown neighborhood of Washington D.C. It is a place of warmth and intellect and those qualities are elements that I tried to incorporate into every paragraph of this book. Many of the thoughts in this volume were formulated for the first time in response to questions asked of me by "Kesherites". The support of the congregation for an effort like this was simply invaluable.

So too the faculty and support staff of Baltimore Hebrew University, beginning with President Rela Mintz Geffen, deserve my gratitude for their assistance and encouragement. Their excitement at my completing the manuscript was truly heartwarming.

My thanks to those who read the manuscript in whole or in part and who offered valuable comments. In this context I would single out three people: David Barak, Carrol Cowan, and Jay Garfinkle, who thoroughly critiqued what I had to say and made it significantly better.

Mrs. Rivkah Blau, a friend and Jewish educator who more than deserves the exceptional reputation she has, worked on the choice of sources that appear, in connection with each of the chapters, so too Samuel Groner and Rozzie Liss did yeoman work in creating the book's indices. Most profound gratitude to the two of you for all that you did.

There is of course my family to whom I first owe the debt of time stolen from them to do this work. Second to my children Dan, Jo Jo, and Arielle. There has been much joy in watching you grow to adolescence, and part of that fatherly pride has come in trying to answer your questions. Some of those questions and some of those answers found their way into the chapters that follow. It thrills me to watch each of the three of you developing an inquisitive mindset that helps in your individual exploration of the universe in both its Jewish and secular manifestations. Third, to my parents, who showed me by living example how Jewish values are intrinsic at every moment and stage of life. Finally, to my wife Sharon, who was a partner in this and in all that I do: there is a debt that cannot be repaid and that can only very poorly be expressed.

To Bernie Scharfstein and his cajoling and kibbitzing, which kept me on track through this entire endeavor, I owe thanks for the opportunity to express myself and my understanding of Orthodox Judaism.

Finally there is my recognition of God's gifts to me that guide me and bless me throughout my life, generally, and in offering this volume, specifically. I originally wanted to title this book with the words from Exodus 33:21 , 'Hiney makom iti' — *there is a place with Me*. I have found in my life that whoever you are, whatever your circumstances, there is a place with God. This book is about finding a place with God and for God in the world that we know. If it succeeds in any small way in accomplishing that for even one person, much less if it impacts in more significant ways on more people, I make that my Thanksgiving offering to the Master of all things.

Washington D.C.
May 2003

Chapter 1
God

We begin with the essence of what we are all about. No section of this book was more difficult to write than this one. Yet in a very real way this chapter is the most central and most important. As with any theological system that constructs its worldview around an immanent and all-powerful God, everything begins and ends with that central fact. For this reason the subject is too big, and any possible description too small, to do it justice.[1]

Further, hovering over the process are approaches such as that of Moses Maimonides (1138–1204), the foremost Jewish philosopher of the Middle Ages, who postulated that one could discuss only God's negative attributes[2] and not his positive ones. Mortals should not say that God is powerful, only that nothing is beyond God's capability to instantly accomplish. Nor should we say that God is good, only that he does not act in ways that are evil. Maimonides, along with several other medieval thinkers, including Saadiah Gaon (882–942), Bahya Ibn Paquda (11th cent.), and Judah Halevi (1075–1141), was concerned that affirmative labels put God, as it were, in a definitional box. Man's categorizing of God creates a picture with borders, which from a divine perspective is limiting and thus unacceptable. While most modern thinkers do not conceptualize the world and God in this way, the concern about understatement in describing God is real.[3]

1

Similarly medieval thinkers, particularly those most influenced by Aristotle, such as Maimonides and Abraham ibn Daud (1110–1180), struggled with what seems to be God's changing relationship with the world and with the Jewish people. At times we appear to be in His favor, while at other times unfortunately, the divine and the human seem completely at odds with one another. For Aristotle and those who were influenced by him, change meant decay, and decay meant death. Only things that remained forever the same could be eternal. For this reason, God could never be different at any given moment than He was at any other given moment.[4]

If this is true, God's love for His people at one point in history and his anger at another point had to be explained in some way other than by saying that God had changed His relationship with us. Usually, this was done by claiming that God was the same but we had changed our perception of our relationship with Him because we were acting differently. Our different behavior brought us into contact with a perceived different aspect of God. That aspect was always there as part of the totality of God, but it was hidden from our view as long as we interacted differently with God. Now that we had, so to speak, chosen a different function from the God menu, this "new" feature of God's divine essence made its appearance to us.[5]

In addition, the very idea of ascribing emotionality to God is troubling to some philosophers. Emotions are aspects of the human personality that often operate at odds with the intellect. They are remarkably volatile and changeable. The medievals in particular viewed ascribing emotions to God as a terrible impediment to developing a proper understanding of the Almighty.[6]

Moderns do not see these issues in the same way. First, our physics is not as restrictive. Change does not necessarily mean death. Matter and energy can change their forms; thus, matter can be changed into energy and energy into matter, but the sum total of matter and energy in the universe is always the same. Similarly, our understanding of psychology makes us value emotions much more than did the medievals. This has led to an evolving perception of God even as we adhere to the principles and premises that are part of our eternal beliefs about the Almighty.

One can, and perhaps should, list the various attributes that we associate with God. Often, this was the way medieval thinkers approached the question, and it remains a valid way to proceed to this day.[7] It is here, however, that one must be careful not to either overstate or, more likely, underestimate the subject.[8]

Though there is some debate, especially with respect to nuance,[9] a list of God's attributes as generally accepted in the traditional Jewish community would include God's existence, His unlimited power, and His status as creator. He is one, singular, unique, eternal. His wisdom is all-encompassing.[10] His compassion touches all,[11] and His divine providence reaches down even to each grain of sand tossed about by wind and sea.[12] He is ruler of all, eternal, ethical, fair (when all the accounts are settled), and good. For Jews He has developed a special category of existence and a unique relationship embodied in a covenant that commingles our fate with His, insofar as this world is concerned.[13]

Obviously, each of these attributes is deserving of discussion, and some do receive analysis elsewhere in this book. However, a thorough treatment would require several volumes and would be far larger in scope than this present work.

For this reason we will leave the list of God's attributes here, but with a challenge to the reader. Each of these attributes needs to be understood not only in terms of what it means as a statement about God but also as regards its implications for us. Most of our thinking and talking about God involves questions on the order of whether God can make a rock that He Himself cannot destroy.* Issues of this type focus only on God.

A much more thoughtful and profoundly life-changing line of inquiry is to try to understand the implications for oneself personally in God's attribute of, say, unlimited power. As a first approach to this question, does this aspect of God not, perhaps, offer an answer, here and now, to much of the despair and depression so prevalent in the world? Would it not be better to call on God's limitless capacity to help us confront life's problems than to sink into desperation and helplessness? Other attributes can be approached in the same way with truly life-changing results. This type of effort means engaging with God directly and personally in a manner that may be foreign to our experience but can, be truly meaningful.[14]

Moderns tend to speak of God not in absolute categories, but more in terms of the roles in which we find Him—in the Bible, the Talmud, and elsewhere in our religious literature. As such, one might focus on God as builder and laborer, given His role in the story of creation.[15] This emphasizes the importance of the work ethic and of the dignity associated with gainful employment, both of which are essential Jewish values.[16]

So, too, a rich trove of inspiration awaits us in the stories telling how God, as Abraham's friend[17] and confidant, responded to his concerns about being childless with support and sympathy, protected Sarah, his wife, from the likes of

---

*For the record, there is an answer to this question. It becomes obvious once we restate the question to reflect what we are really asking: Can the power which is defined as "that power in the universe for which there can be no greater or equivalent power" create a power greater than itself? The answer is no, and the question is self-evidently silly. It is no limitation on this greatest power that it cannot violate the terms of its own existence. The only limitation is on our power of speech, which allows us to frame so foolish a question without realizing how absurd it is.

Pharaoh and Abimelech, and allowed for a lengthy negotiation over the fate of the wicked city of Sodom.[18] This last event begins because, as the Torah tells us, God cannot bear the thought of destroying that evil place without confiding in Abraham that He is contemplating such an overwhelmingly important act.[19] I would hope that my friendships could be anywhere near as strong as this.

The danger in this approach is precisely the opposite of that which we encountered in discussing the medieval period and its understanding of God. While there was an eventual limit to the list of attributes that the medievals could associate with God, there is no limit, except the limits of our scholarship, creativity, and imagination, to the way we moderns can describe God's relationship with us and our world. So, too, these characterizations, almost by definition, deal with the relevance of God's functioning to our lives. However, without the restriction and rigor of the earlier structure, the more modern analysis can and occasionally does describe God in most ungodly and inappropriate roles. There are examples in modern literature that present God in ways that would be demeaning to human beings and even more so to the Almighty. Some balance needs to be struck between the two. This will bring the best of both approaches together to help us better ponder the mystery and meaning for us of the Creator of all that is.

One thing common to both approaches is the effect that God has on those who accept His reality and understand Him on even the most basic level. God makes every single thing I do far more meaningful and significant—both for good and for bad. God being all-seeing means that nothing I do can be hidden.[20] God's eternal existence means that what God sees is remembered forever.

As such, anything terrible that we do will echo through the centuries unless we can do teshuvah (repentance) and thus remove the stain.[21] However, and this is critical, the good that we do is also remembered eternally. For this reason, God is the greatest guarantor of ethical behavior. As I understand the world, it is hard for me to imagine what arguments can be presented for following any objective moral standard without God at the center of that rationale. After all, a hundred or a thousand years from now, no one will remember what I did and whether it was good or bad. That is, unless God is in the equation.

So, too, our hopes, dreams, heartfelt feelings, innermost thoughts, and deepest concerns are also remembered. Rather than being an infinitesimal dot in a virtually limitless universe,[22] rather than having a life that is no more than an eye blink as against eternity—sure formulas for feelings of insignificance—we have the guarantee of an eternal, all-knowing God to ensure that what is and has been significant to me remains so with God for all eternity. Accepting this reality can alone begin to bring meaning back to so many in this society whose existence seems otherwise filled with emptiness, loneliness, evil, and meaninglessness.[23]

1. An interesting treatment of God, though not from a traditional perspective, appears in Jack Miles, *God: A Biography* (New York, 1995). For a more traditional approach, see David Shapiro, "God, World and Man," *Tradition* 14:3 (1974), pp. 37–47, and idem, "God, Man and Creation," *Tradition* 15:1–2 (1975), pp. 25–47.

2. Maimonides, *Guide for the Perplexed* 1:51, 54, and 60.

3. See Sebastian Matczak, *God in Contemporary Thought: A Philosophical Perspective* (New York, 1977).

4. Cf. Internet Encyclopedia of Philosophy, s.v. Aristotle—Overview (http://www.utm.edu/research/iep/). Also, Maimonides, *Guide* 1:55.

5. Cf. *Guide* 1:53.

6. Ibid. 55. Rabbinic literature was sensitive to this to a certain extent as well; cf. Genesis Rabbah 49:8.

7. The mystical system of the *Zohar* or the Kabbalah, follows this pattern. See generally Gershom Scholem, *Major Trends in Jewish Mysticism* (New York,

1995). In that system God is progressively more manifest to the world through ten *sefirot* (appropriately translated and understood as emanations, numbers, or garments) which embody God's major attributes, such as His loving-kindness, His justice, His wisdom, and His eternity. See below, Chapter 16.

8. For talmudic sensitivity to this issue, see Berakhot 33b.

9. Julius Guttmann, *Philosophies of Judaism* (New York, 1973). See especially the views on this issue of Levi ben Gershon (Gersonides), pp. 238–239, Hasdai Crescas, pp. 262–265, and Joseph Albo, p. 285.

10. Even Maimonides would seem to have accepted some of these attributes. In fact, he includes God's existence, unity, eternity, and omniscience in his thirteen principles of the faith (see below, Chapter 11).

11. Psalm 145:9, see the eleventh line of the thrice-daily Ashrei prayer.

12. Cf. David Shlomo Aibeshits, *Sefer Arve Nahal* (Jerusalem, 1991), Ki Tissa 1, and Hullin 7b. On this there is actually quite a bit of debate among Jewish thinkers; for a brief survey, see the *Encyclopaedia Judaica,* s.v. Providence.

13. See below, Chapter 8.

14. Many kabbalistic and hasidic works deal with these issues in terms of understanding the *sefirot* or directing the intent of one's actions toward one or another of them. For a discussion of the development of this approach, see *Encyclopaedia Judaica,* s.v. Commandments, Reasons for: subsection "In Kabbalah."

15. Genesis 1–2.

16. Cf. the editor's introduction to Israel Weisfeld, *Labor Legislation in the Bible and Talmud* (New York, 1974).

17. God calls Abraham "My beloved" Isaiah 41:8.

18. Isaiah 41:8, Genesis 15:1, 12:10–20, 18:17–33, 20.

19. Genesis 18:17–19.

20. This is the theme of many of the High Holiday prayers; e.g., Le'e-l Orekh Din; see Philip Birnbaum, *High Holiday Prayer Book* (New York, 1979), p. 261.

21. See below, Chapter 7.

22. See below, Chapter 5.

23. For further discussion of meaning as a fundamental need that human beings have, see Joseph Fabry, Reuven Bulka, and William Sahakian, *Finding Meaning in Life: Logotherapy* (Northvale, N.J., 1995), and Reuven Bulka, *Work, Love, Suffering and Death: A Jewish/Psychological Perspective Through Logotherapy* (Northvale, N.J., 1998). The classic in the field is Viktor Frankl, *Man's Search*

for Meaning (Boston, 1992). Much of Frankl's work involved studies of Holocaust survivors and how they endured, survived and recovered from the horrors they experienced.

Chapter 2
The Bible

For traditional Jews second only to God, it all begins and ends with the Bible—the revealed word of the Creator.[1] That act of revelation has shaped the course of Jewish behavior, thought, and world outlook from the moment it became a miraculous reality to today. In a real sense it puts a structure on the God idea and makes it accessible to me on a day to day, minute by minute basis. This chapter will explore the various belief statements that you have just read in the three preceding sentences.[2]

First, a definition: What do we mean by the Bible and by the term "Torah" when it is used as synonym for "Bible"?[3] Actually, these words can mean any of a number of things depending on the context. In their most limited meaning, they refer only to the Five Books of Moses, or Pentateuch ("Torah" can be even more limited to the specially prepared parchment scrolls found at the center of our synagogue life). However, the two terms can also refer to the entire Written Law.[4] This body of literature consists, in our present arrangement, of twenty-four books,[5] beginning with Genesis and ending with Chronicles.[6] Actually, one could easily come to a number other than twenty-four without changing the Bible's content. The number twenty-four is found in the Talmud, and it embodies a traditional way of counting the books that accepts no divisions, such as First and Second Samuel, treats Ezra and Nehemiah as one book, and counts the twelve minor prophets as one.[7] These twenty-four books are divided into three sections known as Torah, Nevi'im, and Ketuvim, or Bible, Prophets, and Writings. The Hebrew acronym for this way of describing the Bible is *Tanakh*, which derives from the first letters of the terms *Torah*, *Nevi'im*, and *Ketuvim*.[8]

At this point we have reached the limit of the term Bible in a Jewish context. Obviously, Christians will include the books that they refer to as the New Testament. Some Christian Bibles also include the Apocrypha.[9] These books, covering greatly divergent themes and written in many different styles, were composed in the so-called intertestamental period. While many of them emulate biblical style, and while some, explicitly or implicitly, make the claim for inclusion in sacred scripture, the Rabbis determined that these books were not divinely inspired.[10] As such, they find no place in the Jewish Bible, though some are quoted approvingly by some rabbinic authorities.[11] Finally, Torah can also mean the entire body of traditional Jewish learning, including both the Written and the Oral Law. (see below)

The division of the Torah into the threefold Tanakh speaks, among other things, to differences in the revelatory nature of the material. Moses was our greatest prophet.[12] The medieval Spanish commentator Don Isaac Abravanel (1437–1508) explained that Moses, unlike other prophets, was able to suspend his own personality and the natural tendency we all have to edit or interpret what we experience.[13] As such he served as a pure vessel to receive the unadulterated word of God, which he then transmitted in written form to the first Torah scrolls, writing them himself.[14]

For this reason, traditional Judaism believes that it is only the five books of the Pentateuch that may be used as a legitimate source for divinely inspired biblical law. Subsequently, when other halakhic requirements were added, such as the reading of the Book of Esther on Purim, the Rabbis took great pains to show that their true origin was not in later revelation, not in the Prophets or the Writings, but in the five books.[15]

Only purely Rabbinic decrees, which are less stringent in a number of ways, could originate outside the Pentateuch.

This belief served as an important buffer against the claims of Christianity and Islam that their founding "prophesies" had replaced the revelation of Torah. Judaism has a ready answer to such claims. As no prophecy could equal the one given to Moses, no future revelation could replace or supersede even one letter of the words God spoke to him.[16]

While the Prophets and the Writings also contain revelations from God, these do not achieve the level of the Mosaic revelation,[17] and, as we have said, are not sources of law.[18] Rather they tell us of our history,[19] exhort us to follow God's commands,[20] and offer insight into Judaism's understanding of the human condition. These insights appear most dramatically in such books as Ecclesiastes, Job, and Proverbs.

There may also be some revelatory differences between the Nevi'im and the Ketuvim. Some suggest that the Nevi'im occupy a higher revelatory niche than the Ketuvim.[21] Others suggest that the messages contained in the Nevi'im were given to the prophets with the charge that they be transmitted orally, in a public-speaking forum, to the people.[22] The Ketuvim, on the other hand, were given with the specific instruction that they be written down to be studied from a text. It is also true that the Ketuvim section was open for a longer period of time than the other sections, and that the final determination of what was or was not to be included in this part of the Bible was made later in history than the closing of either the Torah or Nevi'im sections to any further additions. [23]

The revelatory character of the material in the Bible serves as a rationale for the many-faceted and multiple-level analysis of these texts that one finds in rabbinic literature, called the Oral Law.[24] The Bible represents miraculous communication.[25] As such, while it can and should be read on its most idiomatically understandable level (what we call *peshat*),[26] other levels of interpretation are also available because of the very nature of the origin of the text. These other levels of analysis are called *derash*, or deeper analysis;[27] *remez*, or hints,[28] which includes such things as *gematria* (numerological parallels)[29] and *notarikon* (words whose deeper meaning is revealed by the abbreviations hidden behind their letters);[30] and *sod*, or secret analysis, meaning esoteric or mystical interpretation.[31]

All of these, even the most basic level of *peshat*, can and do involve a great deal of intellectual effort and debate before one arrives at a final conclusion. This conclusion may then be challenged by others which may start the process of analysis over again. It is also, often true that more than one understanding is legitimate. But any interpretation must be consistent with the rules of exegesis and must not be at odds with the rest of our sources.[32] It is said that the Torah has seventy faces.[33] The number seems not to be an exaggeration but an understatement.[34]

Because of the miraculous nature of the material, proprieties of context cease to be important once one moves beyond the level of *peshat*. Each verse, each phrase, even each word, letter, and nuance is a miracle of God's revelation. Hence it is assumed that each, standing alone, has something important to say to us.[35] Many midrashim, many statements of rabbinic analysis, simply substitute an alternative meaning for one or more words in a phrase or sentence.[36] While these alternative meanings would make no sense in context, and therefore could never be part of *peshat*, they are perfectly legitimate in an analysis of other levels of meaning. It is here that the teachers of the oral tradition that surrounds the text find one of their most important mechanisms for associating their thoughts with or deriving their teachings from the written words.[37]

We come finally to the question of the earthly aspect of the origin of the books of the Bible. The Talmud provides the following list of authors who were inspired by God to write the various books they are credited with composing:

Moses wrote his own book and the portion of Balaam (Numbers 22:2–24) and Job. Joshua wrote the book which bears his name and [the last] eight verses of the Pentateuch. Samuel wrote the book which bears his name and the Book of Judges and Ruth. David wrote the Book of Psalms, including in it the work of the elders, namely, Adam, Melchizedek, Abraham, Moses, Heman, Yeduthun, Asaph, and the three sons of Korah. Jeremiah wrote the book which bears his name, the Book of Kings, and Lamentations. Hezekiah and his colleagues wrote Isaiah, Proverbs, the Song of Songs, and Ecclesiastes. The Men of the Great Assembly wrote Ezekiel, the Twelve Minor Prophets, Daniel, and the Scroll of Esther. Ezra wrote the book that bears his name and the genealogies of the Book of Chronicles up to his own time. This confirms the opinion of Rab, since Rav Judah has said in the name of Rab: Ezra did not leave Babylon to go up to Eretz Yisrael until he had written his own genealogy. Who then finished it [the Book of Chronicles]?— Nehemiah the son of Hachaliah.[38]

While the Talmud itself modifies this list somewhat,[39] as do later authorities,[40] a number of items have been the subject of serious differences between traditionalist and secular scholars.[41] However, none of these debates carry the doctrinal implications of the question of the origin of the Five Books of Moses.[42] For this reason we will focus our discussion on that issue after making one more brief comment.

The historical debates as to author and origin are interesting, but, ultimately, they may obscure the fundamental issue: the question of the reality of prophecy as a phenomenon that occurs in this world.[43] In the final analysis, it does not matter all that much whether Isaiah was composed by one author, by two Isaiahs, or by three or four people of the same name. What matters ultimately is whether the author or authors wrote under the influence of divine communication or not. This is in no way meant to suggest that the book of Isaiah had more than a single author.[44] It is, however, meant to focus us firmly on the crucial issue.

Turning to the Pentateuch, it must be recognized that no one is ever truly objective about the question of its origin. Too much is riding on the outcome. For believers, if the Bible was found to not be of divine origin, the structure they have placed around their lives might well collapse into meaninglessness and abject futility. For nonbelievers, proof of the divinity of the Bible would force them to radically alter virtually every element of the way in which they function. Too much is at risk in this question for objectivity to find an easy or comfortable home.

There is, however, a further complication. If you do not believe in God, God effectively ceases to exist for you. The Bible is different. It is still the world's best-selling book, and you can find one in every hotel room you visit as well as in many other places. Even if you disbelieve the Bible, it still exists. It is clearly a book of high moral character that makes a claim of divine origin for its source. If you reject that claim, you must provide an alternative theory of the Bible's origins.

At present, the scholarly world's best-known alternative is called the Documentary Hypothesis. This theory assumes that the Torah comes from a number of literary antecedents that were melded together to form one coherent whole. Classically, these sources numbered four. They are known as J, E, P, and D. The first two letters represent two of the names used for God in biblical writings. The J stands for the four-letter name of God that is traditionally not pronounced as written, as an act (or non-act) of reverence by observant Jews. In Hebrew it is spelled yud, heh, vav, and then another heh. So too E symbolizes the Elo-him name of God. These names appear frequently in the Bible. The theory claims that sources which contain the J name come from a different origin than those which contain the E name.

The P means Priestly and refers to the parts of the Torah that deal with priests, levites, the Temple, and the sacrificial order. Finally, D refers to Deuteronomy, which is claimed to be of later origin than the other books of the Pentateuch. In fact, it is specifically associated with the Biblical tale of a remarkable discovery that occurred during the reign of King Josiah.[45] Josiah became king as a very young man at a time when the Jews had all but abandoned God to pursue paganism. Shortly thereafter, when his servants were busily renovating the Temple to make it a home for idolatry a scroll of the law was found by them in the Temple wall. The scroll was presented to Josiah, and it so impressed him that he not only returned to the Lord, but ordered the land cleansed of idolatry thus instituting a national revival and return to Judaism.

When the Bible tells this story it specifically mentions the presence of blessings and curses in the scroll as having impressed Josiah.[46] Despite the presence of a section that meets this description at the end of Leviticus, scholars have focused on the somewhat longer section of this type in Deuteronomy and posit that this story refers to the discovery of "new" book of Deuteronomy rather than the entire Bible. They, thus, claim that Deuteronomy made its first appearance in the time of Josiah.

A number of significant problems confront the Documentary Hypothesis. First, its origins are suspect. When Christendom was universally (at least in Western Europe) under the control of the Pope, its strictures prohibited direct interaction between the devout Christian and the biblical text. Only papal interpretation was allowed. One of the essential deviations of the Protestant Reformation was a return to individual interaction between scholar and biblical text.

This interaction had not progressed very far before problems were raised concerning the contradictions between the four gospels. These first four books of the Christian Bible tell the story of Christianity's origin. However, they differ in important ways. Protestant scholars attempted to solve the problems this caused by positing a work they called the Q document, from the German word *Quelle,* meaning "source." This document was claimed to be the original written account of the stories of Christianity's beginnings and of the birth, life, and death of its founder. The gospels, in turn, are said to be different elaborations of the original document. It is important to note that no Q document or even any fragment thereof has ever been identified.

When these scholars turned to the Hebrew Bible, an ironic parallel occurred. Where the four gospels had been seen as originating from one source, the Hebrew Bible (in this case the Pentateuch), which is fairly unitary (though there are some apparent contradictions that need explanation), was theorized by these same scholars as coming from four different sources. The one became four, and the four became one.

The theory has other problems as well. Julius Wellhausen (1844–1918), perhaps the best-known of its originators,[47] based his theory on five premises, among which are some that current knowledge tells us are obviously false.[48] For example, Wellhausen assumed that Moses could not have written the Bible because he lived long before writing was invented. We know today from many sources that this is incorrect. So, too, Wellhausen assumed that primitive people have simple rituals, and that anything elaborate must come later in time when their culture has become more sophisticated. There are many pieces of evidence that tell us that this too is not true.

A major foundation stone of the Documentary Hypothesis is, as discussed above, the presence and usage of different divine names in the Torah. As indicated, those sections that have the four-letter name of God are designated J, and those that use the name Elo-him are designated E. The theory works well in the first few chapters of Genesis,[49] against which background it was developed. However, beyond these chapters the structure rarely works. Often, one finds the J and E names together or a string of J names and then an E or the reverse in the same chapter. (There are, of course, explanations offered in traditional Jewish sources, for the use of God's different names in these first chapters of Genesis.)[50]

These inconsistencies are explained by scholars of the Documentary Hypothesis as the work of the Redactor, an unknown scribe who melded the sources together. The anomalies are often seen as pious attempts to harmonize the texts. However, the claimed Redactor, if he existed, was entirely inconsistent and capricious in applying these supposed harmonizing techniques. There are many places where harmonizing would be expected if the theory were true, but there is no sign of it.

Some assume that there was not one Redactor but a redaction process that extended over many centuries. As before, there is no literary evidence of intermediary documents or of separate J, E, P, or D works. (Defenders would argue that these materials are too early to have been preserved.) More important, it is hard to imagine how sacred literature could be melded and emended in this way but still remain acceptable to believing devotées who were attached to it in its original form. Only someone with great authority might be able to get such a thing through people's natural resistance. But, as we have seen, the single Redactor theory also has its problems.

One final challenge to the theory comes from careful study of the biblical text. There seems to have been much literary reliance of one text on another in a way that would be impossible according to this hypothesis. As an example, the first chapters of Kings clearly utilize literary imagery and inspiration taken from Deuteronomy. As Solomon builds and dedicates the

Temple of the Lord that he has built in Jeruṣalem, the book, and
Solomon in his speeches and prayers, draw significantly and
appropriately on earlier biblical material, and in particular on
Deuteronomy. Yet according to the Documentary Hypothesis,
the text of Deuteronomy, supposedly dating from the time of
Josiah, is of much later origin than Solomon and Kings.
Interestingly, some contemporary secular scholars have opted
out of the Documentary Hypothesis, claiming instead a single
early Second Temple date for the Bible's composition. This
approach is challenged by the extensive details of the First
Temple period preserved in the Bible. Not surprisingly, this
school has been forced to deny almost every aspect of the Bible's
historical account of the First Temple period. However, far too
much supportive evidence exists for this claim to stand.

Of course, the belief in revelation avoids many of these
problems. Nonetheless, it too has its challenges. First among
them is the miraculous nature of the communication with God.
Modern, rational man has difficulty accepting the idea that the
Almighty would speak in such a way. Whether one accepts or
rejects this phenomenon is ultimately dependent on something of a leap of faith or the lack of faith. One's belief system
will in all likelihood determine one's view of the possibility of
such an event.

Second, a challenge is often raised on the basis of the different literary styles one finds in different parts of the Five Books
of Moses. However, Shakespeare wrote tragedies, sonnets,
comedies, and love stories, and yet he was one author. Different
styles are appropriate for different types of material. Since the
Bible contains many different types of materials, different styles
are to be expected. Also, if we take the entire Bible, God's words
were filtered through different prophets with different back-
grounds, personal histories, and ways of expressing the visions
they had seen.[51] Some years ago, someone developed a computer program that, when fed the text of the Pentateuch, divid-

ed it into the four divisions predicted by the Documentary
Hypothesis. However, when the works of classical and modern
writers were also fed into the computer, the program divided
each author's work into the same four categories.

The third challenge to the Bible's divinity is the question of
its historicity. This is an area in which the study of archaeology has become quite important. Before discussing its impact
on our question, two things should be said. First, Wellhausen
opposed the use of archaeology for biblical study. Concern
that archaeological discoveries will contradict what one
believes, is a source of anxiety not only for the traditionalist.

Second, archaeology is neither an exact nor a perfect science, though it is sometimes treated that way. The possibility
of missing or misinterpreting something certainly exists, and
must be taken into account.[52] Finally, fashion prevails in
archaeology as it does in perhaps every area of study. Hence,
the pendulum swings from periods when challenging the biblical narrative is in vogue to times when supporting the text is
the fashion.

All of this said, there are some archaeological findings that
raise serious questions. Nonetheless, as the years have passed
and as more and more has been discovered, respect for the historicity of the biblical text has grown. A prime example is the
attitude of two Protestant commentaries, written from a scholarly perspective, to the Book of Esther. The *International
Critical Commentary* of the early twentieth century saw the
book as a mythical tale of new Persian gods (Mordechai-
Marduk and Esther-Ishtar) defeating and replacing the older
Babylonian deities.[53] This mythical tale was dressed up in
Jewish garb, probably to justify religious acceptance of a festi-
val that had pagan roots, but which had been accepted by the
Jews as something they wished to commemorate.

In contrast, the *Anchor Bible*, published in the 1960s and
1970s, calls the Book of Esther "an historical novel with the

accent on the first word."[54] This is quite a different judgment. After decades of study and archaeological research, especially in Shushan, or Susa, the capital of Persia, conclusions that are vastly different than the original assumptions have been reached. The direction of the change has, obviously, been toward the side of tradition.

One last item is the question of the integrity of the biblical text. Scholars of the historical school spent much time and effort suggesting emendations that, in total, would produce a text vastly different than the one we have, and they effectively claimed that what we now possess was significantly corrupted over the centuries.

On the other hand, some in the traditional community assume that no errors have ever appeared in the biblical text. Support for this position has been found, among other places, in Maimonides' thirteen principles of faith;[55] in Nachmanides' introduction to his Bible commentary, in which he makes the mystical claim that if the text was read with different breaks between the letters, it would spell out a continuous stream of God's names; and in the recent popularization of what are said to be secret codes in the Torah. However, at least insofar as our medieval authorities, Maimonides and Nachmanides, are concerned, their comments deal with the Torah as given at Sinai (or in the alternative talmudic opinion, throughout the forty years in the desert)[56] and not with the question of whether the text has been preserved inviolate to this day.

Maimonides, in discussing the laws of the Torah text, refers to different schools of Masoretes, the eighth-century scholars who worked on correcting and restoring the biblical text to one that was as close to the original as possible.[57] Maimonides tells us that the accepted text of the Ben Asher school is superior to the others. He does not claim, however, that it is perfect.[58]

Many talmudic and midrashic passages indicate that the Rabbis were aware of textual problems in the Bible. We are told that the Rabbis were unsure of exactly which words are to be written to include or exclude silent letters, such as vavs and yods.[59] Ezra the Scribe, who in a far earlier era than the Masoretes, also worked on the textural integrity of the Bible, encountered a number of difficult passages where even he could not determine with absolute certainty what the original text was meant to be.[60] Finally, Ashkenazic (Western European) Torah text differs in one letter from the Sephardic (Spanish and Mediterranean) text.[61] Obviously, only one can have the original reading.

Tradition magazine published an interesting debate on this subject some years ago. Zvi Yehuda and Shneur Leiman took up opposite sides of the following intriguing question: If archaeologists were to discover Moses' Torah, would we change our Torahs to conform?[62] In the course of their discussion, they marshaled most if not all of the sources indicating rabbinic awareness of textual difficulties in the transmission of the biblical word from generation to generation.

However, the story here is not the errors in the text, it's the lack of such errors. The discovery of the Dead Sea Scrolls pushes the date of our earliest extant Bibles back from the eighth or ninth century C.E. to the second and third century B.C.E. The remarkable correlation between those ancient documents, particularly in the Pentateuch, and our texts is simply remarkable.[63] The halakhic practice of removing a Torah scroll from use for even the slightest imperfection, until it is fixed has obviously stood us in good stead.[64] It has preserved God's word virtually intact for three and a half millennia. This means that we can approach the Torah text with a high degree of confidence about its genuineness and authenticity.

Even the small errors that have crept in are not legally consequential. While they might affect in a very small way our understanding of *peshat*, Jewish law is rooted in *derash* and, more important, is always considered against the literary record of centuries of rabbinic analysis of relevant texts. We no longer go directly from analysis of nuances in the Bible to required behaviors and have not done so for hundreds of years. In short, we are not fundamentalists, and so these minor discrepancies are legally unimportant.

One last point needs to be made that ties together much of what has been said above. At the very least, this point overarches the entire discussion. We must take note of the moral superiority of the Bible. We say this not as a source of arrogance or chauvinism, but as an important historical reality. What has challenged people about the Bible down through the centuries, what suggests to readers and students that the claimed divine origin is real, what impresses the objective reader as the central integrating factor of the text, is the embodiment in its confines of remarkable moral and ethical sensibilities. These values lead to a meaningful lifestyle embodying those ideals that is unparalleled, certainly in the world where it was born and, in my view, unmatched to this day. The Bible's influence is unrivaled in world literature, and the challenge of its vision has remained both cogent and ennobling over the three thousand–plus years of its existence. When we start from this reality, the reason for people's continued life-transforming commitment to the Bible becomes clear. The power of its message makes divine origin its obvious source, and all the counter-arguments and competing theories tend to pale into insignificance.

1. Many biblical verses and sources attest to this belief; e.g., Exodus 20:1, if one understands the phrase *kol ha-devarim ha-eleh* ("all these things" or "all these

speakings") to mean the entire Torah. See the discussion of dogma below in Chapter 11.

2. There are few comprehensive works on the Bible that are both scholarly and traditional, and they must be read with care because many of the issues they raise cut close to the line of acceptable theology versus heresy. A valuable source is Moses Hirsch Segal, *Mavo ha-Mikra* (Jerusalem, 1964). In addition, a good overview is given by the introductory discussions in the various volumes of *Da'at Mikra* (Mosad Harav Kook edition). Some important comments will also be found in the essays following the various books of the Pentateuch in J. H. Hertz, *The Pentateuch and Haftorahs* (London, 1960). For discussion of medieval commentary on these issues, see Eric Lawee, "Don Isaac Abarbanel: Who Wrote the Books of the Bible?" *Tradition* 30:2 (1996), pp. 65–73.

3. See next note.

4. The terms "Torah" and "Bible" part company here. The oral tradition may still be properly referred to as "Torah." It is never, however, called "Bible."

5. This is the traditional number; cf. Ta'anit 5a, and see especially Numbers Rabbah 14:4 and Ecclesiastes Rabbah 12:11. Josephus, *Against Apion* 1:39–41, has, interestingly, only twenty-two books, but this may mean that Ruth was counted with Judges, and Lamentations with Jeremiah.

6. Actually, a number of different orderings exist. Compare Bava Bathra 14b to any Hebrew Bible and note the differences. See *Encyclopaedia Judaica*, s.v. Bible: Canon, Text, and Editions, subsection, The Order of the Books. Christian Bibles also have the books in a different order.

7. See Segal, *Mavo ha-Mikra*, chap. 1, sec. 6.

8. Ibid., secs. 1–5.

9. Ibid., sec. 7; *Encyclopaedia Judaica*, s.v. Apocrypha and Pseudepigrapha (which includes a valuable chart); George W. E. Nickelsburg, *Jewish Literature Between the Bible and the Mishnah* (Philadelphia, 1981). For the texts themselves, see Robert Henry Charles, ed., *The Apocrypha and Pseudepigrapha of the Old Testament* (Oxford, 1963–64).

10. Mishnah Sanhedrin 10:1, Sanhedrin 100a–b.

11. Cf. Hagigah 13a quoting Ben Sirah.

12. Numbers 12:6–8, Deuteronomy 34:10, Yevamot 97b, Exodus Rabbah 2:6, Leviticus Rabbah 1:14, but see Numbers Rabbah 14:19, which says that the

gentile prophet Balaam was his equal. For further discussion of the status of Moses in Judaism, see below, Chapters 4 and 11.

13. For Abravanel's life and career, see Benzion Netanyahu. *Don Isaac Abravanel, Statesman and Philosopher* (Philadelphia, 1968); Jacob S. Minkin, *Abarbanel and the Expulsion of the Jews from Spain* (New York, 1938).

14. See Abravanel's commentary to Deuteronomy 34:10 and Numbers 12, and his introduction to Deuteronomy. See also Deuteronomy Rabbah 9:9.

15. Hullin 139b, Megillah 2b–3a et passim.

16. See below, Chapter 11.

17. The Talmud distinguishes between the different sections of the Bible in a number of ways and in many different sources; see Mo'ed Katan 18b, Hullin 139b, Megillah 2b, Hagigah 10b.

18. Megillah 2b et passim.

19. The biblical books that deal primarily with history include Joshua, Judges, Samuel, Kings, Ezra, Nehemiah, and Chronicles.

20. The literary prophets, such as Isaiah, Jeremiah, and Ezekiel, fill this role.

21. Maimonides, *Guide for the Perplexed* 2:45; see also J. D. Eisenstein, *Otzar Yisrael*, s.v. *bikoret kitvei ha-kodesh*.

22. This is true at least in the case of the books of the literary prophets, such as Isaiah, Jeremiah, and Ezekiel. Some primarily historical books are included in this section (Joshua, Judges, Samuel, and Kings) because they tell stories involving these prophets or events occurring during their lives.

23. None of the books in the prophetic section are as late in history as the Second Temple works, such as Daniel, Ezra, and Nehemiah, included in the Ketuvim. Moreover, the first appearance of the name Ketuvim appears much later than the time when the use of the the name Nevi'im came into vogue. See Segal, *Mavo ha-Mikra*, chap. 1, and *Encyclopaedia Judaica*, s.v. Bible: Canon, Text and Editions.

24. Shabbat 88b et passim.

25. Cf. Maimonides, *Mishneh Torah*, Hilkhot Yesodei ha-Torah 7:1; Judah Halevi, *Kuzari* 1:13–25.

26. Shabbat 63a et passim; Eisenstein, *Otzar Yisrael*, s.v. *peshat*.

27. *Otzar Yisrael*, s.v. *derash*.

28. Ibid., s.v. *remez*.

29. Ibid., s.v. *gematria*. For example the word tzitzit (fringes) totals 600 when one substitutes the numerical values for the letters. If one then adds the 8 strings and five knots that are traditionally used to make each of the fringes

the Gematria is 613 and the tzitzit become reminiscent of the 613 commandments.

30. Ibid., s.v. *notarikon*. An example of notarikon is the suggestion that "amen" embodies the phrase "E-l Mekekh Ne'eman"—"God is the faithful King."

31. For a discussion of Jewish mysticism, see below, Chapter 16. The earliest mention of the four modes of interpretation can be found in Isaiah ben Abraham Halevi (1565–1630), *Shenei Luhot ha-Berit*, Ki Tetze.

32. There are several listings of the rules of interpretation. See Eisenstein, *Otzar Yisrael*, s.v. *middot ha-torah*. These include a list of seven associated with Hillel, of thirteen by Rabbi Ishmael (included in the standard siddur), of thirty-two by Rabbi Eliezer ben R. Yose ha-Gelili, and a rather artificial list of 613 in the introduction to the commentary on Sifra in the *Ayelet ha-Shahar* of Meir Loeb ben Jehiel Michael (Malbim).

33. Abraham Ibn Ezra (1089–1164) was one of the first Jewish thinkers to use this phrase; see his commentary on Numbers 10:28. See also n. 24 above.

34. See M. Kasher, *Torah Shelemah*, for a sense of the breadth of biblical exegesis.

35. There are innumerable examples. For instance, compare Rashbam's commentary on Genesis 1:8 to the usual understanding of the verse.

36. This may be the basis for the rabbinic idea that the word *et* (usually used as part of the direct object) implies that something is to be added to the verse (Genesis Rabbah 1:14). The word *et* can mean "the" and can also mean "with" (see Exodus 1:1). Substituting "with" for "the" implies that something needs to be added. This despite the fact that in context the word cannot possibly mean "with." Nonetheless, under this rationale if *et* appears, it must always imply some addition (Bava Kama 41b).

37. See, the next chapter.

38. Bava Batra 14b–15a.

39. Ibid.

40. See Lawee, "Don Isaac Abrabanel"; Malbim, *Ayelet ha-Shahar* introduction to Psalms, both cited above.

41. See any secular or scholarly introduction to the Bible.

42. See below, Chapter 11.

43. Maimonides, *Mishneh Torah*, Hilkhot Yesodei ha-Torah 7:1.

44. For the best argument on this issue, see Rachel Margalioth, *The Indivisible Isaiah* (New York, 1964). This work, using scholarly methodology argues for a unified book and a single author.

45. II Kings 22. He lived from 640–609 B.C.E. and began his reign when he was only eight years old.

46. Ibid., v. 16.

47. Wellhausen first laid out this structure in detail in *Die Composition des Hexateuchs* (1889).

48. See Umberto Cassuto, *The Documentary Hypothesis* (Jerusalem, 1961).

49. Even in these first chapters there are some inconsistencies; see Genesis 3:5

50. Cf. R. Joseph Dov Soloveitchik, my great teacher, *The Lonely Man of Faith* (New York, 1992).

51. Hagigah 13b.

52. As an example, see James B. Pritchard, *Gibeon, Where the Sun Stood Still* (Princeton, N.J., 1962), esp. p. 136. Gibeon is described as "a great city" (Joshua 10:2) at the time when the Jews entered Canaan after the exodus. Pritchard, no traditionalist, reports, "In this period pottery was elaborately decorated with paint in distinctive designs on forms that were at home in Greece and in Cyprus. Imported ware appears in the Late Bronze period along with local imitations of it. In our first three seasons [meaning three years of excavations], this well-known type of ware had been conspicuously absent among the several hundred-thousands of sherds that had been retrieved and examined. Consequently, at the end of the 1959 campaign we had been forced to report that as yet not a trace of evidence had been found for any occupation of Gibeon during the Late Bronze period. From a fairly representative sampling of the mound at el-Jib it looked as though no material basis existed for 'a great city' having been there at the time of Joshua. "This seeming discrepancy between the biblical record and the actual remains at the site was suddenly resolved in 1960, when we opened two tombs to find in them a rich assortment of Late Bronze Age pottery. . . . These richly furnished tombs of the Late Bronze period indicate that Gibeon was in existence in the period immediately before the time of Joshua."

Had the tombs been missed during the fourth year as well, or if there had been no fourth year of excavation, the scholarly conclusion would have been that the biblical account was wrong. With the fourth year and a little bit of luck, there is corroboration. Compare this to the scholarly conclusion that the biblical story of Joshua's destruction of Ai, a neighboring city to Gibeon, is a fabrication because there is no archaeological evidence. Is it at all possible that this too is a case of something being missed? See Pritchard, *Gibeon,* pp. 23, 137, and Joshua 7–8. The linkage between Ai and Gibeon is made explicit in Joshua 9:3.

53. The Esther volume in the *ICC* was authored by L. Paton in 1908.

54. The Esther volume in the *Anchor Bible* was edited by C. Moore in 1971.

55. See below, Chapter 11.

56. Gittin 60a.

57. *Mishneh Torah*, Hilkhot Tefillin, Mezuzah, ve-Sefer Torah 8:4. See also *Encyclopaedia Judaica*, s.v. Masorah.

58. For further discussion, see Eisenstein, *Otzar Yisrael*, s.v. *bikoret kitvei ha-kodesh*.

59. Kiddushin 30a.

60. Numbers Rabbah 3:13; see also Shabbat 115b–116a, Yalkut Shimoni Numbers 10:729.

61. They disagree as to whether the last letter of the word *dakah* in Deuteronomy 23:2 is a heh (Sepharad) or an alef (Ashkenaz).

62. Yehuda, "Hazon Ish on Textual Criticism and Halakhah," *Tradition* 18:2 (1980), pp. 172–180; Leiman, "Hazon Ish on Textual Criticism and Halakhah: A Rejoinder," ibid. 19:4 (1981), pp. 301–310

63. For a good discussion, see Lawrence H. Schiffman, *Reclaiming the Dead Sea Scrolls* (New York, 1994), pt. 3.

64. Y. Shtainer, *Dinei Sefer Torah she-Nimtse'ah Bo Ta'ut* (Jerusalem, 1984).

Chapter 3
Halakhah, the Oral Tradition, and Legal Debate

Halakhah, the Jewish legal system, chose for its name a word that implies traveling a path.[1] Also implied in the name is the all-encompassing nature of the system. Wherever one goes, whatever one does, in all aspects of even the most mundane parts of one's life, Jewish law speaks and provides structure, obligation, and guidance.[2]

The name also connotes a path to a destination.[3] Though different thinkers debate whether commandments are ends in themselves[4] or only means to an end,[5] all agree that living a halakhic lifestyle brings one closer to God.[6]

The term Halakhah, as used in Jewish discourse, actually has two different meanings. It can refer, as indicated, to the entire system of Jewish law, or it can mean an individual decision reached by application of that system to a specific circumstance or problem.[7] In either case its great advantage is that it defines, by limitation, prohibition, and affirmative requirement to act in certain ways, a settled patch of ground on which to stand and make sense of a confusing and complex world. Part of the faith we have in the halakhic system is that it will provide an appropriate answer to the legal and moral questions great and small that we all encounter in our human existence. This faith is a corollary of the belief that the system has its roots in God and His eternally authoritative divine revelation.

This leads us to a discussion of the sources from which Halakhah is derived. The Bible and prophecy are treated in other chapters of this book, and our discussion of divine revelation can be found there. For this chapter, suffice it to say that the system always assumes a divine revelation at its core and never loses sight of that event and that belief.[8]

Around this revealed text called the Bible an oral tradition, at least some of which was given by God, came into being. Whether this oral material was entirely revealed at Sinai, as maintained by Abraham Ibn Daud (ca. 1110–1180),[9] or whether along with some settled law, methods of interpreting the text were revealed, with the Rabbis then being allowed to use these methods to derive answers to new questions that arose over time, as maintained by Maimonides (1138–1204),[10] is a matter of scholarly debate. In addition, new laws created by the Rabbis either to prevent violations of Torah law or to meet specific societal needs appeared. All of this is part of the oral tradition.

Evidence for the antiquity of this tradition has grown over time. First, we know that authoritative texts always develop such traditions. Terms like "the wall of separation between church and state"[11] and "our traditions of gun ownership"[12] are nowhere to be found in the U.S. Constitution. Without attempting to agree or disagree with these oral accretions to the Constitution, one must take note of their often effective use in defense of certain public policy positions. Obviously, these oral traditions have garnered some measure of support and acceptance over the years.

Second, the written Torah itself leads the way to the Oral Law. We are told at one point that we are to "slaughter [the animal] as I have commanded you."[13] However, no details of ritual slaughter appear in the biblical text. From the very first time this verse was read by anyone, an oral explanation would have been needed to make the sentence intelligible.

Third, the law of *hazakah* substantiates a tenant's claim to ownership of property under his control, even without a deed or other proof of purchase, if he claims to have purchased the property and has occupied it for three or more years consecutively without challenge by the previous owner. This law appears nowhere in the Bible but does find a place in our oral tradition and is codified in the Mishnah.[14] Interestingly, a similar law appears in the ancient Mesopotamian legal document known as the Code of Hammurabi.[15] Chronologically, this law code predates Abraham. This is not to say that our law was borrowed from Hammurabi's code, only that it existed long before our oral traditions were committed to writing, and that the concept survived for two millennia before being written down in a Jewish context.

The discovery and recent complete publication of the Dead Sea Scrolls has taken us even further. The inhabitants of Qumran, where the scrolls were found and many were written, had their own "oral" traditions that embodied ideas not explicitly stated in the Bible. They committed them to writing, often as commentary to the biblical text, centuries before the Rabbis did. Unlike the Rabbis,[16] they apparently saw no prohibition in doing so.[17]

Analyzing these materials reveals that, although their conclusions were often dramatically different, their methods were quite similar to those of the Rabbis. Oral tradition and biblical interpretation in light of those traditions were, therefore, a reality in the ancient world long before the destruction of the Second Temple.[18] That national tragedy has long been understood in scholarly circles as the real beginning of the Oral Law period.[19] This is not what our tradition says,[20] and the newest evidence tends to support the side of tradition.

Most intriguing in this regard is a scroll known as Miktzat Ma'asei Torah.[21] This scroll is, in effect, the breakaway letter written by the Dead Sea sect to those who remained loyal to the Temple in Jerusalem as that sect left what it viewed as a corrupt and theologically evil institution. They went from there to found their community in Qumran.

The letter contains twenty-two examples of how ritual in the Temple differed from what the Dead Sea Scroll sect thought Temple practice should be. Given these "violations" the sect felt it could not remain in Jerusalem.

Intriguingly, all twenty-two examples appear in the Talmud as debates often between the Rabbis and what the Talmud calls the sectarians (*minim*). In twenty-one of the twenty-two cases, the position that the Qumran sect insists is correct is described by the Talmud as the view of the *minim*. In twenty-one of the twenty-two cases, the view described as the one wrongly holding sway in the Temple is described in the Talmud as the position of the Rabbis.

One of the twenty-two cases is reversed in the Talmud so that the Rabbis and sectarians appear to say the same thing. As the scroll is older and was written in what we today would call real time, we must find an appropriate explanation for the report that appears in the talmudic text. There as yet no generally accepted theory that deals with this one problem.

In any case, twenty-one of twenty-two is a strong enough batting average to corroborate the talmudic claim that rabbinic law held sway in the Temple.[22] It also shows that the oral tradition was around and in good health more than two hundred years before the Temple's destruction when the Qumran breakaway occurred.[23]

This again poses a significant challenge to the belief mentioned above that the oral tradition was in largest part produced by the Rabbis after the destruction of the Second Temple in 70 C.E. The Conservative movement, in particular, bases many of its assumptions about rabbinic authority on this now apparently repudiated premise.[24] It will be interesting to watch the reevaluation that should now occur.

It is true that after the Temple's destruction and after the failed Bar Kokhba rebellion some sixty-five years later, a decision was reached to commit the oral tradition to writing.[25] The Bar Kokhba rebellion is important here because at least some Rabbis thought he was the Messiah.[26] The Second Temple was rebuilt seventy years after the First Temple's destruction.[27] This may have been a contributing factor to Bar Kokhba's messianic claim, for his success, had it come, would have repeated the sequence in the same seventy-year timeframe.

In any case, once the rebellion failed, while the belief in a Messiah remained, the immediate anticipation of his coming passed. The Rabbis needed to prepare the people for the long night of diaspora history. Further, the loss of the Temple also meant the loss of the seat of the Sanhedrin, the supreme court, the repository and final decisor of the Oral Law.[28]

Without a living human governing body, a textual authority was accepted as the necessary and appropriate replacement. In this way a determination was made to commit the oral tradition to writing.[29]

It is likely that the first attempt was a halakhic commentary of the Pentateuch, excluding Genesis, which has very few laws. The schools of Rabbi Akiva and Rabbi Ishmael produced two different versions of this commentary, known as Midrash Halakhah.[30] This was necessitated by their somewhat different approaches to analyzing biblical texts. In general, Rabbi Akiva was willing to go further in exploring nuances of the text than was Rabbi Ishmael. Stylistic differences existed as well.

Ultimately, this arrangement of the oral law proved unsatisfactory. The law of the Sabbath appears numerous times in the Bible. To which of these references should one turn to find a particular oral law? Also, many oral traditions, including rabbinic laws, have no obvious link to the text. Where would one put them?

A generation after the students of Rabbi Akiva and Rabbi Ishmael compiled the beginnings of the Midrash Halakhah, Rabbi Judah the Prince produced the Mishnah.[31] Topically arranged, succinct in its wording, it became the next authoritative work for Jews after the Bible. The prestige, power, and pure talent of its author certainly helped in that process.[32]

Discussions grew around the Mishnah in both Palestinian and Babylonian academies of learning. These were added to the Mishnah to produce two Talmuds, the Yerushalmi, or Jerusalem Talmud, and the Bavli, or Babylonian Talmud. For a variety of historical reasons, the Babylonian Talmud was accepted as the one which is to be considered more authoritative. The Babylonian Talmud was completed sometime between 600 and 800 C.E.[33]

Later generations wrote commentaries to the text and responsa to answer halakhic questions that arose throughout the Jewish world. Beginning in the early Middle Ages, codes of Jewish law were written to organize this expanding body of material and derive appropriate conclusions from it. The great sage Maimonides (1138–1204) played an important role in this development with his topical codification of all of Jewish law as it existed in his day.

The process reached its culmination in the sixteenth century with the work of Joseph Caro (1488–1575) and Moses Isserles (1525–1572), also known as Rema. Caro wrote the *Shulhan Arukh* (literally the "set table," usually called the Code of Jewish Law in English) covering the rules of Jewish life as lived by diaspora Jewry. He based his work primarily on the earlier codes of Maimonides, Rabbi Isaac Alfasi (1013–1103), also known as Rif, and Rabbenu Asher ben Yehiel (1250–1327), also known as Rosh. As Rif and Rambam as well as Caro himself were Sephardic, or Spanish/ Mediterranean, Jews, the Code of Jewish Law reflected the Sephardic approach. Isserles' *Mappah* (or "tablecloth"), known today as glosses to the text of the *Shulhan Arukh*, provided the Ashkenazic, or Western European, way of doing things.

No work of comparable authority has emerged since that

time, although the process of responsa, interpretation, commentary, and even the authoring of codes has continued to this day. All these works can and are consulted to determine what the Halakhah requires in any situation. The library of sources is huge, and there is no limit to the range of subjects that can be addressed.

There is another way to approach the question of the origins of Halakhah. That is to discuss authority centers rather than literary sources. From this perspective, one can view Halakhah as three concentric circles, each distinct but influencing the others. The central circle is the material that comes from revelation. This includes the Five Books of Moses and the parts of the oral tradition that derive from Sinai. As we have seen there are maximalist opinions, such as those of Ibn Daud (ca. 1100–1180) and Nachmanides (1194–1270), and minimalist opinions, such as that of Maimonides, on the question of how much of our oral tradition falls into this category.[34]

Around this central core is the ring of rabbinic interpretation. The Talmud tells of a particular halakhic argument in the course of which one scholar invokes a heavenly voice in support of his position. Led by Rabbi Joshua and quoting the verses "it is not in heaven"[35] and "you shall follow the majority,"[36] the Rabbis rejected that voice and followed their own majority opinion.[37] Divine revelation in legal matters stops at a certain point and cannot operate any further in the halakhic system.[38]

The third circle is that of community custom, or minhag.[39] "If the Jews are not prophets they are sons of prophets," says the Talmud.[40] Their actions carry a divine spark. For this reason, the Talmud tells us with confidence that in some specific cases where the law was unclear to the Rabbi being asked for his response we are to be guided halakhically simply by seeing what the people do and following that practice.[41]

Most intriguing in this regard is the requirement that a new rabbinic law does not take effect unless a majority of the peo-

ple accept it. Non-acceptance by a majority of the nation is ultimately a veto that cannot be overridden.[42]

One can look at the fundamental ideological differences
between the contemporary movements in Judaism as deriving
from the different emphases they place on these circles. It is the
emphasis on rabbinic interpretation and the less powerful
impact of the other circles that underlies Conservative
Judaism, the emphasis on the community in the aggregate and
the deemphasis of the other sources of authority that defines
Reconstructionism, and the emphasis on individual behavior
rather than divine or rabbinic imperative that is the hallmark
of Reform. From an Orthodox perspective, our disagreement
with these movements comes from our insistence on recognizing what we see as the proper authority of each of the circles.

One frequent element of the halakhic system, even when it
is functioning in all its aspects, is the prevalence of debate.
Different theories exist to explain why debate is so ubiquitous.
Some claim that it emerges from the fact that parts of the tradition were lost. This view follows the opinion that all of the
oral tradition was given to Moses at Sinai, but persecution,
memory loss, and inattentiveness to detail caused some of the
tradition to be forgotten. Debate reflects attempts to replace
what is missing.[43]

Others see debate as built into the system. According to their
approach, diversity serves to give the system strength. Some
hold that God revealed all sides of every debate to Moses at
Sinai, leaving the scholars of each generation to decide which
view to accept.[44] Others, like Maimonides, hold that God
revealed the biblical text and thirteen different methods of interpretation. A natural consequence of this theory is that different
legitimate interpretations of the text would then emerge[45] as the
sages began to use these different interpretive methods.

Certainly, these last two theories imply that more than one
truth exists in Halakhah. Some scholars, such as Rabbi Isaac

Hutner (1907–1980), even find multiple truths in the first theory in the sense that the system produces the various opinions while trying to recreate what has been lost.[46] Hence they are truths of the system. These multiple-truth theories are expressed in the phrase "These and these are the words of the living God."[47] It is a hallmark of the system that different opinions are respected in this way. However, not all possible opinions contain truth. The most important limitation on the range of these multiple truths is that the opinions emanate from within the rules of the system. For this reason non-Orthodox positions often are not recognized as achieving the same level of truth, as they are frequently not derived from within the system, but come instead from contemporary secular morality. From a traditional viewpoint, borrowing from secular culture in this way is only legitimate if that which is borrowed is not in violation of pre-existing halakhik norms, and not if what is borrowed is used to change Jewish law in ways not allowed by the system of Halakhah.

The description of the halakhic system presented here should convey a sense of its resilience, vibrancy, and dynamism. That is why it has served for millennia and continues to do so as an effective way to help us lead our lives and make sense of our existence.

1. Cf. J. D. Eisenstein, *Otzar Yisrael*, s.v. *halakhah*.

2. Hayim Donin, *To Be a Jew* (New York, 1972), pp. 29 ff.

3. Ibid. See Exodus 18:20 for the possible source of the concept.

4. Shem Tov ibn Shem Tov, *Kevod Elohim* 21b ff. Some take this position for laws other than those that are logical and obvious, e.g., the prohibitions against theft and murder. See Saadiah Gaon, *Emunot ve-De'ot* 3:5, 1–3; Bahya Ibn Paquda, *Hovot ha-Levavot* introduction and 3:3. Logical laws on the other hand are followed because one must be true to one's intellect.

5. Much of the third section of Maimonides' *Guide for the Perplexed* deals with this subject and his opinion that rationality is the hallmark of all of the laws; see 3:26–32.

6. There is a great amount of published material on the subject of this chapter, far more than can be summarized here. Two particularly rich sources are Moshe Sokol, *Rabbinic Authority and Personal Autonomy*, a volume in the Orthodox Forum series (Northvale, N.J., 1992), and Menahem Elon's classic *Mishpat Ivri* (Jerusalem, 1978).

7. Aaron Lichtenstein, "Does Jewish Law Recognize an Ethic Independent of Halakhah?" in *Modern Jewish Ethics: Theory and Practice*, ed. Marvin Fox (Columbus, Ohio, 1975).

8. Cf. the first few sentences of Maimonides' introductions to both his *Mishnah Commentary* and his *Mishneh Torah*.

9. See his *Sefer ha-Kabbalah*, introduction.

10. See his *Mishnah Commentary*, introduction.

11. The phrase about the wall of separation originated with Thomas Jefferson, but James Madison's "line of separation" seems to more accurately reflect the constitutional wording.

12. Often referred to by those who oppose gun control legislation.

13. Deuteronomy 12:21.

14. M. Bava Batra 3:1, Baba Batra 28a ff.

15. See James Pritchard, *The Ancient Near East: An Anthology of Texts and Pictures* (Princeton, N.J., 1971), pp. 142, #31, Hammurabi lived in the 18th century B.C.E.

16. Gittin 60b.

17. For discussion of the Dead Sea Scrolls and the relationship of a number of them, at least conceptually and methodologically, to rabbinic Oral Law compositions (midrashim and law codes), see Lawrence Schiffman, *Reclaiming the Dead Sea Scrolls* (New York, 1994), esp. p. 222.

18. The scrolls in question are from the second and perhaps even third century B.C.E. That puts them within 150 years of the traditional date of the closing of the Bible.

19. Many scholarly and popular texts that deal with the rabbinic period take this approach; see Judah Goldin, *The Jewish Expression* (New Haven, 1976), chap. 3.

20. Yoma 19b, see also Sukkah 48b.

21. Schiffman, *Reclaiming the Dead Sea Scrolls*, pp. 83 ff.

22. See above, n. 20.

23. See Schiffman, *Reclaiming the Dead Sea Scrolls*.

24. *Encyclopaedia Judaica*, s.v. Conservative Judaism.

25. Much of the literary activity of the Oral Law is credited to the students of R. Akiva in the post–Bar Kokhba era (Sanhedrin 86a). However, many scholars associate this with concern expressed by the Rabbis as they entered the "vineyard at Yavneh" after the destruction of the Second Temple (Shabbat 138b, Tosefta Eduyyot 1:1). This would make the decision even earlier. Also, Tractate Eduyyot, which many consider to be the first tractate redacted, is mentioned as having been taught at Yavneh (Berakhot 28a). Perhaps some of the work took place earlier than the Bar Kokhba revolt, but the literary activity may well have been given new impetus and urgency by the tragic outcome of that revolt and the Hadrianic persecutions that followed it.

26. Maimonides, *Mishneh Torah*, Hilkhot Melakhim 11:3.

27. II Chronicles 36:21.

28. *Mishneh Torah*, Hilkhot Sanhedrin 1:3 and Hilkhot Mamrim 1:1.

29. See above, n. 25.

30. Sanhedrin 86a and see *Encyclopaedia Judaica*, s.v. *Midreshei Halakhah*. The texts as we have them contain later additions as well.

31. Cf. Bava Metzia 33b, 86a; Rosh Hashanah 7b.

32. See Aaron Hyman, *Toledot Tanna'im Ve'amoraim* (Jerusalem, 1964), s.v. *yehudah ha-nasi*.

33. An important source on the history of the oral tradition is the *Iggeret Rav Sherira Gaon*; see the edition of Binyamin Levin (Jerusalem, 1972).

34. See above, nn. 9–10; also, the first two *shoreshim* ("roots") of Maimonides' *Sefer ha-Mitzvot*, and Nachmanides' critique of these comments.

35. Deuteronomy 30:12.

36. Exodus 23:2.

37. Bava Metzia 59b.

38. See Maimonides' introduction to his *Mishnah Commentary*. Note also the non-acceptance of even Elijah the prophet's opinion as against that which has been accepted as halakhically correct (Pesahim 34a, Yevamot 102a, Menahot 32a). See also Shabbat 104a, Yoma 80a, Megillah 2b, Temurah 16a, and Maimonides, *Mishneh Torah*, Hilkhot Yesodei ha-Torah 1:1.

39. Cf. J. D. Eisenstein, *Otzar Yisrael*, s.v. *minhag*.

40. Pesahim 66a; the context of the comment is the famous Hillel allowing the people to display their knowledge of what is the proper behavior to solve a particular halakhic question that he could not answer.

41. Berakhot 45a, Eruvin 14b, Menahot 35b, and see Pesahim 54a, where the

people's practice is offered as support for a halakhic position.

42. Maimonides, *Mishneh Torah*, Hilkhot Mamrim 2:5–6.

43. See above, n. 9, and Jair Hayyim ben Moses Samson Bacharach, *Havot Yair*, responsum 192.

44. *Havvot Yair*, loc. cit., cites this view. For sources, see Moshe Halbertal, *People of the Book* (Cambridge, Mass., 1997), p. 63. I disagree with Halbertal's reading of the medieval sources in this regard and do not believe that this position exists in the places he sees it, but it does appear in early modern sources, possibly because of the same misreading that Halbertal is guilty of, which also appears in *Havvot Yair*, so I include it here.

45. See n. 10 above.

46. Isaac Hutner, *Pahad Yitzhak*, Kuntros Ve-zot Hanukkah, ma'amar gimel.

47. Eruvin 13b.

Chapter 4
Prophecy

Though many of the elements that might go into this chapter were covered in our discussion of the Bible, a number of important issues remain. Fortunately, the subject of prophecy has always intrigued scholars, both medieval and modern, and their discussions thoroughly examine the biblical and rabbinic sources. In actuality, there are so many sources that some of them seem contradictory. In addition, some of our greatest scholars approached the question of prophecy from within their own philosophies of Judaism. As a result, a number of different approaches to the questions we will explore can be found in our literature.[1]

Who is a prophet, and how does one qualify for this distinction? For Moses Maimonides (1138–1204), also known as Rambam, perhaps our greatest philosopher and halakhist, prophecy is a matter of personal perfection.[2] In each person there is, as it were, a receiver ready and able to tune into the prophecy of God that emanates from Him. This receiver acts through the imaginative faculty, but it is only activated in a person who has perfected himself morally, ethically, intellectually, and emotionally.[3] At this point, unless God acts to prevent it, prophecy becomes a reality.[4] When this occurs, the person becomes another type of human being, qualitatively different than he or she was before.[5]

For the poet and philosopher Judah Halevi (ca.1075–1141),

prophecy is what we might today call a genetic trait that for most of history can only be found in Jews.[6] From the time of Adam on, some human beings have had this divine element whereas others do not. After successive refinements, and the expulsion from the Jewish community of the line of those without this capacity, such as Ishmael, Esau, and Noah's sons Ham and Japheth, only Jews retain this ability. Therefore, since all Jews are potentially prophetic, the choice of a particular individual to be a prophet is determined by circumstances and God's preference.[7]

Saadiah Gaon (882–942), the first medieval Jewish philosopher, also saw the prophet as the product of God's choice and the need of the moment, but like all other Jewish thinkers, he rejected the "genetic" theory subsequently expounded by Judah Halevi. For him it is simply God's choice at the moment as needed by the circumstances.[8]

How does the prophet establish him- or herself? Maimonides has the most elaborate description of this process.[9] For him the simplest method is to be acknowledged as a true recipient of God's word by an already accepted prophet.[10] In the absence of such a predecessor, Rambam requires that we first look to the prophet's message to make sure that it does not promote idolatry or in some other way permanently attempt to undermine or alter the Torah.[11]

Second, the person's character and righteousness must be clearly established. As mentioned, according to Maimonides, only someone who has achieved this type of perfection can qualify.

Third, the prophet must predict in great detail a series of good events, and they must come true in every aspect. Prophecies for evil may be rescinded by God's mercy. Not so prophecies for good.[12]

For others, the capacity of a prophet to perform miracles and foretell the future would be enough as long as the message brought by the individual is not violative of the Torah's own rules.[13]

If one hears voices, should one seek psychological help, or should one believe that they are a manifestation of divine communication? Ultimately, the prophet knows the truth, whether because of the personal transformation described by Maimonides or because miraculous events begin to occur in the prophet's presence.[14]

The prophet has extraordinary power. Disobedience of him is punishable by death.[15] This is true even when the prophet orders a temporary violation of any Torah law other than idolatry,[16] as Elijah did in offering a sacrifice on Mount Carmel.[17] Since the Temple was standing in his day, sacrifices outside its precincts would normally have been illegal.[18] But Elijah needed to strike a blow for God and expose Ba'al as a false deity. For this reason he proved that he could call down fire from heaven to consume his sacrifice. Though the prophets of Ba'al tried as well they were unsuccessful. This showed the Jewish people who was in communication with a Diety and who was not.

Can there be prophets today? Maimonides certainly thought so.[19] I sometimes think that he may have expected prophecy to emerge within himself and did not fully understand why it did not.[20] However, his theory does allow for God to intervene and not allow prophecy to reach someone even when that person is worthy of divine communication.[21]

Other thinkers held that prophecy ceased to be a possibility after the deaths of the last of the biblical prophets, Haggai, Zechariah, and Malachi.[22] Presumably the mission of prophecy had been successfully completed. Perhaps its task was to combat the Jewish flirtation with idolatry which was such a major factor in the history of the First Temple period. The Second Temple period saw much less of this involvement with false gods, and thus, the miraculous connection to God represented by prophecy may no longer have been necessary.

In any case, although it is sometimes said that *ruah ha-kodesh* ("divine spirit") accrued to certain postbiblical figures,[23] no claim of prophecy has ever been made of anyone in the traditional community since the close of the twenty-four books of the Bible. At most, the claim of *ruah ha-kodesh* refers to an almost miraculous intellectual ability that enables the individual in question to make very precise distinctions in order to respond to a given issue.[24] Even so, in the analysis of such issues, it is up to the scholar as a scholar, and not as a prophet, to develop appropriate conclusions.[25] Other scholars remain free to and, in fact, do argue against the conclusions reached by individuals said to possess *ruah ha-kodesh*.[26]

Finally, it is important to remember that after Moses, who was unique in his prophecy,[27] no prophetic vision can determine Halakhah.[28] Jewish law, after the first revelation at Sinai, is a matter of logical analysis and not of divine supernatural communication.

Finally, we take up the question of the task of the prophet. The term *navi* in Hebrew does not mean "future teller," as is implied by the English word "prophet." When Moses went to Pharaoh, he was made master (*elohim*) over the Egyptian ruler, and Aaron his brother was made Moses' *navi*.[29] Clearly, Aaron was not a future teller in this context. He was Moses' spokesman. So, too, the prophet was God's spokesman. He came forward with God's word to His people or to other nations. As part of this responsibility the prophet would frequently be called on to condemn, criticize, and exhort the people and its leadership.[30] Often those who were the subject of the prophecy were far less than thrilled to hear it. Sometimes,, the situation might prove uncomfortable, dangerous, or even fatal to the prophetic messenger.[31]

Adding to the necessary heroism of being a prophet, distorting God's message was prohibited on pain of death.[32] So, too, refusing to deliver a prophecy was unacceptable.[33] The biblical story of Jonah's reluctance to prophesy to Nineveh and the difficulties he faced as a result make the point eloquently.

The prophet had one other job that at times was also very difficult. He or she was to defend the Jewish people before God even when His anger was legitimate.[34] Moses praying for the Jews, even when doing so appeared to be defying God's orders that Moses remove himself from the people so that God could destroy them, is a classic example of fulfilling this mandate.[35]

However, even Moses slipped at one point. During his encounter with God at the burning bush, his repeated insistence that the Jews would not listen to him is seen by some as an improper attack on the people before God.[36] When God turns Moses' flesh leprous as a sign that he should undertake to lead the Jews out of Egypt, this divine act can be understood as punishment for his unfair doubting of the Jews. Interestingly, the Jews, in fact, did not listen to Moses.[37] However, he was still culpable because he had expressed his doubts before the people actually failed.

Similarly, when Elijah abandons his people for Mount Sinai and a vain and unavailing spiritual solitude, he is castigated by God for doing so and for defending his actions by claiming that the Jews had repudiated the covenant with God.[38] This incident actually appears to have been a prelude to Elijah's removal from this world in a fiery chariot.[39] Since he had given up his task of protecting the Jews, it was time for his successor, Elisha, to take over. In Jewish mystical tradition, Elijah is required to be present at every circumcision to be witness to our reaffirmation of the covenant and to learn that abandoning the Jews was wrong.[40]

In the end, the prophetic tradition of Israel is a tradition of social critique and challenge, of speaking uncomfortable moral truths to power and of shaking people from their ethical complacency while defending the good that exists, and preserving the people. Whatever the reason for its absence today, we are poorer for its passing but far richer for the literary record of its activity that the Bible preserves.

1. Perhaps the best modern philosophical treatment of this subject is Abraham Joshua Heschel, *The Prophets* (New York, 2001), introduction. See also David Bakan, *Maimonides on Prophecy* (Northvale, N.J., 1991).

2. Maimonides, *Mishneh Torah*, Hilkhot Yesodei ha-Torah 7:7; *Mishnah Commentary*, introduction; *Guide for the Perplexed* 2:32, 36.

3. The passages cited in the previous note from the *Guide* give the fullest treatment of this issue.

4. *Guide* 2:32.

5. Hilkhot Yesodei ha-Torah 7:1, based on the Bible's description of the effect of prophecy on King Saul in I Samuel 10:6.

6. *Sefer ha-Kuzari* 1:88–95.

7. Ibid., 98–99.

8. *Sefer ha-Emunot ve-ha-De'ot*, sec. 3.

9. Hilkhot Yesodei Ha-Torah 8:1–3, 10:1–3. Compare with Saadiah, loc. cit.

10. Hilkhot Yesodei ha-Torah 10:8.

11. See the sources cited above in n. 9.

12. Based on Jeremiah 28, especially vv. 8–9. See also Maimonides, Introduction to his *Mishnah Commentary*.

13. Saadiah, loc. cit.

14. Ibid.

15. Deuteronomy 19:18, Hilkhot Yesodei ha-Torah 9:3.

16. Yesodei ha-Torah 9:3–4.

17. I Kings 18

18. Mishnah Zevahim 14:4–8.

19. That is the clear implication of the sources from the *Guide* cited above. See Abraham Joshua Heschel, *Prophetic Inspiration After the Prophets: Maimonides and Other Medieval Authorities* (Hoboken, N.J., 1996).

20. According to Heschel, Maimonides may have believed that in some measure and at certain times he did achieve prophecy.

21. *Guide* 2:32.

22. Yoma 9b et passim. See discussion in Heschel, loc. cit. "Prophetic Inspiration."

23. Such a claim is sometimes made about Rashi; see Zevi Elimelech Dynow, *Igra de-Kallah* (Lemberg, 1868), 142b,

24. Tosafot Eruvin 60b, s.v. *ein eilu*.

25. Cf. Maimonides, *Mishnah Commentary*, introduction.

26. For example, Tosafot, Nachmanides and Abraham Ibn Ezra debate with Rashi at many points in their respective commentaries.

27. Maimonides, Yesodei ha-Torah 7:6.

28. Yoma 80a et passim; see also Bava Metzia 59b and Maimonides, Hilkhot Yesodei ha-Torah 9:1.

29. Exodus 7:1.

30. Heschel, *Prophets*, introduction.

31. Cf. II Chronicles 24:19–22.

32. Deuteronomy 18:20, Maimonides, Hilkhot Yesodei ha-Torah 9:3.

33. Ibid.

34. Heschel, loc. cit.

35. Cf. Exodus 32:1

36. Exodus 3–4; Rashi to Exodus 4:6, based on Midrash Tanhuma; Exodus 25:23. See also Shabbat 97a.

37. Exodus 6:9.

38. I Kings 19, esp. vv. 10, 14.

39. II Kings 2.

40. Jacob ben Asher, *Tur*, Yoreh De'ah, 265 end.

Chapter 5
Humankind's Place in Creation

Perhaps no aspect of theology distinguishes Judaism from Christianity more than its view of the place occupied by human beings in the spiritual universe.[1] This difference makes its presence felt in many areas, most dramatically in discussions of the nature of humankind, of sin, of repentance, and of the goal and purpose of existence. Traditional Christianity assumes a flawed and sinful humanity.[2] Judaism does not.[3] For Judaism, while the potential for the most extreme human depravity is as much within the realm of philosophical possibility as it is within the historical record, it is neither the assumed state of the human condition nor a necessary consequence of a human being acting alone without God or Judaism to guide him.[4] Judaism may help significantly in the moral quest but moral people can exist without it, because homo sapiens, by their nature, have so much innate potential.

In Judaism's view of the cosmos, man is the most important being in the created universe.[5] After God Himself, nothing and no one is more significant. Even angels, in the mystical description of their origin, come from a lower place in God's metaphysical universe than does the soul of man.[6]

This valuing of the human being makes its presence felt in a number of ways. The Bible records many covenants between human beings and God.[7] Only if we are significant in God's eyes could such covenants make sense. God is not generally described as entering covenantal relationships with animals or inanimate objects, and where something of this sort does appear in biblical or rabbinic literature,[8] it occurs only for the purpose of advancing God's plan for human beings generally or for Jews specifically.[9]

This is in line with the biblical picture of man as ruler over God's creation. While restrictions and the requirement to act responsibly limit what man *should* do, human power and ingenuity expand the potential for what man *can* do to the limits of imagination. Man is to treat this world as if he were its constitutional monarch.[10] Whether he is obedient to that constitution or not, he remains the monarch unless and until God actively steps in.

This is not a frightening state of affairs for Judaism. While many fear man's destructive power, Judaism is optimistic about man's creative power and seeks to properly manage man's darker side.[11]

I recently had first-hand experience with this difference in approach. I testified before Congress, along with a Roman Catholic cardinal and a Protestant theologian, on the subject of human cloning. Technology exists, or may shortly be developed, that will make cloning human beings not just a possibility, but potentially an everyday reality. The technology involves taking an egg cell from a woman, removing its DNA, and replacing it with DNA from another individual, which will be induced to begin the process of reproduction. The egg will be implanted in a recipient mother's womb, and barring an unforeseen accident, a baby will emerge that is the genetic twin of the DNA donor.

Several writers have discussed this issue from a traditional Jewish perspective.[12] All agree that while questions of family relationships must be resolved, cloning may, in some circumstances, prove very valuable. It is, after all, a mechanism for managing infertility. One authority cites the example of a Holocaust survivor whose entire family was wiped out and who was made sterile by the terrible Nazi medical experiments.[13] Such an individual might well want to continue his genetic line, and cloning might be the only way to accomplish this. It would seem to be entirely appropriate to use all the mechanisms of God's world that He has given into our care and control, absent a specific halakhic prohibition, to meet so touching a human request.[14]

At the congressional hearing, I expressed this position and specifically stated that while there are questions and concerns, there are uses of this technology that could be valuable. In contrast, the Cardinal was opposed to the entire technology on the grounds that cloning constituted "playing God in the work of creation."

It struck me as remarkable that crediting someone with an act of the same description, *na'aseh shutaf le-ha-kodesh barukh hu be-ma'asei bereshit* (literally, "becoming a partner with God in the works of creation"), was regarded by the sages of the Talmud as one of the finest compliments any human being might receive.[15] These two diametrically opposed attitudes dramatically embody the essence of the different world views that Judaism and Christianity have concerning the place of humankind in the universe.

The same opposition, expressed in very different terms, was the centerpiece of the Protestant theologian's presentation. He, too, opposed cloning, on the grounds that "being created through cloning is a violation of human dignity and people have a right not to be created in this way."

Not being an expert on Protestant theology, I am not sure to this day what exactly that means. From a Jewish perspective, human existence is the most dignified and valuable experience in God's universe,[16] and the procedure by which that existence begins would not seem to affect its dignity.[17] Even a *mamzer*, the product of a clearly sinful incestuous or adulterous relationship,[18] should he become a Torah scholar, is entitled to more honor than an ignorant high priest.[19] Life is measured by what one is and what one becomes, not by where one comes from.

Judaism, in keeping with its teaching of ultimate human significance, has a long tradition of people arguing with God when human perception senses injustice on God's part.[20]

From Abraham arguing that God must act justly, as befits the Judge of the entire world,[21] to Moses demanding to be erased from the Torah if God would not forgive His people,[22] to Levi Yitzhak of Berdichev bartering forgiveness for the Jews' sins against "forgiving" God for his supposed inattentiveness to His people's needs,[23] to Elie Wiesel's demand for God's "face" to appear somewhere in the darkness of the Holocaust,[24] Jewish tradition has always confronted God when this was seen as appropriate. Only our standing as human beings allows us to do so.[25]

In this connection we should mention *kiddush hashem* (sanctification of God's name)[26] and *hillul hashem* (profanation of God's name).[27] As one might imagine simply from hearing the terms, these are important concepts in Judaism. Among their various colloquial and halakhic meanings, they are often used to designate conduct, especially in public, that brings credit or discredit to God.[28]

Perhaps this is man's most important capacity. God has no representative and no visible presence in this universe more important than humans and their behavior.[29] Jews in particular, as the people of God, bear a special burden, and observant Jews even more so than others.[30] Our behavior and how others react to it determine, in large measure, how people assess God and His message to the world. It is as if God's fate on earth rested in our hands.

Hillul hashem, using the root meaning of the term *hillul*, connotes creating, as it were, a hole or vacuum in God.[31] When an outwardly observant Jew, supposedly someone living by God's word, murdered the prime minister of Israel, the absence of God in the person and the act was palpable to the entire world. God's reputation suffered accordingly.

Conversely, when a possible presidential candidate who is an observant Jew acts with integrity, sensitivity, and morality, when the story is told that on first being nominated to the Senate he did not directly address his own nominating convention on a Friday night because it was Shabbat, God's felt presence in the world grows with each day of his service to his country and his God. Only human beings can control the sense of the Divine Presence in the world in this way.

Idolatry is one of the worst, if not the worst, of all sins in the Bible.[32] Obviously, worshipping another god violates our oath to God and our covenant with Him.[33] Less obviously but very significantly it also diminishes man. After all, has not the idolater raised a stone, an animal, a piece of wood, or even the sun, moon, and stars, above himself?[34] To Judaism this is anathema, both because of its doing fundamental violence to God's plan for the hierarchy of the universe and because many misdeeds are done by human beings out of a sense that they and their actions are not really important enough to matter.[35] In Judaism's understanding of the world, human beings always matter because we matter so much to God.

The uniqueness of mankind may well be embodied in the Biblical claim that we were created in God's image.[36] In itself that statement is significant.[37] Jewish thinkers have debated which human quality is the true manifestation of the divine element in human beings. Opinions range from Maimonides' belief that intellect is the God-like asset,[38] to Martin Buber's claim that it is our capacity to love,[39] to S. R. Hirsch's assertion that it is our ability to make moral choices.[40] Certainly these three qualities are, at least potentially among the most noble and ennobling within any human beings capacity. Our challenge is at a minimum, to use these and any other characteristics unique to human beings in ways that bring credit to the God whose essence they may reflect.

1. The subject of this chapter is discussed by Mordecai Roshwald, "Man and Universe in Greek and Hebrew Perception," *Judaism* 38:1 (1989), pp. 63–73; Jeremy Cohen, "The Bible, Man and Nature in the History of Western Thought: A Call for Reassessment," *Journal of Religion* 65:2 (1985), pp. 155–172; Bernard Mandelbaum, "The Human Being: A Jewish Perspective," *Christian Jewish Relations* 15:2 (1982), pp. 8–16.

2. In addition to the passage from the Christian Bible cited in the opening dis-

cussion of repentance in Chapter 7, see Romans 3:9–20.

3. Cf. Judah Loewe (Maharal) of Prague, *Sefer Netivot Olam*, Netiv ha-Tzedakah 2.

4. The concept of *hasidei umot ha-olam* ("pious gentiles," cf. Joseph Albo, *Sefer ha-Ikkarim* 1: 23, 25) and the acceptance of the idea that a non-Jew may have a place in the world-to-come (see Chapter 18) lend themselves to this conclusion; so, too, does the choice in Jewish literature, of gentiles as the paradigms for honoring one's parents. In the biblical world this is Esau (Cf. Shmot Rabbah 46:4) who is not otherwise seen as someone we would want to emulate. In the rabbinic world it is Damah b. Nethinah (Kedushin 31a). In both cases a non-Jew is projected as the role model for how we are to treat our parents, despite the fact that honoring parents is not a gentile requirement (see Chapter 8). Obviously then, these gentiles must have been self-taught.

5. Cf. Genesis Rabbah 8:3–9, Avot de-Rabbi Natan 1:31.

6. Cf. Genesis Rabbah 21:5, Numbers Rabbah 19:3, Sanhedrin 93a, Hullin 91b; see Peter Schafer, *The Hidden and Manifest God* (New York, 1992), for discussion of human vs. angelic roles in early Jewish mysticism.

7. Cf. *Encyclopaedia Judaica*, s.v. Covenant; Ecclesiastes Rabbah 7:28.

8. As a model, see Genesis 9.

9. Ibid., v. 15

10. This is implicit in the phrase *le-avdah u-le-shamrah* in Genesis 2:15, and the imperative *vekhiushuhah* in Genesis 1:28, which describes man's mission in this world. See also Genesis Rabbah 8:3–9

11. Cf. Abraham Ibn Ezra's criticism of the builders of the Tower of Babel for attempting to limit humankind's dominion over the world to only one location (commentary to Genesis 11:7). See also the source cited in n. 3 above.

12. Michael Broyde, "Cloning People: A Jewish Legal Analysis," *Jewish Spectator* 63:4 (1999); John Loike, "Human Cloning and Halakhic Perspectives," *Tradition* 32:3 (1998); Avraham Steinberg, "Human Cloning: Scientific, Ethical and Jewish Perspectives," *Assia–Jewish Medical Ethics* 3:2 (1998). See Chapter 22 on Beginning of Life and Ethics.

13. Rabbi Moses Tendler of Yeshiva University (personal communication).

14. Procreation is, after all, the first mitzvah in the Torah, and at least four different imperatives push us to produce the next generation (see Yevamot 62a, 62b, 63b, and 65b).

15. Shabbat 10a, 119b. Though the contexts are different, the sentiment is the same.

16. The debate between Bet Hillel and Bet Shammai (Eruvin 13b) on the ques-

tion of whether it was easier for mankind (*no'ah lo le-adam*) to have been created than not, in which the sages voted that it was not easier, is open to a number of interpretations. Sources describing the infinite value and importance of the human being would seem to be more definitive of the Jewish attitude. See, for instance, Avot 3:15 and 4:17 (especially), Sanhedrin 37a, and the sources cited above in n. 5.

17. All human existence begins in ignoble fashion according to Avot 3:1.

18. For sources, see *Encyclopaedia Judaica*, s.v. Mamzer.

19. Mishnah Horayot 3:8.

20. Cf. Anson Laytner, *Arguing with God: A Jewish Tradition* (Northvale, N.J.), 1990.

21. Genesis 18:25.

22. Exodus 32:32.

23. See Samuel Dresner, *Levi Yitzhak of Berditchev: Portrait of a Hassidic Master* (New York, 1974), pp. 77 ff.

24. Cf. his *Night* (New York, 1960).

25. Job's victory over his friends in God's verdict confirms this (Job 42:7). One does not find this type of confrontation in Christian literature. There the stance is much more one of acceptance of whatever comes as God's will.

26. See J. D. Eisenstein, *Otzar Yisrael*, s.v. *hillul hashem*.

27. Ibid.

28. Cf. Maimonides, *Mishneh Torah*, Hilkhot Yesodei ha-Torah 5:11.

29. Cf. Judah Loewe, (Maharal) of Prague, *Tiferet Yisrael* 70; Isaac ben Moses Arama, *Akedat Yitzhak* 67.

30. Cf. Hilkhot Yesodei ha-Torah 5:11.

31. See A. Evan-Shoshan, Hamilon Hachadash, (Jerusalem, 1977).

32. It is condemned many times in the Bible in the harshest terms; cf. Jeremiah 2:13.

33. A covenant implies exclusivity.

34. Deuteronomy 4:28 (which becomes a refrain in Deuteronomy 28:36, 64, 29:16). See also Psalms 115:4 ff.

35. The example of King Saul and his sin is a good one. See I Samuel 15, and Samuel's criticism in v. 17.

36. Genesis 1:27.

37. M. Avot 3:14.

38. Cf. *Guide for the Perplexed* 1:1.

39. Cf. his "I and Thou."

40. See his commentary to Genesis 1:27.

Chapter 6
Theodicy:
The Problem of Evil

Religion alleviates all the great problems of existence except one, and that one it appears to make worse. The exception is the existence of evil in the world.[1] If God is all-good and all-powerful, how can evil occur? This question, phrased in different ways, is as old as religious thinking and certainly as old as Judaism. Abraham demands of God that He, the "judge of the entire world . . . do justice.[2]" Jeremiah demands to know "why the path of the wicked is so joyous?"[3] In this vein, the Rabbis saw the problem of the tragic righteous and the prosperous wicked as the meaning of the insistent "Show me your glory" with which Moses confronts the Lord.[4] Finally, there is the biblical Book of Job, which mounts its naked challenge to the usual biblical theology—that good behavior nets you "rain . . . in its season" and abundant harvests, while the opposite produces barricaded heavens and barren fields[5]—with the story of history's most righteous man and his terrible suffering.[6]

Confrontation with evil produces two types of questions. We think first of the grand philosophical challenges, of asking why God allows these things to happen and of how they are to be understood in a universe claimed to be ultimately good. It is here that the challenge to religion in general, and to traditional Judaism specifically, can be found. Certainly, the questions are legitimate.

However, a second set of concerns also arises, and these are often not discussed as they should be, despite the profound impact they have on the lives of those who survive tragedy or are witness to it. For this reason we will deal with these issues first. These questions center on the aftermath of tragedy and the challenge of what to do next. People are often in such shock after a terrible experience that they are distorted internally, in some cases for years. They may have difficulty moving on with any constructive response whatsoever. Writing in the aftermath of 9/11 and the continuing flood of terrorist attacks in Israel makes this discussion even more important. Here proper application of traditional Jewish law and belief can be extremely helpful.

Modern researchers have defined a number of important psychological stages in the grieving and mourning process.[7] Though they were created long before such formal analysis, Jewish *avelut* (mourning) rituals meet those emotional needs quite dramatically.[8] Beginning with the requirement to physically, and by hand, tear one's clothing,[9] which allows an outlet for one's anger, many emotions and internal feelings are given appropriate expression. A further example, Jewish law requires actual burial in the ground in the presence of the mourners and others who are there to pay their respects.[10] The awful sound of the earth and stones hitting the casket is usually enough to end denial and allow the painful process of healing to begin.

Similarly, placing oneself low to the ground whenever one sits for seven days after the burial of a relative, expresses the feeling of being diminished.[11] So, too, the visits paid by friends and members of one's community during this period help overcome the natural feelings of isolation and aloneness that come with personal tragedy.[12] Finally, standing in the congregation to recite Kaddish signifies both acceptance of the reality of what has occurred and reaffirmation of and reconnection with God, one's faith, and one's community.[13] Where the evil or tragedy is not the death of a relative, though no formal mourning rituals exist, exploring the process of *avelut* and the symbols of mourning in Jewish ritual which express one's emotions may inspire an individual to find an answer to the problem of what to do to move away from the tragedy and not be consumed by it.

Many other elements of our mourning laws and customs also provide similarly therapeutic symbols and behaviors. Above all, these things provide the survivor with a roadmap and a blueprint. The roadmap guides us through the overwhelming questions "What is my first step?" "What is my second step?" "What do I do next?" At the same time, the blueprint provides direction as to how we can begin to rebuild our lives, at least internally and emotionally.

Returning to the "why" questions, while remaining for a moment with the "What do I do?" problem, we have here the formula for Judaism's ultimate approach to the reality of evil. However adequately or inadequately we answer the "why" questions, the ultimate challenge is what we do after the tragedy. If we live meaningfully against the tragedy, if we rebuild what was lost, if we learn something important from the tragedy and make the world better because of what we have learned, if we memorialize what is gone in something that works for the good of the world, if we somehow, in some way, find a mechanism to bring light out of the dark, then we have responded as Judaism has historically wanted us to do.[14]

The destruction of the First Temple somehow brought about the end of idolatry as a theological force in the Jewish community,[15] though it would have been easy to see the event as the triumph of idolatry, since the destroyers were pagans. The destruction of the Second Temple led to the writing of the

Oral Law—the Mishnah and later the Gemara—and the deepening of commitment to Jewish knowledge and observance, though it could easily have led to capitulation to the Greco-Roman culture of the conquerors. The expulsion from Spain led to the deeper spirituality that came with the popularization of Jewish mysticism and to great codifications of Jewish law. It could easily have led to the acceptance of the more militarily powerful religious cultures of the time, Christianity and Islam. Finally, the Holocaust was followed by the creation of the State of Israel and, hopefully, by a greater awareness of the importance and preciousness of every single Jewish soul.

It is important to stress here, and not to misunderstand, that these developments in no way justified or paid for the tragedies that preceded them. They were, however, pivotal departures from the former norm that Jews found to be meaningful and through which they were able to make positive, significant, and important changes in their way of living in the aftermath of the tragedy. I believe that we survive today, after all the bad things we have experienced, only because of our ability to function in this way.

One last comment before focusing fully on answering the "why" questions. There are those who say that the inadequacy of the answers Judaism offers for these questions caused them to leave their faith. "How can I be Jewish or believe in God after the Holocaust?" is the usual refrain for such decisions.

I must admit to never having understood this conclusion. If God does not exist, does the problem get any easier? Indeed, it seems to me to get harder, at least in an emotional sense. With God in the equation, the possibility of an explanation exists. Without God, we have an uncaring universe. Everything that occurs is random and without purpose. Is that really a better or more satisfying answer? At least when we acknowledge the existence of God, there is some address at which to hurl the challenge, and one can demand an explanation even if it is not immediately forthcoming. Without God one can shake one's fist at the sky and rail at the heavens, but no one and nothing is there to hear.

"Why?" Some would say that the only possible response is "because." Fortunately, Jewish tradition provides other answers—and they are, thankfully, often quite a bit more emotionally satisfying.

Actually, there are many Jewish answers, and we will be able to survey only a few. The presence of many suggested solutions, tells us that no one approach is sufficient to cover all situations. However, a mosaic made up of all the theories may touch most human circumstances with at least one response that will be meaningful to each particular situation. For those ultimately painful events still not covered, at least the search for proper closure continues. In fact, because any tragedy is experienced individually, one's own answer may require a personal quest that can take many years before one fully resolves the challenge that life has presented. Perhaps the quest alone is valuable and may, in itself, be a part of the ultimate resolution.

Why is there evil in the world? Some possible suggestions:

1. *Evil is a response to sin.*[16] Certainly, the Bible takes this approach over and over again.[17] Moderns are often uncomfortable with this explanation. We don't like to deal with terms like "sin," preferring psychological rationalizations that explain away what we have done wrong. However, God's providence and His justice are still operative principles in the Creator's running of the universe.

On the other hand, those who facilely explain a specific tragedy involving other people as being the result of a specific sin (as in the claim that a terrible bus crash in an Israeli town was caused by the prior opening of a movie theater on Friday nights in that same town) are misusing the concept. That is, unless they can show that God speaks to them and explains completely His reasons for doing the things He does.

Nonetheless, as a self-explanatory tool this can be very useful. Our literature advises examination of one's own deeds as a first approach to tragedy.[18] This is not a call to wallow in guilt, but if we can find a connection between our actions and the things that have happened, we can use this as a springboard for self-exploration, for change and for living meaningfully against the tragedy.

It is important to note that the call for self-examination comes with recognition from as early as Talmudic times that it may not yield a satisfactory or complete answer.[19] This opens the door to other responses, including those listed below.

2. *Most, if not all evil, is the result of acts by human beings.*[20] God grants us free will.[21] In fact, without free will we would not be human.[22] Absent free will God would be a puppeteer pulling our strings and not a true God or king. Evil is the price paid for human freedom.

3. *Existence is only possible because God, as it were, limited Himself and allowed room for the world to come into being.* This limitation of God's presence (however we understand it) creates evil.[23] While this mystical formulation seems to be a metaphysical expansion of approach number 2, it is really much more far-reaching and profound.

All evil can be understood as a limitation of some kind. Our knowledge and technology are limited, so we cannot find every medical cure or predict every natural disaster. This leads to tragedy. Our moral capacity and decision-making ability are often terribly limited. Many evils come from this limitation. Sometimes the limitation that causes the evil is simply living in a certain time, a certain place, or a certain way. Being born today as an average citizen in Ethiopia brings with it evil and tragedy that are not incurred by being born in the United States or Israel. Similarly, I will never sing solo in Carnegie Hall because I was not born with the talent to do so. For some, people such a limitation may be a real palpable evil.

In any case, the act of divine limitation creates challenges in this world. However, it is also, perhaps surprisingly, an act of love. All love is limitation. To love a spouse is to make room for that person in one's life. One must compromise on many things from important life decisions, to perhaps being unable to get into the bathroom whenever one wants in order to sustain a relationship.

Loving a child, in particular, is an almost daily act of self-limitation by parents. As the child grows, he or she needs more room for his or her personality to emerge and to develop his or her own life. Eventually parents find themselves in full retreat.[24] However, if the child is to become an adult he or she must leave the nest and fly on his or her own.[25]

Basing themselves on these understandings of the metaphor of God's act of self-limitation in creating the universe, the mystics view tragedy as both an act of evil and also as an act of love. As a father or mother must allow a toddler to skin a knee if the toddler is to grow up, we, too, find our knees bruised or far worse. God's love allows Him to hold back his intervention so that we can live our own lives and not be overwhelmed by His presence.

4. *When all things are considered, this is really the best of all possible worlds.*[26] While momentary aberrations may appear, a long-term view finds just and appropriate outcomes almost everywhere. The few discrepancies that remain unexplained reflect situations where our knowledge of all the circumstances is incomplete.

5. *Evil presents a challenge for human beings to meet in this world.* The next world will redress any shortcomings in appropriate reward and punishment that occur in this life. However, it will lack the great challenge and satisfaction of transforming evil into good.[27]

6. *Evil is an affliction of love that purifies us from the sins we have*

committed in this world.[28] In doing so it increases our reward in the next world and serves as a mechanism for a degree of personal and even (when visited on Jewry as a whole) national growth that would not otherwise be achievable·

7. *Occasionally, as punishment for our collective sins, God hides His face from us.*[29] When this occurs we perceive the world as a series of random occurrences. These "natural" processes can create tragedies. Nonetheless each event has a purpose and is part of God's plan.[30]

As indicated the foregoing list is not meant to be comprehensive, only representative.

Finally, to conclude the discussion of theodicy, we must take up the Book of Job. To my mind, its challenging presence in the Bible is one of the most powerful indications that our holy book is divinely inspired. No man-made corpus, certainly not one created in the ancient world, would contain a work so overtly at odds with its God and its basic philosophy, at least as one reads superficially through most of the rest of the Bible.[31] Yet the Bible would be incomplete without it. It would not adequately represent the breadth of human experience without this book.[32] Job's presence validates the belief that a higher power's words and inspiration can be found in our most holy texts precisely because the challenge it poses is so disconcerting and so real.

There are many opinions as to the meaning of the Book of Job.[33] I add my hand here, first because Job is so important a part of the Bible and of our subject, and second because, having taught the book for seven years as part of my synagogue's adult education institute, I hope to have something valuable to contribute.

Job is both a complex and a fascinating study.

As indicated, Job is the enemy of the usual biblical formulation of how the world operates. Even his Hebrew name,

Iyov, sounds suspiciously like *oyev*, meaning "enemy" (both words are made up of the same Hebrew letters).

Iyov is a wonderful man.[34] The description of his piety far exceeds even the nice things the Bible has to say about such heroes as our patriarchs or Moses.[35] Job lives his pious life to the hilt, even offering weekly sacrifices in case his children,[36] who seem quite nice themselves,[37] have inadvertently blasphemed against God.

Meanwhile, God's independent prosecutor (referred to in the book as "the satanic angel," not as a personage named Satan) appears in heaven and reports that he has visited the whole world.[38] I understand this to mean that the angel is reporting on having found moral outrages everywhere.[39]

Implicit in this is the demand that God exact justice.[40] God responds by holding Iyov and his righteousness up as the world's redeeming social feature.[41] The angel, as he is tasked from creation to do, challenges Job's piety,[42] attributing it to the fact that Job has only experienced God's bounty and has been protected from tragedy.[43] "Remove that protection," argues Satan "and he will sin against you big time."[44]

Compelled by this logic, God, in two stages, allows multiple tragedies and afflictions to descend on Job.[45] Between the two stages God rails at the angel in a remarkable verse, saying, "You have seduced me into swallowing Job alive for no good reason."[46] The verse is shocking,[47] but it is essential for the book to make sense.

The answer to the "whys" of Job's afflictions is already present in this summary of the first two chapters. God has set up a system. In it there is an investigator/prosecutor. His task is to prosecute and challenge. With the world in terrible shape morally, punishment must follow if God is going to remain true to His system.

However, an out presents itself in Job's piety. His merit protects the world. But the angel, by the nature of the task and the rules set down by God, must challenge, and so Job, through no fault of his own, suffers.

The rest of the book is Job's search for "why." He demands a debate with God, interestingly with God, himself, serving as arbiter as well.[48] Job's friends assume that Job has sinned (they are, presumably, unaware of the heavenly dynamic). Job refuses to accept this explanation asserting that he doesn't deserve the tragedy that has befallen him. (I often wonder if in fact he knows what has happened in heaven.) He seeks a deeper and different explanation of why he must be a victim. Assuming he knows what has transpired in heaven, he is seeking to understand why this dynamic has caused him pain. Even if he does not know the heavenly story, he will receive an answer to this question at the end of the book that will help him to understand that other dynamics than the one described in Deuteronomy are operative in God's universe.

Finally, Job is given an answer. God explains that the rules which have caught him in their web were set down at creation.[49] Job was not there, nor does he have anything near the breadth of knowledge and understanding to fathom their whys and wherefores.

Many people stop here and see this final answer as a call to faith.[50] To me that denies the power of the book. Job demands an answer and seems entitled to one that does not beg the question.

I believe that God tells Job more than just the fact that he was not there at the beginning and therefore does not and cannot understand. Job is also told about the animals and plants that live by God's largess and love.[51] This is part of God's message precisely because it is the most direct answer to Job's question.

God is telling Job that he and all human beings could live in a universe where life was a product only of God's benevolence. In such a world there would be no primordial rules, no laws of universal functioning to explore, to question, or to answer. If that were true, human beings would be no different than animals. Further, if God's reward and punishment followed immediately and in direct proportion to our actions, we would be Pavlovian animals whose behavior was the result of training and largely dependent on immediate rewards and punishments.

However, we are part of something much larger. If we are to be human beings, rational, eternal laws must hold sway. It is only in such a universe that man's finest features—his intellect, his reason, even his moral judgment can function.[52] God is not just a God of benevolence and power. He is primarily a God of laws. Even if His laws cause pain at times, and even if the pain seems unfair, those tragedies are justified by the greater value of a universe made accessible to human reason. In other words, law is ultimately more important than benevolence.

As such, Job's pain is part of the divine plan. So, too, all human suffering. Even if we cannot find a reason here and now for the pain we suffer, the rationality of the universe promises that a reason does exist and can be known in the fullness of time. Especially when one accepts the possibility that the reason may not relate to strict reward and punishment, but may involve other dynamics as well, one may well find the closure one seeks. With searching and investigation, proper understanding may become accessible to the one who searches for it.

Job is ultimately consoled by this.[53] Job has now had the interaction with the Almighty that he sought, and has had God's decisions sufficiently explained to him so that his problem is resolved internally. A corresponding resolution of his existential situation follows, for all that he lost, and more, is restored to him.[54]

Perhaps simply knowing that his suffering is part of God's plan and that it derives from God's underlying structure of the universe is enough. This knowledge gives the tragedy a purpose and a meaning. When people find purpose and meaning that is larger than themselves in an encounter with evil, their personal philosophical struggle will likely diminish or end—and end satisfactorily, in the sense that what they have gone through, even the bad, will be seen by them to have served a larger calling.

1. There is a great deal of literature on the subject. Two studies of interest are Anson Laytner, *Arguing with God* (Northvale, N.J., 1990) and David Birnbaum, *God and Evil* (Hoboken, N.J., 1989).

2. Genesis 18:25.

3. Jeremiah 12:1.

4. Exodus 33:18; see Exodus Rabbah 45:5.

5. Deuteronomy 11:14.

6. Not all scholars read Job this way (cf. Maimonides, *Guide for the Perplexed* 3:22), but I do because of the long description of his positive qualities in Job 1:1, 8, and 2:3. No other biblical character is credited with so many positive attributes.

7. Most well-known is in the work of Elisabeth Kübler-Ross; see her *On Death and Dying* (New York, 1993).

8. See Maurice Lamm, *The Jewish Way in Death and Mourning* (New York, 1969); Jack Riemer, *Jewish Reflections on Death* (New York, 1974).

9. *Shulhan Arukh*, Yoreh De'ah 340.

10. Lamm, *The Jewish Way in Death and Mourning*, p. 64.

11. Ibid., p. 111; *Shulhan Arukh*, Yoreh De'ah 387.

12. Lamm, *The Jewish Way in Death and Mourning*, p. 111.

13. Ibid., p. 153.

14. This was the approach of my teacher of blessed memory, Rabbi Joseph Dov Soloveitchik. See his *Kol Dodi Dofek* (Jerusalem, 1976; English trans., 2000), and see Shalom Carmy, *Jewish Perspectives on the Experience of Suffering* (New York, 1999).

15. See Yoma 9b, 69b and J. D. Eisenstein, *Otzar Yisrael*, s.v. *avodah zarah*.

16. This is a central theme of the holiday Musaf prayers, which read,

"Because of our sins we were exiled from our country." Birnbaum, *God and Evil*, p. 613.

17. The historical books from Joshua to Kings repeatedly take this approach.

18. Berakhot 5a.

19. Ibid.

20. Maimonides appears to take this position; see *Guide for the Perplexed* 3:10–12 and *Mishneh Torah*, Hilkhot Teshuvah 5:1–4.

21. Berakhot 33b, et passim.

22. Maimonides, *Shemonah Perakim*, chap. 8.

23. See the discussion of mysticism in Chapter 16.

24. Sotah 49a.

25. Genesis 2:24.

26. I find this to be the approach of Saadiah Gaon (882–942); see his *Emunot ve-De'ot*, chaps. 4–5, 9. The phrase "best of all possible worlds" is most closely associated with Gottfried Wilhelm Leibnitz (1646–1716). See also Paul Weiss, "God, Job and Evil," in *The Dimensions of Job*, ed. Nahum Glatzer (New York, 1969), p. 193.

27. Avot 4:17. I find this to be perhaps the most profound comment in all of rabbinic literature. Many religious belief systems assume that life in the next world is dramatically superior to life in this world. But it is virtually unheard of to see this world as better than the next in any way. For Judaism this world does have this element of superiority, and, therefore, while we are here we are to keep focused on the tasks of this world.

28. Berakhot 5a. For some of the different approaches to the concept, see Bahya ben Asher ben Hlava; Rabbenu Bahya to Exodus 5:22; Meir Loeb Malbim, Commentary to Proverbs 3:11; Rashi, Berakhot 5a, s.v. *yisurin shel ahavah*; Menahem Meiri, Commentary to Avot 4:19; Jacob Joshua ben Zevi Hirsch, *Penei Yehoshuah*, Berakhot 5a; Isaiah Horowitz, *Shenei Luhot ha-Berit*, Be-Asarah Ma'amarot 5; and Nissim ben Reuben Gerondi, *Derashot ha-Ran* 10.

29. Deuteronomy 31:18.

30. For presentations of this approach, see Rashi, Hullin 139b, s.v. *le-ma'aseh ester*; Meir Simhah ha-Kohen of Dvinsk, *Meshekh Hokhmah*, Deuteronomy 31:17; Yitzhak Isaac Chaber, *Sefer Beit Olamim*, 137a.

31. For example, Job clearly challenges the passage on reward and punishment recited in the daily statement of our faith, the Shema, Deuteronomy 11:13–21, esp. vv. 14–17.

32. Interestingly, there is no indication in rabbinic literature that anyone ever challenged Job's place in the canon in the way that some other books were challenged. See above, Chapter 2.

33. N. Glatzer, *Dimensions of Job* (New York, 1969) presents some thirty-two different approaches to the book.

34. Job 1:1.

35. Job is described with four terms of praise; no other biblical character receives more than one or at most two.

36. Job 1:5.

37. Job 1:4.

38. Job 1:7.

39. I assume that the satanic angel goes where there is evil to be found. This reading is supported by God's response in the next verse and by Job's cataloguing of the world's evils in chap. 24.

40. This is the assumption of the source from Deuteronomy cited in n. 31.

41. Job 1:8.

42. The satanic angel fulfills this role in several places in the Bible; e.g., Zechariah 3:1, I Chronicles:21:1.

43. Job 1:9–10.

44. Job 1:11.

45. Job 1:12–19 and 2:7.

46. Job 2:3

47. See R. Yohanan's comment in Bava Batra 16a.

48. See Laytner, op. cit.

49. Job Chap. 38 ff.

50. Glatzer has an entire section entitled "Job as a Lesson in Faith" that includes six different articles.

51. Cf. Job 38:25-27.

52. Cf. Job 39:26–40:2, 40:13–15, 42:1–5. See also Elihu's comments to Job, which say the same thing, Job chaps. 32–37 especially chaps. 36–37.

53. Job 42:1–5.

54. Job 42:10–16.

Chapter 7
Teshuvah

We know that the law is spiritual; but I am not: I am unspiritual, the purchased slave of sin. I do not even acknowledge my own actions as mine, for what I do is not what I want to do, but what I detest. But if what I do is against my will, it means that I agree with the law and hold it to be admirable. But as things are, it is no longer I who perform the action, but the sin that lodges in me. For I know that nothing good lodges in me—in my unspiritual nature, I mean—for though the will to do good is there, the deed is not. The good which I want to do, I fail to do; but what I do is the wrong which is against my will; and if what I do is against my will, clearly it is no longer I who am the agent, but sin that has its lodging in me.

I discover this principle, then: that when I want to do the right, only the wrong is within my reach. In my inmost self I delight in the law of God, but I perceive that there is in my bodily members a different law, fighting against the law that my reason approves and making me a prisoner under the law that is in my members, the law of sin. Miserable creature that I am, who is there to rescue me out of this body doomed to death?[1]

When I as a Jew read this passage from the Christian Bible, I want to reach out and yank Paul, the author, by his lapels and say one word, "teshuvah." From my perspective, Paul has simply missed this most important of Jewish principles, that of the capacity for and power of repentance.

The process of teshuvah (repentance and return) is a very simple one to describe, though it can be very difficult to accomplish.[2] It is presented differently by different scholars,[3] but there are certain basic elements that must be there for it to succeed. We begin by owning our own actions and taking responsibility for them.[4] A sense of regret over past misdeeds will naturally emerge as we accept personal responsibility.[5] This will evoke an admission of guilt, which must be expressed out loud and in detail to God.[6] If we have wronged another human being, we need to make restitution and offer apology to him or to her.[7] In such a circumstance or even if the matter involves only ourselves and God, we may need to make significant alterations in our lifestyles and behavior to avoid repetition of the sin.[8] Finally, the penitent must firmly resolve never to engage in these negative activities again.[9]

Ultimately, the process allows you to see yourself as, in effect, a new person ready to start over again. Maimonides (1138–1204) describes complete repentance as being back in the same situation but this time resisting the same temptation to sin.[10] While repentance can be performed without this,[11] and while it often may not be advisable or possible to experience this test, it is nonetheless true that if you successfully pass through such a moment of truth, you will, once and for all, know that you have reached a very different and much more positive place in your life. You will not need to endure the spiritual and existential angst that Paul describes in his heart-rending outpouring of guilt cited here. Even without Maimonides' test, we have God's promise that the honest returnee will find a home with God,[12] and, therefore that one can feel confident that one is not eternally or fundamentally flawed.

I have encountered a second example of the same divergence between the Jewish and Christian understandings of the capacity for personal repentance on the rare occasions when I have been approached by evangelical Christians interested in challenging my Jewish beliefs. Their opening question often follows these lines, "Doesn't the Bible require an atonement sacrifice for the removal of sins?[13] How then can you achieve atonement now that the Temple is gone?" The intent, of course, is to present Jesus as the replacement for the atonement sacrifice.[14]

Though I would rather not be bothered with these attempts to convert me, answering the question is not very difficult. The Bible tells us that "we can pay for the bulls with our lips."[15] This means that prayer can and does substitute for sacrifice. Further, many sacrifices other than atonement offerings are biblically required,[16] and these, too, can no longer be offered. Yet we continue to function. Christianity does not claim to offer a replacement for these offerings.

However, a more profound answer is also available. The Bible tells us over and over again that God is not interested, ultimately, in sacrifices. They are required when the Temple is standing, but their purpose is to spark the offering of oneself to God through repentance and renewed commitment.[17]

This is the crucial point, and it begins with the Jewish attitude on what it means to be human.[18] Judaism takes a positive, optimistic view of mankind. It has an unshakable faith that all, except perhaps those who have led ultimately evil lives or those with mental impairment (who are not culpable), have the capacity to transform themselves through repentance.[19] Critically essential to this process, and despite many important outside influences on it, are one's own actions, one's own self-inspired transformation. No outside factor is necessary for that repentance, and no outside factor can grant absolution. My teshuvah is the key.[20]

The same is true on a smaller scale when one is repenting not the entire direction of one's life, but the all-too-common

everyday transgressions that come from carelessness and negligence. Again, it is up to the one who committed the negative
acts to repent and make amends.[21]

The power of the act of repentance is truly remarkable.
While some scientific theories and some philosophical belief
systems posit that the future is determined and therefore that
it cannot be changed, Judaism teaches that through teshuvah
even the past can be recreated. The Talmud tells us that repentance motivated by fear (for example, fear of punishment) will
erase past misdeeds. However, "if one's repentance comes out
of love of God, then the wrong actions of the past will be considered as positive acts."[22] In the case of repentance out of
love, the transgression and what one learned from the history
and experience of the misdeed must have played a part in the
eventual transformation. In fact, the change might not have
occurred unless the wrongdoing had preceded it. For this reason, the sin is redeemed by the repentance that follows from it
and ultimately counts in God's economy as a good act.

It is no wonder that our sources see teshuvah as necessary
for the world to survive.[23] Without it the sins of the past would
weigh us down, as they did Paul. Also, all the wrongdoing
that anyone did would remain forever unrecompensed. With
teshuvah there is the opportunity for a clean slate.

This process can take a very long time or can happen virtually instantaneously. Occasionally, people will agonize over a
life change for years. In other situations a single event or a single moment can be the catalyst for a total transformation.
Pragmatically, if we are talking about a lifestyle change, it is
usually psychologically healthier to make the alterations slowly and gradually. Our minds need to develop new psychic
structure to integrate the changed reality in which we now live
so that we can make ourselves comfortable in it.

There are far too many people who, having been exposed to

Sabbath observance, precipitously decide to keep Shabbat. As they have not gradually become familiar with the practices of the holy day, they run out of appropriate activities by early Saturday afternoon on their first attempt at observing the Sabbath and sit for hours doing nothing, waiting for the day to be over. Often, this can lead them to abandon the enterprise of observance completely. They would have been far better served by taking on the Sabbath obligations gradually.

The Talmud credits three different people with being the first Jew to initiate teshuvah.[24] They are Reuben, Judah, and David.[25] Further analysis shows that these three followed very different paths in their repentance. Reuben is pictured as continuously "in his sackcloth and ashes," Judah admits his sin very publicly once, in no uncertain terms, and never seems to return to it, David spends much time on his teshuvah but seems to want to bring it to an end.[26]

Some of our medieval authorities parallel these three in their respective philosophies of repentance. Jonah ben Abraham Gerondi (Rabbenu Yohah, 1200–1263) speaks of repentance as a continuing process and holds that it is appropriately done as ongoing activity.[27] Maimonides (Ramban), on the other hand, boils the teshuvah process down to the moment of confession.[28] While he recognizes other methodologies and elements,[29] the single act of confession, or *viddui*, dominates Maimonides' version of the return from sin. Other scholars, such as Sa'adiah Gaon (882–942) and Bahya Ibn Paquda (11th cent.), speak of a completable process of teshuvah.[30] Their description of the process has a beginning, a middle, and an end. It is longer than Maimonides' version and shorter than Rabbenu Yonah's. Reuben, who repented forever, Judah, who did penitence in a moment, and David, who took some time for the process but sought an end to it, appear, respectively, in Rabbenu Yonah, Rambam, and Sa'adiah/Bahya.

At the end of our brief discussion, it is clear that every step of the process is profoundly individual. No single blueprint exists for return, repentance, transformation, or repair of misdeeds. Only one thing is universal: our belief that with desire and effort we can change ourselves for the better. Some outside the Jewish world deny this capacity. For us it is central to who we are and how we view the world and our place in it.

1. Romans 7:14–24.

2. Some suggestions for reading on this subject are R. Joseph Soloveitchik, *On Repentance* (Jerusalem, 1980); Abraham Isaac Kook, *Rabbi Kook's Philosophy of Repentance* (New York, 1968); Yehoshua Blau, "Creative Repentance: On Rabbi Soloveitchik's Concept of Teshuvah," *Tradition* 28:2 (1994), 11–18; Pinchas Peli, "Repentant Man: A High Level in Rabbi Soloveitchik's Typology of Man," *Tradition* 18:2 (1980), 135–159; and Michael Wyschogrod, "Sin and Atonement in Judaism," in *The Human Condition in the Jewish and Christian Tradition* (Northvale, N.J., 1986), pp. 103–128, among many others.

3. Compare Maimonides, *Mishneh Torah*, Hilkhot Teshuvah 1:1 and 2:2, with the chapter headings in Rabbenu Yonah of Gerona's *Sha'arei Teshuvah*, and with the section on teshuvah in Bahya Ibn Paquda's *Hovot ha-Levavot*. The process is described differently in each, but the purpose and outcome are the same.

4. Maimonides, Hilkhot Teshuvah 1:1.

5. *Hovot ha-Levavot*, Sha'ar ha-Teshuvah 4. This is called *harata* in Hebrew.

6. Maimonides and Bahya, ad loc. This is called *viddui*. Maimonides focuses on this in the first paragraph of his discussion of teshuvah, Bahya presents it third.

7. Maimonides, Hilkhot Teshuvah 2:9. Setting things right only with God is not enough.

8. Ibid. 2:1, See also Rabbenu Yonah's *ikrei ha-teshuvah* (root principles of repentance) discussed throughout the first section of Sha'arei Teshuvah.

9. Maimonides, Hilkhot Teshuvah 2:1; Bahya and R. Yonah, ad loc. This is called *kabbalah*.

10. Maimonides, loc. cit.

11. Ibid. 2:2.

12. Deuteronomy 30:1–10.

13. Presumably this is a reference to the Yom Kippur (Day of Atonement) sacrifice described in Leviticus 16; note the Christian Bible's reference to that annual sacrifice in Hebrews 9:26.

14. Hebrews 9:23–28.

15. Hosea 14:3.

16. See generally Leviticus and Numbers.

17. Cf. 1 Samuel 15:22–23. Interestingly, the same sentiment appears in the Christian Bible, Mark 12:33.

18. See above, Chapter 5.

19. The Pharaoh of the Exodus appears to have had his capacity for repentance taken away when God repeatedly hardened his heart. Exodus, chaps. 7–14

20. See generally Maimonides, Hilkhot Teshuvah, esp. 1:3, 2:2.

21. Ibid 1:1.

22. Yoma 86b.

23. See A. Cohen, *Everyman's Talmud* (New York, 1949), p. 104, for this conclusion and for the sources that he sees as supporting it.

24. Cain appears to have been the first human being to repent, Leviticus Rabbah 10:5.

25. Reuben: Genesis Rabbah 82:11 and 84:19; Judah: Sotah 7b; David: Mo'ed Katan 16b (see Rashi, s.v. *sheheikim*).

26. Reuben: Genesis Rabbah 84:19, Targum Jonathan to Genesis 37:24, Midrash ha-Gadol to Deuteronomy 100.26; Judah: Genesis 38:26, see also Exodus Rabbah 30:19; David: Sanhedrin 107a, Shabbat 30a, Midrash on Psalms 17:2.

27. Cf. Sha'arei Teshuvah, Gate I, secs. 15–17.

28. Hilkhot Teshuvah 1:1.

29. Ibid. 2:4.

30. Saadiah Gaon, *Emunot ve-De'ot* 5:5; Bahya, *Hovot ha-Levavot*, loc. cit.

Chapter 8
Gentiles

In Jewish thought there are two categories of Gentiles: idolators and Noahides (who are sometimes also called Righteous Gentiles and who qualify as resident aliens in a Jewish state were it to be run according to Halakhah (Jewish Law). In our discussion of the afterlife,[1] we will mention the talmudic teaching that righteous gentiles have a share in the world-to-come.[2] As opposed to idolaters, righteous gentiles are non-Jews who live by the seven Noahide laws.[3] What those laws consist of and how they affect both the gentile world and Jewish relationships with that world are the subjects of this chapter.[4]

We begin with a modern cultural conundrum. As society has accepted the values of diversity, multiculturalism and tolerance, it has downplayed, and perhaps done away with, the goal of the melting pot. For a long time, American society envisioned all the different strains of our population—racial, ethnic, religious, and so on—melting together into one consistent culture. This vision has come to be seen as insensitive to minorities, because their identities tend to get lost in the cultural melding.

While tolerance and appreciation of diversity seem like good values, these ideals also evoke a very serious concern. Any society, no matter how diverse, must have some shared ethical principles if it is to survive. Where can the cultural similarity be found in the emphasis on diversity?

Judaism handles the problem of unity within diversity by means of the 613/7 solution. By Torah law, Jews are required to keep 613 commandments.[5] However, non-Jews are only required to keep seven basic societal laws. This leaves great room for diversity, for in the remaining 606 laws that are not applicable, non-Jews are essentially free to choose their own way (which may, but need not correspond to Judaism's).

To be fair, this is an oversimplification. Many scholars read the seven laws expansively, seeing them as principles encompassing general categories of law and thus drawing in other requirements.[6] However, even the most expansive reading of the seven does not impose anywhere near 613 obligations on a gentile.[7] This leaves plenty of room for diversity once one gets beyond the fundamental unity.

What are the seven commandments, and where do they come from? The Noahide code consists of the following seven laws:

1. Not to kill
2. Not to steal
3. Not to engage in sexual immorality
4. Not to eat meat taken from a live animal, but to kill the animal first
5. Not to engage in idolatry
6. Not to curse God
7. To create a court system for legal redress[8]

Some of these need additional explanation. The fourth law, which obviously touches on cruel treatment of animals, makes commitment to this value something of an economic burden. Primitive tribes would make their animals into a replenishable food source through a practice almost too painful to describe. By removing a portion of the animal's flank and using it for food, one could leave the animal to heal and then repeat the process. This could be done several times in an animal's lifetime. The Noahide code prohibits this procedure, and thereby makes the eating of meat much more expensive, as it entails the death of the animal. In so doing, this law teaches that material concerns are secondary to avoiding cruelty—even if the cruelty is only to animals.

The seventh commandment is seen by some as requiring much more than a court system. Obviously, it would be difficult to run any society using only these seven laws. Some, therefore, including Rabbi Moses Nachmanides (1194–1270), also known as Ramban, the great Spanish philosopher and biblical exegete, see this requirement as including the imperative for gentile society to create other laws of its own that would allow it to function in a just and moral way.[9]

Finally, even the prohibition against idolatry needs explaining. The pagan idolatry of the Bible, with its human sacrifice,[10] bodily mutilation,[11] and fertility rituals,[12] was unalterably objectionable on many, many levels.[13]

Maimonides presents a somewhat different criterion for idolatry. For him, it was the belief in multiple gods that defined an idolater.[14] Thus a true monotheist is not included in this category. On this basis, Maimonides, and others, declared that Islam was not idolatrous.[15] Other authorities made a similar determination about Christianity.[16] This is particularly true because that religion has moved from more trinitarian expressions, which saw the father deity, the son deity, and the spirit deity as three separate entities, to more unitarian expressions that see all three as different manifestations of the same single God. Over the centuries, the unitarian approach has come to be the dominant Christian understanding of the Godhead. This latter approach is not entirely dis-similar to our understanding of God as sometimes manifesting Himself from within His aspect of mercy, and other times from within His aspect of justice.[17]

Understanding the difference in Jewish law between a Noahide, or righteous gentile, and an idolater is critical, and not just for entry into the world-to-come. Non-Noahides are suspected of engaging in murder, theft, and immorality.[18] We are, therefore, subject by Jewish law to impose serious limita-tions on our business dealings with such individuals, and on our relations with them in other areas of social inter-course.[19]This would obviously create hardships for Jews living in countries where the dominant culture was idolatrous.

On the other hand, Noahides are to be embraced.[20] We are commanded to sustain and help them.[21] Maimonides expects us to advantage Noahides to a small but significant degree in their business dealings with Jews. Thus, he requires that their laws be followed in our financial dealings with them when they are a minority population living under Jewish majority rule.[22]

The origin of these seven laws (and therefore their name) come from the verses in the Bible that describe God's first com-munication with Noah and his family after they leave the ark.[23] The seven laws are found in the Torah text as analyzed by the Rabbis.[24] Presumably, they are God's prescribed pro-phylactic against the world collapsing into the type of moral chaos that existed before the coming of the flood. Maimonides certainly takes this view of the seven laws.[25]

According to midrash, Adam, too, was given six of the seven laws (the law protecting animals would not have been applicable because Adam was prohibited from consuming meat).[26] This approach takes the view that human beings can-not survive without some structure of laws to guide them.

Intriguingly, there are people today living consciously as and calling themselves Noahides, some in groups and some as individuals.[27] I have one in my neighborhood. His frequent questions about Noahide law have taken me into a new area of Halakhah that I never thought I would enter and have expanded my own knowledge and interest in this subject.

1. Chap. 18.

2. Cf. Tosefta Sanhedrin 13:2. Maimonides codifies this opinion in *Mishneh Torah*, Hilkhot Teshuvah 3:5.

3. For further discussion, see Joseph Munk, "Non-Jews in the Light of Halakhah," *Le'ela* 37 (1994), pp. 27–32; Yehudah Levi, "Israel and the Nations of the World," in *Encounter: Essays on Torah and Modern Life*, ed. H. Chaim Schimmel and Aryeh Carmell (Jerusalem, 1989), pp. 41–44; Dov Frimer, "Israel, the Noahide Laws and Maimonides: Jewish-Gentile Legal Relations in Maimonidean Thought, *Jewish Law Association Studies* 2 (1986), pp. 89–102; Nahum Rakover, "The Law and the Noahides," *Jewish Law Association Studies* 4 (1990), pp. 169–180; Michael Wyschogrod, "The Law, Jews and Gentiles: A Jewish Perspective," *Lutheran Quarterly* 21 (1969), pp. 405–415.

4. For the fullest discussion of these laws, see Aaron Lichtenstein, *The Seven Laws of Noah* (New York, 1981). See also *Encyclopedia Talmudit*, s.v. *ben noah* and s.v. *ger toshav*, and the discussion at the end of the latter section about the requirements for acceptance of such an individual by a Jewish court before the Noahide designation may apply. This section discusses the applicability and scope of the designation "Noahide" today. Since the biblical Jubilee year (Yovel), which occurs according to the Bible every half-century, is inoperative in our reality, acceptance of righteous gentiles may also be halakhically inoperative. There are scholars who offer solutions to the problem.

5. The number 613 is somewhat problematic, as it is based on a midrash, Makkot 23b–24a, that both Maimonides and Judah Halevi openly disagree with. Nonetheless the idea that there are 613 biblical commandments has become sacrosanct, and all listings of the commandments, including Maimonides' presentation of them accept it, even as they differ on what is to be included and excluded in that number. See Aheron Kahan, *The Taryag Mitsvos*, (New York, 1987); H. Lipkin, *Taryag Mitzvot* (1962–1967); and A. Rabinowitz, *Taryag* (Jerusalem, 1967).

6. Cf. Lichtenstein, *Seven Laws of Noah*, introduction and conclusion.

7. Lichtenstein finds something in the neighborhood of 65 of the 613 laws as being applicable to non-Jews.

8. See either Lichtenstein or *Encyclopedia Talmudit*, loc.cit.

9. Nachmanides, commentary to Genesis 34:13.

10. Leviticus 20:2, Deuteronomy 12:31.

11. Leviticus 21:5; Maimonides, *Mishneh Torah*, Hilkhot Avodat Kokhavim 12:13.

12. Deuteronomy 23:18

13. Maimonides describes the "great error" of idolatry in Hilkhot Avodat Kokhavim 1:1–3.

14. Maimonides, Hilkhot Avodat Kokhavim 2:1 and *Guide for the Perplexed* 3:29, 32.

15. Joseph Caro, *Bet Yosef*, Yoreh De'ah 124 and 146; Rema, Yoreh De'ah 146:5; Maimonides, *Mishneh Torah*, Hilkhot Ma'akhalot Asurot 11:7.

16. For the fullest treatment, see Jacob Katz, *Exclusiveness and Tolerance: Studies in Jewish-Gentile Relations in Medieval and Modern Times* (Westport, Conn., 1980). From the Jewish perspective, some aspects of Christianity, such as the belief in God's incarnation in a human being and the iconography used by some denominations, seem to touch on idolatry.

17. Cf. Genesis Rabbah 12:15.

18. This assumption is made on the grounds that one who does not accept these laws is suspected of violating them. Moreover, the Rabbis regarded idolatry/paganism as a doctrine that brought out the worst in human beings. There are a number of ways to understand this, but perhaps the simplest is to point out that a belief system that raises animals or pieces of wood and stone above human beings has obviously opened the door to a great deal of human degradation.

19. Cf. *Shulhan Arukh*, Yoreh De'ah 152–156

20. Cf. Maimonides, *Mishneh Torah*, Hilkhot Zekhiyah u-Matanah 3:11.

21. Ibid., Hilkhot Avodat Kokhavim 10:2.

22. Ibid., Hilkhot Melakhim 10:12.

23. Genesis 9:1–4.

24. Sanhedrin 56a ff.

25. Compare Genesis 6:11 and Maimonides, *Mishneh Torah*, Hilkhot Melakhim 10:11.

26. Genesis Rabbah 34:13.

27. For information on these groups and related sources, see Kimberly Hanke, *Turning to Torah: The Emerging Noachide Movement* (Northvale, N.J., 1995); David Davis, *Finding the God of Noah: The Spiritual Journey of a Baptist Minister from Christianity to the Laws of Noah* (Hoboken, N.J., 1996); Yirmeyahu Bindman, *The Seven Colors of the Rainbow: Torah Ethics for Non-Jews* (San Jose, Calif., 1995).

Chapter 9
Israel

The trend in contemporary Western culture has been to downplay any sense of nationalism or of the importance of a strong association with a particular piece of territory.[1] Many factors have contributed to this change that has taken us away from the traditionally very strong connection between land, peoplehood, and personal identity. Among these factors are our urban society, so alienated from land and nature, and rapid air travel, which makes the entire world accessible in a day and in a way that one could not have accomplished in a lifetime in earlier generations. The Internet, which allows for virtually instantaneous communication with anyone, anywhere, as long as they are online, has also helped to diminish the sense of importance associated with any particular place.

Nonetheless, in the face of these powerful trends, traditional Judaism continues to declare a specific corner of the Middle East sacred and precious.[2] This, without regard to centuries of exile from that land and the continuing difficulties of terrorism and neighboring enemies—which remain despite the current peace process. As that process has proceeded, the divide over the importance of land between traditionalists and secularists has played itself out in the debate over the issue of land for peace. In general, traditionalists have opposed trading land for promises of peace, while secularists have supported that policy. Even among those few secularists who oppose the peace process and those few traditionalists who are in favor of it, the attitude toward the land is often less reflective of a political position and far more a matter of religious perspective. If the debate were only theological and not also political and strategic, the traditionalist/secularist divide would be even clearer and more pronounced.

Our task is, then, to investigate the roots of the continuing connection between the traditional Jew and the land of Israel, its implications for the way Jews live their lives, and the effect and meaning of this connection for the observant Jewish community. This is especially important and troubling today because of the many acts of violence taking place in the holy land.

Most discussions of this issue, appropriately, begin with God's promise to Abraham when He called our founding father to his sacred mission: "To your descendants have I given this land."[3] But the promise of Israel is even more far reaching than that. It is part of the blessings and heritage bequeathed by Abraham to Isaac,[4] by Isaac to Jacob,[5] and by Jacob to his children and descendants.[6] Also, it is the "Promised Land" of the Exodus.[7] Most important, it is, after the Jew's relationship with God, the most significant unifying theme and subtext of the Bible, Judaism's central book.

If one were to summarize the story of the Bible from Abraham until the end of the Five Books of Moses in one sentence, that sentence would arguably be, "The history of the Jewish people from the promise that the land of Israel would be theirs, to the moments just before fulfillment of that promise."[8] As for the rest of the Bible, with the exception of the wisdom literature[9] and the psalms,[10] its one-sentence description would be, "The history of the Jews in the land of Israel through the First Temple period, the destruction, the exile, and the return." Essentially, the written Torah ends with the second entry into the land and the rebuilding of the Temple.[11] One's central book, one's defining story, cannot be so focused on a land without that focus having a lasting and profound effect.

After the destruction of the Second Temple, Judaism survived in large measure because of the belief in a Messiah.[12] This belief gave the people the strength to carry on, faithful to their commitment to Judaism, despite terrible acts of persecution.

Although there is significant divergence of opinion as to his ultimate mission and meaning, it was always understood that the Messiah would bring about the return of the Jews to the land of Israel.[13] Each day in the thrice-daily services,[14] each year at the pivotal celebratory points of Yom Kippur[15] and Passover,[16] and throughout the sacred sources of Jewish literature beyond the Bible, such as the Talmud and the Midrash,[17] the theme of the importance of the land appears over and over again.

Our most important thinker in this area was Nachmanides (1194–1270), also known as Ramban, the great Spanish philosopher, kabbalist, and biblical commentator.[18] For Nachmanides, the Torah is the law of the God of the land of Israel. Unlike other thinkers, Nachmanides held that no mitzvah (commandment) could ever truly be fulfilled except in the Holy Land. In his view, the traditional distinction between laws dependent on one's being in the land of Israel and those not dependent on one's location is really a matter of needing commandments while in exile to keep in practice, as it were, for the true fulfillment of all of God's laws once we return to Israel.[19]

Nachmanides also held that the requirement for Jews to live in Israel applies to our time as well as to all past and future eras.[20] True to this belief, he left the affluence and "quality of life" of the Golden Age of Spain for the relative desolation of the Israel of his time.[21] When he reached Jerusalem he discovered that two Jewish clothes dyers were the totality of the permanent Jewish community in the holy city.[22] Through his efforts he managed to revitalize Jewish life in Jerusalem.[23] A copy of a letter to his son describing his work and success can be read on a commemorative monument that stands outside the synagogue he founded during his time in the city.[24] The synagogue still functions as a house of prayer, despite its partial demolition during the Jordanian occupation of 1948–67.[25]

While other medieval scholars did not see *yishuv eretz yisrael* ("settlement in Israel") as a contemporary requirement,[26] and while there are many situations that allow for exceptions to that requirement, such as danger[27] or inability to make a living,[28] even when the imperative is in force, all authorities agree that living in Israel is a positive religious experience and may well fulfill a mitzvah even if an imperative is not in place.[29] The wide circulation and interest in tales of travelers to the Holy Land[30] and the large amount of charitable financial support that messengers from Israel have gathered in diaspora communities throughout the two thousand years of exile[31] indicates that those who visited Israel and those who chose to live in the Holy Land were always viewed as heroes by the Jewish people.

Modern Zionism, though clearly a secular, even at times an anti-religious movement, owes a debt to our religious tradition.[32] Aside from the obvious parallel to the expressed desire of our prayers and Bible for Jews to live as a sovereign people in our homeland, one need only recall the dramatic outcry of protest that swept the nascent Zionist movement when its founder, Theodor Herzl,[33] entertained the suggestion that Uganda might serve as the Jewish homeland instead of Palestine.[34] Even secular Jews could not give up on the ancestral homeland.

The story of secular Zionism is not the subject of this work, but it has clearly been both a remarkable success and an abject failure. Theodor Herzl, the assimilated aristocratic Viennese journalist, was witness to the Dreyfus affair and its attendant antisemitism.[35] Troubled by this phenomenon, Herzl came to the conclusion that anti-Jewish hatred was a result primarily of the Jews' unusual situation in gentile society. Where the German had his country and the Frenchman his, the Jew was a pariah precisely because he lived the life of the perpetual stranger, a person without a country. The "final solution" for the Jews, therefore, was a homeland which would normalize them in the world community.

As part of this dream, Herzl and his followers believed that all Jewish ritual laws and other elements that might serve to alienate us from the family of nations should be eliminated in the new Jewish state. In this way we would become like all others and achieve normalcy. It is important to note that, contrary to the general belief often voiced by Zionists, Herzl never saw his Jewish state as a refuge for Jews in the face of an event like the Holocaust. It was only the occurrence of the Holocaust, long after Herzl's death and before the state's creation, that brought this argument to prominence.

Herzl's dreams achieved remarkable success. His announcement in 1900 that a Jewish state would be a reality within fifty years was the height of hubris and fantasy, given the world situation at that time. In beating the deadline by two years, Herzl proved that "if you will it, it is no dream,"[36] and no amount of revisionism can take that triumph away.

On the other hand, his goal of Jewish normalcy supposedly attendant on creating a Jewish state never became a reality. The Jew and the Jewish state to this day remain international pariahs in far too many circles. The current post-Zionist movement,[37] the active de-judaizing of the state and particularly of the secular school system curriculum in Israel, along with the calls for a new Middle East that have appeared in Israeli political discourse,[38] are a continuation of the desire to be "normal." Despite going far beyond Herzl and the other early secular Zionists, even rejecting and condemning their work, the central thesis is the same. If the Jewish component of the state is eliminated, Israel will be like all the rest, and normalcy, along with a respite from the hatred of the nations of the world, will have been achieved.

While this last desire may be understandable on an emotional level, given our blood-stained history, the process has not been, and will not be, successful. The hatred of Israel in the Arab world is only remotely related to its Jewish character. Instead, its sources are twofold. First, there is the claim by the enemies of Israel that it is illegitimate because it is a European and American incursion into the region which causes untold hardships, human displacement, death, and grief.[39] Second, there exists a tenet of at least some strains of Islam that rejects as defilement any situation in which land once held by Islam returns to the control of non-Muslims. Since Israel was once under Islamic control, the presence of its non-Muslim government is anathema.[40] Whether these can be overcome to create a real and lasting peace is the central question of the peace process, on which no judgment will be passed here. However, the issues as stated have little or nothing to do with the Judaic quality of the state.

Further, and perhaps more importantly, removing the Judaic quality of the state removes much of the rationale for its existence and for people continuing to put their lives on the line to maintain it. After all, why risk the dangers of terrorism and of enemy states potentially armed with weapons of mass destruction to maintain Israel unless there is an ideological component challenging people to make so great a sacrifice? The rate of emigration by secular Israelis from the state is testament to this.[41] So, too, the fact that the only significant aliyah (immigration) to Israel from Western society comes from the observant community indicates this as well.[42]

Measuring Zionism's success against the criterion of the Jewish state being treated as normal forces one to conclude that it is a failure in these terms. So, too, by the test of sustained ideological commitment of secular Zionists to the Zionist ideal, the evidence may well be tending in the wrong direction. By this last measure, only religious Zionists, whose commitment comes from the Bible, Talmud, and Halakhah, seem to get a passing grade.

Mentioning the large number of observant *olim* (Jews who immigrate from the diaspora to Israel) draws us to the question of our tradition and its response to the Zionist movement. When Herzl and his followers first made their appearance on the Jewish scene, the religious establishment was almost universally negative in its reaction to the new movement.[43] Its secular, even anti-observant origins and its vision of a state without religious rituals were enough to engender strong and impassioned opposition, embodied in such works as *Ikvesa de-Meshiha* ("The Epoch of the Messiah") by Rabbi Elchanan Wasserman (1875–1941), one of the most important leaders of the European rabbinic establishment in that period.[44] In addition, this type of political activism was foreign to the experience of Jews in Europe and stood in opposition to the general quietism with which Jews attempted to avoid angering the often hostile majority among whom they lived. This quietism fueled by historical necessity, combined with contemporaneous Jewish religious ideology and the influence of mysticism as then understood, added up to a powerful negative reaction to Zionism and Zionists.[45]

However, a small group of Rabbis, including most notably Rabbi Abraham Isaac HaKohen Kook (1865–1935), the first Ashkenazic chief Rabbi of modern Israel, saw the Zionist movement not only as valuable, but as an important step in the fulfillment of God's ultimate messianic plans. Embodied in organizations such as Bnei Akiva[46] and Mizrachi,[47] these groups and personalities gave ideological expression to religious Zionism. To a very great extent the religious Zionism they founded was the philosophical ancestor of the *kippah serugah* (crocheted kippah) ideology,[48] with its hesder yeshivot,[49] its religious schools and kibbutzim, and its unflagging commitment to "the people of Israel in the land of Israel observing the Torah of Israel."[50]

Important ideological offshoots of this segment of the Jewish community have led to the settler movement,[51] Gush Emunim,[52] and the dramatic contributions of Yeshivat Har Etzion.[53] Though significantly different in some aspects of their ideologies, they all emerged from the same roots.

Contemporary Israel is a cutting edge issue in the debate between more modern and more yeshivish expressions of Orthodoxy.[54] In Israel, it is in fact *the* dividing issue. In short, for many people in Israel, one's attitude toward the state reflects one's ideological place in the Jewish community. Even outside Israel it is an important component in making that determination.

Phrasing the question more succinctly, what is the theological meaning of the creation of the State of Israel (and the Jewish return to Jerusalem) in our day? Jews have prayed for two thousand years at least three times daily and said, "May our eyes behold [the moment] as you return mercifully to Zion."[55] Is the State of Israel, in any way, a fulfillment of that prayer? So, too, we make our frequent request to God that "to Jerusalem Your city may You in mercy return."[56] Again, were the events of 1967 a positive divine reaction to that request?

Responses to questions like these range across the ideological spectrum. On one end, the theology of Satmar/Neturei Karta sees the state as the very opposite of a divine act.[57] For them, the appearance of a Jewish state before the coming of the Messiah is anathema. Basing themselves on a talmudic statement describing two oaths taken by the Jews at God's behest, not to "go up as a wall [i.e., in military formation] to capture the land of Israel" and not to "disobey the gentile nations,"[58] they declare the state and its activities outside the pale and support for its existence essentially heretical.

While most segments of traditional Judaism view this source as a midrash or rabbinic story,[59] and therefore not as halakhically binding, these groups view this talmudic tale as the most essential in all of Jewish religious literature. For them these oaths of God take precedence over all other contradictory sources or events.

In much of the rest of the hasidic or yeshivish world, the presence of many Jews and much Torah learning in any place is significant. The fact that this occurs in the Holy Land is certainly important. However, for this community the judgment of the state depends on the halakhic quality of its leadership.[60] As the government is not made up of people whose fidelity is to Torah, as the policies of the state are not governed by Jewish law, and as the direction of the state, far more often than not, is secularist, accepting the state as a theologically important development is simply impossible. Though some in this group celebrated its birth as a miracle, the reality of its existence has never come close to meeting the potential of that moment for them.

Finally, there are those who continue to see the state as theologically significant. Fueled by the teachings of the aforementioned Rav Kook and Rav Joseph Dov Soloveitchik,[61] who served for decades as president of the American branch of Mizrachi, the Religious Zionists of America, and who frequently proclaimed himself a religious Zionist, this group focuses on the dramatic historic changes represented by the emergence of the state. It sees the process initiated by this historic miracle as, at least, a potential prelude, if not a definite first step, to the final coming of the Messiah.

Further, from a purely Torah perspective, the opportunity that Israel provides, not just for learning, but for practical implementation and further development of halakhic principles, is impossible anywhere else.[62] The computerization of classic Jewish sources, the ongoing analysis of problems that never arise in a state not run by Jews, the expansion of our understanding of the agricultural laws that comes from dealing with them in the only place where they are required to be kept—all this has dramatically expanded the borders of Torah.

In addition, while any traditional Jew ultimately wants a Jewish state run according to halakhic principles, we must also recognize that Halakhah may not have been ready to run a state in 1948. As a diaspora community, we did not face many of the questions that are essential to running a modern country. How does one run a power plant, a hospital, or an army on the Sabbath according to Halakhah? What are the Jewish legal parameters governing foreign relations with countries that murder their citizens in immoral and illegal ways? What is the state's obligation in terms of such things as health care, privacy, and the management of poverty? How much leeway does Halakhah allow for the government to answer these public policy concerns on its own?

Responses to these and many similar questions, both from a halakhic and a technological vantage point, were not available in 1948. Yet it would have been impossible to wait for the answers to be researched before proceeding with establishing the state. Though the answers can be found in Halakhah, many of the questions simply had gone unasked while we were in diaspora. Careful re-exploration of our sources and partnerships between Rabbis and secular experts are necessary for this process to proceed to a successful conclusion.

With the emergence of the state, halakhic thinkers in and out of Israel have begun to analyze these types of questions.

The hope is that the day will come when this newfound legal creativity will link up with a more responsive Israel, and a halakhically run state will emerge. In the meantime, for those on the religious Zionist end of the spectrum, the reality of a Jewish state in the territory promised to Abraham and the reunification of Jerusalem under Jewish control are events that are unquestionably seen as theologically significant answers to our prayers.

A microcosm of this broad spectrum can be seen in the liturgical reaction to Yom ha-Atzma'ut (Israeli Independence Day). In the Jewish community one can find those who fast and say extra penitential prayers (Selihot) on that day.[63] One can also find those who say the normal penitential prayers (Tahanun) and do not either fast or celebrate.[64] There are those who recite the prayers as usual except for the omission of Tahanun.[65] This prayer is omitted for even the most minor of celebrations. Some recite the prayers of praise (Hallel) which appear in the liturgy on days commemorating miraculous events that touch the entire people of Israel, especially those that occur in Israel itself.[66] Some say this Hallel without its blessings,[67] and some say it with the blessings.[68] Some, especially among those in the last category, add other celebratory prayers developed by the Israeli chief rabbinate for the day.[69]

Ending on a personal note, my custom is to recite Hallel with the blessing. Along with my halakhic reasons for doing so, I often imagine my response to God's inquiry if I do the wrong thing on this day. If I do not say Hallel, if I do not say the berakhah, and I am wrong, I presume God will ask me something like this: "You merited to live at a time prayed for and yearned for daily by your ancestors for two thousand years. How could you not respond with words of praise in their fullest expression?" To that question I can imagine no answer.

On the other hand, if saying Hallel and the blessings is wrong, I presume God will want to know why I said an unnecessary blessing or prayer. At least in this case I can respond that I thought I was reacting to God's fulfillment of our prayers.

Finally, we must take note of the talmudic passage that tells us that after miraculously vanquishing the Assyrians who were besieging Jerusalem and threatening to destroy it some twenty-seven hundred and fifty years ago, God desired to make the king of Judah, Hezekiah, the Messiah. God did not do so, says the Talmud, because Hezekiah failed to sing songs of praise in response to the miracle of salvation that occurred at that time.[70] I, for one, do not wish to repeat that mistake today.

1. The literature on this subject is too vast to summarize here. The Harvard University Library online catalogue (Hollis) lists more than three hundred titles in this area. One important thinker in this area is the first chief Rabbi of Israel, Rabbi Abraham Isaac Hakohen Kook. A summary of some of his teachings can be found in D. Samson and T. Fishman, *Eretz Yisrael: The Teachings of HaRav Avraham Yitzchak HaCohen Kook* (Jerusalem, 1996). A powerful statement of the importance of Israel appears in Abraham Joshua Heshel, *Israel: An Echo of Eternity* (New York, 1969). For an important philosophical treatment of the emergence of Israel in its larger historical context, see Emil Fackenheim, *The Jewish Return into History: Reflections in the Age of Auschwitz and a New Jerusalem* (New York, 1978).

2. Cf *Encyclopedia Talmudit*, s.v. *eretz yisrael*.

3. Genesis 12:7.

4. Presumably in Genesis 25:5.

5. Genesis 28:1–4.

6. This was presumably part of his request to be buried in Israel and not in Egypt, where he died. In making this request he reminds his sons of Abraham's purchase of the family plot. Clearly, this was in a land where he expected his descendants to live. Genesis 49:28–32.

7. Exodus 6:8.

8. I would suggest that the first point made by Rashi in his biblical commentary is meant to express something similar. He explains that the inclusion, in a book of laws like the Torah, of the biblical narrative from creation to the appearance of the first legal section in Exodus 12, is to justify why the Jews are entitled to take the land of Israel from the seven indigenous peoples who had original possession of it.

9. Such as Proverbs and Job.

10. Some of which do speak of Israel, cf. Psalms 126 and 137.

11. See the very last verses in Chronicles, their parallel in the first verses in Ezra, and the narrative in the rest of Ezra and Nehemiah.

12. One indication of the importance of the messianic idea to Judaism is the fact that no less than four of the eighteen or nineteen blessings of the daily Amidah deal with the subject. Since the first three and last three blessings are formulaic, i.e., they appear in all recitations of the Amidah, this means that four of the thirteen penitential blessings deal with this subject, a very large percentage.

13. Isaiah 27:13; Maimonides, *Mishneh Torah*, Hilkhot Melakhim 11:1

14. This can be found in the introduction to the Modim prayer, which reads *ve-tehezenah ainenu be-shuvekha le-tzion be-rahamim* ("May our eyes see when You return with mercy to Zion").

15. This is recited at the very end of the day, at the close of Neilah, the final prayer service of the day, recited just before dark.

16. This is said immediately after the last integral section of the Seder. The songs that appear subsequently in the Haggadah are later additions to the structure of the Seder ritual.

17. Cf. M. D. Gross, *Otzar ha-Aggadah* (Jerusalem, 1977), s.v. *eretz yisrael.*

18. See Aryeh Newman, "The Centrality of Eretz Yisrael in Nachmanides," *Tradition* 10:1 (1968), pp. 21–30. See also N. Rabinovitch, "Conquest of the Land of Israel According to the Ramban," *Crossroads* 2 (1988), pp.181–187.

19. Newman, Ibid."

20. See his glosses to Maimonides, *Sefer ha-Mitzvot*, at the end of his commentary to that work; also, his biblical commentary, Numbers 33:53.

21. Cf. *Encyclopaedia Judaica*, s.v. Nahmanides, Moses. In truth, Nahmanides also left to escape a threat from the church and the government. However, his choice of Israel as his destination was in keeping with his overall approach to the importance of living in that land.

22. Ibid.

23. For further details, see Charles Chavel, *Ramban: His Life and Teachings* (New York, 1960).

24. It can also be found in the *Siddur Minhat Yerushalayim* (Jerusalem, 1963).

25. It is known as the Ramban shul. It is located in the heart of the Jewish Quarter of the old city of Jerusalem and houses at least three different congregations at the present time.

26. See *Encyclopedia Talmudit*, loc. cit., subsection *yeshivatah yishuvah u-she'ar dinehah*.

27. In addition to the discussion in the *Encyclopedia Talmudit*, see Tosafot Ketubot 110b; Medina, *Responsa Maharashdam*, Even ha-Ezer 123; Trani, *Responsa Mabit* 3:131; Zahalon, *Responsa Maharitatz* 1:5, Eliezer Waldenberg, *Responsa Tzitz Eliezer* 7:48; Moses Feinstein, *Responsa Iggerot Mosheh*, Even ha-Ezer 1:102.

28. See discussion in *Encyclopedia Talmudit*, loc. cit.

29. Cf. Feinstein, *Iggerot Mosheh*, Even ha-Ezer 1:102.

30. Cf. *Encyclopaedia Judaica*, s.v. Benjamin of Tudela; and s.v. Literature, Jewish, subsection: Geography and Travel.

31. From the decree of Cyrus allowing the Jews to rebuild the Second Temple (Ezra 1:4), through the Second Temple period and on into medieval and modern times, contributions have come from the diaspora to Israel to support Jewish life in the Holy Land. Halakhically, the poor of Israel are considered to be the same as the poor of one's own city in implementing the principle "the poor of your own city take precedence." Moses ben Mordechai Galanti, *Responsa Maharam Galanti* 76.

32. Again, there are far too many works on the subject to detail here. One important article is C. Waxman, "Messianism, Zionism and the State of Israel," *Modern Judaism* 7:2 (1987), pp. 175–192.

33. Herzl's ideas were expressed most completely in his book *Der Judenstaat*, which he published in 1895.

34. *Encyclopaedia Judaica*, s.v. Uganda Scheme.

35. Ibid., s.v. Herzl, Theodor.

36. The watchword of the movement, used by Herzl as its motto in his *Altneuland* (1902).

37. Criticized most forcefully in the writings of Yoram Hazoni.

38. Cf. S. Peres, *The New Middle East* (New York, 1993).

39. Again, much literature exists on this subject; see the writings of Edward Said or Hanan Ashrawi.

40. Many sources discuss this concept. In light of the events of September 11, 2001, I will cite B. Dart, "What Drove Middle Class Terrorists?" *Atlanta Constitution*, September 29, 2001.

41. Cf. Y. Leket, "The Problem of Yerida," *Jewish Frontier* 48:7 (1981), pp. 38–43.

42. Two relevant articles by C. Waxman, "American Aliya: Dream and Reality," *Morasha* 2:3 (1987), pp. 1–7, and "In the End Is It Ideology? Religio-Cultural and Structural Factors in American Aliya," *Contemporary Jewry* 16 (1995), pp. 50–67.

43. *Encyclopaedia Judaica*, s.v. Zionism, subsection Religious and Secular Anti-Nationalism.

44. See E. Wasserman, *Ikvata de-Meshiha* (Los Angeles, 1985).

45. *Encyclopaedia Judaica*, loc. cit.

46. Bnei Akiva is the youth movement of Ha-po'el Mizrachi, founded in Jerusalem in 1929 under the spiritual leadership of Rav Kook.

47. It was founded in 1902 as a religious faction in the World Zionist Organization.

48. The term comes from a famous article by Ephraim Kishon, which can be found in his *Ha-Kippah ha-Serugah: Ve-od Kamah Satirot Pro-Yisre'eliyot* (Bet El, 1993).

49. For discussion, see S. Cohen, "The Hesder Yeshivot in Israel: A Church-State Military Arrangement," *Journal of Church and State* 35:1 (1993), pp. 113–130; Aaron Lichtenstein, "The Ideology of Hesder," *Tradition* 19:3 (1981), pp. 199–217; A. Cohen, "On Yeshiva Men Serving in the Army," *Journal of Halachah and Contemporary Society* 23 (1992), pp. 5–31.

50. This is the slogan of Mizrachi, coined by Rabbi Meir Berlin (Bar-Ilan).

51. See Y. Goldstein, "The Settlement Ethos in Jewish and Zionist Thought in Eretz-Israel, Israel and the Jewish Diaspora, 1991, pp. 80–92, and D. Penslar, "From Degania to Kiryat Arba: The Ideology of Zionist Settlement," *Zionist Ideas* 16 (1987), pp. 11–20.

52. "Jewish Messianism, Religious Zionism and Israeli Politics: The Impact and Origins of Gush Emunim," *Morasha* 3:2 (1988), pp. 39–47.

53. See their "virtual Bet Midrash" online.

54. See the pamphlet published by Edah on the varieties of Orthodoxy. For a discussion of the Haredi position and its development over the years, see Charles Liebman, "Paradigms Sometimes Fit: The Haredi Response to the Yom Kippur War," *Israel Affairs* 1:3 (1995), pp. 171–184.

55. Philip Birnbaum, *Daily Prayer Book* (New York, 1949), p. 91, part of the daily Amidah.

56. Ibid., p. 89, part of the weekday Amidah.

57. Norman Lamm, "The Ideology of the Neturei Karta, According to the Satmarer Version," *Tradition* 12:2 (1971), pp. 38–53.

58. Ketubot 111a.

59. The source is not codified as law by any of the classical decisors, such as Maimonides, or in the *Shulhan Arukh*.

60. See n. 54 above.

61. Who served for decades as president of the American branch of Mizrachi, the Religious Zionists of America.

62. The periodicals *Crossroads* and *Tehumim* give graphic testimony to this fact in every issue.

63. I am told that some Satmar and Neturei Karta do so.

64. Most in the yeshiva world do this.

65. I know people ranging from the right-wing world to even some in the modern Orthodox world who do this.

66. See the discussion of Hallel, Megillah 14a.

67. This was the view of Rav Soloveitchik and many others.

68. This is the position of the Israeli chief rabbinate.

69. One can find them in the *Rinat Yisrael Siddur* (Jerusalem, 1972).

70. Sanhedrin 94a.

Chapter 10
The Messiah

It is a cardinal principle of traditional Judaism that a Messiah will come, someday.[1] This individual, descended from King David,[2] will, at some point in time arise to bring about the redemption of the Jews from diaspora and persecution.[3] He will also usher in an era of peace and universal morality.[4] The term "Messiah," *mashiah* in Hebrew, means "the anointed one,"[5] and it refers to both the Messiah's mission and the Messiah's status as a king of the Davidic dynasty. Kings from this line were anointed with sacred oil as a symbol of office.[6]

Maimonides lists belief in the Messiah as one of the thirteen cardinal principles of the Jewish faith and requires us to anticipate his coming at all times.[7] So, too, the Talmud reminds us that at our final judgment, we will be asked whether or not we actively anticipated this redemption, and we will be judged favorably in regard to this question only if we can honestly answer that we did.[8]

Though there is broad agreement on the preceding description, the details, the specifics, and even the ultimate meaning of the Messiah's coming are subjects of debate and interpretation. Two main streams of thought on the Messiah arise from differences between the more rational schools of thought and mystical teachings in Judaism.

A major presentation of the former can be found in Maimonides, *Mishneh Torah*, Hilkhot Melakhim chapters

11–12, excerpts of which appear below:

Chapter 11

1. King Messiah will arise and restore the kingdom of David to its former state and original sovereignty. He will rebuild the sanctuary and gather the dispersed of Israel. All the ancient laws will be reinstituted in his days; sacrifices will again be offered; the Sabbatical and Jubilee years will again be observed in accordance with the commandments set forth in the Law.

3. Do not think that King Messiah will have to perform signs and wonders, bring anything new into being, revive the dead,[9] or do similar things. It is not so. Rabbi Akiva was a great sage, a teacher of the Mishnah, yet he was also the armor-bearer of Ben Kozeba [Bar Kokhba]. He affirmed that the latter was King Messiah; he and all the wise men of his generation shared this belief until Ben Kozeba was slain in [his] iniquity, when it became known that he was not [the Messiah]. Yet the Rabbis had not asked him for a sign or a token. The general principle is: This law of ours, with its statutes and ordinances [is not subject to change]. It is forever and for all eternity; it is not to be added to or to be taken away from. [Whoever adds anything to it, or takes away anything from it, or misinterprets it, and strips the commandments of their literal sense is an impostor, a wicked man, and a heretic.]

4. If there arise a king from the House of David who meditates on the Torah, occupies himself with the commandments, as did his ancestor David, observes the precepts prescribed in the Written and the Oral Law, prevails upon Israel to walk in the way of the Torah and to repair its breaches, and fights the battles of the Lord, it may be assumed that he is the Messiah. If he does these things and succeeds, rebuilds the sanctuary on its site, and gathers the dispersed of Israel, he is beyond all doubt the Messiah. He will prepare the whole world to serve the Lord

with one accord, as it is written: "For then will I turn to the peoples a pure language, that they may all call upon the name of the Lord to serve Him with one consent" (Zephaniah 3:9).

Chapter 12

1. Let no one think that in the days of the Messiah any of the laws of nature will be set aside, or any innovation be introduced into creation. The world will follow its normal course. The words of Isaiah, "And the wolf shall dwell with the lamb, and the leopard shall lie down with the kid" (Isaiah 11:6), are to be understood figuratively, meaning that Israel will live securely among the wicked of the Gentiles, who are likened to wolves and leopards. . . . All similar expressions used in connection with the messianic age are metaphorical. In the days of King Messiah the full meaning of these metaphors and their allusions will become clear to everyone.

4. The sages and prophets did not long for the days of the Messiah so that Israel might exercise dominion over the world, or rule over the Gentiles, or be exalted by the nations, or that it might eat and drink and rejoice. Their aspiration was that Israel would be free to devote itself to the law and its wisdom, with no one to oppress or disturb it, and thus be worthy of life in the world-to-come.

5. In that era there will be neither famine nor war, neither jealousy nor strife. Blessings will be abundant, comforts within the reach of all. The one preoccupation of the whole world will be to know the Lord. Hence Israelites will be very wise; they will know the things that are now concealed and will attain an understanding of their Creator to the utmost capacity of the human mind, as it is written: "For the earth shall be full of the knowledge of the Lord, as the waters cover the sea" (Isaiah 11:9).

Maimonides, in these chapters, describes the Messiah as a national-political-religious figure and the redemption as a

national-political-religious redemption. There is no expectation of miraculous occurrences, and no fundamental changes
in nature need occur. The Messiah's coming is an event well
within the ken and experience of the average human being.

Nonetheless, even Maimonides does not know of only this
vision of the messianic era. In his letter to the Jews of Yemen,
he describes a different messianic vision. A brief excerpt follows:

> Did you not know, my brother, that the Messiah will be a
> very great prophet, greater than all the other prophets that
> came after Moses, our Teacher, may his memory be blessed . . .
> and God will single him out with blessings and attributes
> which He did not even give to Moses, our Teacher . . . and the
> signs and the miracles which will appear by his hand will be a
> proof for the truth of his claim and the truth of his lineage . . .
> and God will cause confusion among all the rulers of the earth
> as they contemplate his deeds. Their kingdoms will be lost,
> and they will desist from standing against him, whether by
> sword or by rebellion. What I mean to say is that they will not
> speak against him, nor will they deceive him. Rather, they will
> be frightened as a result of the signs and miracles that will
> appear by his hand.[10]

Apparently, when Maimonides spoke of the Messiah in
terms of minimal halakhic requirements in the *Mishneh Torah*,
he was presenting a purely rational picture. On the other
hand, when he wrote to the Jews of Yemen, whose hearts were
being drawn to a false messiah, he presented a somewhat
more mystical and miraculous description to help them see
that the messianic claims of this individual were a lie.

To approach the more mystical Messiah in a systematic way,
we need to go back nearly half a millenia before Maimonides to

the era of the Talmud. The Midrash and the Talmud contain many sources that speak of a radical change in the nature of things that will occur in the messianic era. These changes are of two types: physical and legal. Physically, we are told that the mountains and valleys will be smoothed out so that transportation will become much easier.[11] Also, trying to pick a fruit on Shabbat will result in the fruit telling you not to do it because it is Shabbat.[12] Many similar examples can be found.

Halakhah (Jewish law) will also undergo significant alteration according to these sources. All the traditional holidays will disappear except for Purim and Yom Kippur.[13] All the books of the Bible will lose their sanctity save the Five Books of Moses, and possibly Esther.[14] Some sources even suggest that nonkosher foods will become kosher.[15] The picture is one of a radical physical and spiritual break with the world as we know it.

The conceptual underpinnings of this vision of an altered world are provided for contemporary Jews by Kabbalah, the Jewish mysticism that was popularized in the medieval period.[16] Its most popular version today is based on the work of the great sixteenth-century mystic Rabbi Isaac ben Solomon Luria (1534–1572), known as the Ari· In the teachings of the Ari, the world first came into existence through ten emanations of God's divine attributes, the garments with which He presents himself to the world, known as the sefirot. The sefirot embody such attributes as God's kindness, God's justice, and God's wisdom.[17]

Opposite the ten sefirot of goodness, and to maintain a spiritual balance in the universe, ten sefirot of evil also came into being in the primordial universe.[18] Initially, these latter sefirot were lifeless, but then a great cosmic cataclysm occurred. Eventually, a cleavage developed between the ninth and tenth of these holy sefirot, and divine sparks were scattered everywhere, even into the sefirot of evil.

This penetration of these living sparks into the husks of evil not only animated them, but also brought on the existence of this world. The mystic believes that if we could see beyond the illusions of physical reality visible to our eyes, we would understand that all things—you, me, the pages of this book that you are reading, the computer used to write it—are really sparks of God embedded in husks of evil.[19]

An important consequence of this belief is that everything in the universe is divinely precious, because everything possesses these Godly sparks. For this reason alone all human beings must be treated with the respect implied by their possessing this hidden divine glow.

This super-reality, or metaphysics, of divine sparks embedded in husks of evil is not a static condition. The sparks yearn to rise upward, to shed their husks and return to their origin. We can help in that process. Doing a mitzvah (a good deed) with an object containing a divine spark, or perhaps even in the presence of such an object, causes the spark to resonate with the spirituality of the action and move upwards.[20] Doing mitzvot, observing Halakhah, keeping God's law, even proper intent in our actions are not simply a matter of moral behavior, as valuable as that is. They are also steps toward the final redemption of all the sparks from their husks of evil.

The final return of all of the sparks will bring about the redemption of the Jewish people and the coming of the Messiah and the messianic era. However, when this happens the nature of the world will have changed. Metaphysically, it will no longer be made up of sparks of God in husks of evil. The sparks will have been redeemed and returned to their source. Further, the husks of evil will have lost their vitality and power. This will be reflected in the changed experiences of fruit reminding us that it is Shabbat, and of smoothed out mountains and valleys. These and the other altered physical realities described in rabbinic literature make the point that for

Jewish mysticism, the coming of the Messiah means a shattering of the existing reality and the creation of a true "new world order."[21]

The door is also open in this formulation to radical alteration of Halakhah, and even to its cessation in the form in which we know it. In mysticism, as we have said, the purpose of Halakhah in this world is to bring about the raising of the sparks and the redemption of the world. Once the world is redeemed, Halakhah will no longer be needed in the same way, thus raising the possibility that it will not function in the post-messianic universe as it does in the pre-messianic world.

The mystical Messiah is obviously radically different from the rational Messiah with which we began our discussion. There will unquestionably be positive national-political consequences for the Jewish people in the messianic era as anticipated by the mystics, for the return of the Jews to Israel and the rebuilding of the Temple are seen, in Kabbalah, as manifestations of the return of the divine sparks to their source and the healing of the primordial breach in the sefirot, a theme thoroughly expounded in the writings of Rabbi Moses Hayyim Ephraim of Sudylkow (1740–1800), the grandson of the founder of Hasidism, the Baal Shem Tov[22] and in other mystical works. Nonetheless, these national-political changes are not the primary purpose or goal of the messianic era as understood by the mystics. They are at most ancillary to the cataclysmic reshaping of reality and existence.

In simplest terms, the mystical Messiah represents a radical break with previous history, whereas the rational Messiah does not. For the mystics, Halakhah and reality will likely, change, while for the rationalist, they do not. For the mystic, life after the Messiah is profoundly different, but for the rationalist, that is not necessarily the case.

Over the course of Jewish history, the vision of the mystical Messiah has been a far more powerful source of ferment and change, both positive and negative, than any expectation that the Messiah would follow the rationalist's more limited blueprint. This pattern was set long before the Ari.

Christianity follows the mystical model precisely. A "messiah" has come and the world is redeemed and altered. Therefore, a "New Testament" is required to replace the old, to explain the new reality and how we are to behave differently in this redeemed world. The old laws were necessary in the premessianic world, but now the new faith is what is needed.[23]

Roughly a century after the Ari's time, the pattern appeared again in the person of Shabbetai Zevi (1621–1676), the "mystical messiah."[24] With Sarah, his wife, and Nathan of Gaza, his prophet, to aid him (or as is often claimed, to trick and mislead him), he persuaded many Jews to believe that the world had been redeemed. In that way, his engaging in strange actions such as marrying a Torah scroll, which would otherwise have been condemned as anti-halakhic, were understood by his supporters as reflecting the "new world order."

Many Jews in Shabbetai Zevi's time believed he was the Messiah and that the redemption was at hand. These Sabbatean followers thought they had come to see the greatest moment of joy in human history. Some of them engaged in anti-halakhic activities as part of this belief and in anticipation of the redemption they thought had come. As a result, when Shabbetai Zevi was revealed as a fraud by his conversion to Islam and then by his death, a great national depression descended on the Jewish people.

Nonetheless, some Sabbatean believers remained. Nearly a hundred years later, a great Torah scholar, Jacob Emden (1697–1776), denounced another great Torah scholar, Jonathan Eybeschuetz (1690–1764), as a Sabbatean. This schism caused great communal acrimony for many years.[25]

Two present-day movements of historical importance that are not usually thought of as messianic actually parallel the mystical messianic model. The first is Reform Judaism. I quote here from the Pittsburgh Platform of 1880, the founding document of the American Reform movement:

> We recognize, in the modern era of universal culture of heart and intellect, the approaching of the realization of Israel's great messianic hope for the establishment of the kingdom of truth, justice, and peace among all men. We consider ourselves no longer a nation, but a religious community, and therefore expect neither a return to Palestine, nor a sacrificial worship under the sons of Aaron, nor the restoration of any of the laws concerning the Jewish State.
>
> We hold that all such Mosaic and rabbinical laws as regulate diet, priestly purity, and dress, originated in ages and under the influence of ideas altogether foreign to our present mental and spiritual state. They fail to impress the modern Jew with a spirit of priestly holiness; their observance in our days is apt rather to obstruct than to further modern spiritual elevation.
>
> We recognize in the Mosaic legislation a system of training the Jewish people for its mission during its national life in Palestine, and today we accept as binding only the moral laws, and maintain only such ceremonies as elevate and sanctify our lives, but reject all such as are not adapted to the views and habits of modern civilization.[26]

Note that all the elements are here. The messianic era is upon us, the world has changed and the rules are different; or at least, that is the claim.

So, too, secular Zionism follows this model.[27] Theodor Herzl did not, as many think, want to found a Jewish state as a haven for Jews in case of persecution. Instead, he understood the "Jewish Problem" to be caused by the fact that the Jews alone among the nations of the world did not have a state. Give the Jews a state, and they would be no different from the French or the Germans. Since the founding of a state would radically alter the nature of the Jewish experience in this world, the Jews must help the process along. All the old laws and rituals had been important to keep Judaism and Jews a distinct group when they lived as minorities in foreign lands, but now that Jews would be normalized in their own land, they must give up their old ways and become a "normal" people within the family of nations. Again, the redeemed world requires different models of behavior.[28]

Whether one sees the contributions of these movements to Jewish history as positive or negative, one thing is clear; their messianic assumptions that the world had in fact radically changed have not held true and they need to or have had to modify themselves accordingly.

We conclude, then, with the poetic restatement of the next-to-last of Maimonides' thirteen principles of faith, which as all of his principles remains operative for traditional Jews to this day:

"I believe with complete faith in the coming of the Messiah, and even though he may delay, nevertheless I anticipate every day that he will come."[29]

1. The coming of the Messiah is one of Maimonides' thirteen principles of the faith; see Chapter 11. There is obviously much material on the subject of this chapter. Especially useful are Joseph Klausner, *The Messianic Idea in Israel* (New York, 1955); Gershom Scholem, *The Messianic Idea in Judaism* (New York, 1955), J. D. Eisenstein, *Otzar Yisrael*, s.v. *mashiah*.

2. This tradition is biblical; see Isaiah 11:1.

3. See Isaiah 27:13.

4. See the quote from Maimonides below.

5. See Exodus 29:7, Leviticus 4:3.

6. See Horayot 11b for discussion of exactly which kings were anointed. The non-Davidic kings of Israel were not anointed, and apparently, anointing

was hereditary in the sense that anointing the father made it unnecessary to anoint the son even in the Davidic line.

7. See below, Chapter 11.

8. Shabbat 31a.

9. This comment became an element in the so-called Maimonidean Controversy, the dispute over whether Maimonides' works were a legitimate expression within the belief system of Judaism. For a brief summary, see *Encyclopaedia Judaica*, s.v. Maimonidean Controversy; for a more in-depth treatment, see Daniel Jeremy Silver, *Maimonidean Criticism and the Maimonidean Controversy* (Leiden, 1965) and I. Dobbs-Weinstein, "The Maimonidean Controversy," in *History of Jewish Philosophy*, ed. Daniel H. Frerich and Oliver Leaman (London, 1997), pp. 331–349. See also David Berger, "How Did Nahmanides Propose to Resolve the Maimonidean Controversy?" *Me'ah She'arim*, 2001, pp. 135–146. The controversy led Maimonides to author the *Ma'amar Tehiyyat ha-Metim* (Treatise on Resurrection) in which he reaffirmed his belief in this principle, although not necessarily as part of the Messiah's establishing himself as Messiah.

10. I. Shailat, *Iggerot ha-Rambam* (Jerusalem, 1987), pp. 154 ff.

11. Genesis Rabbah 23:6–7.

12. Midrash on Psalms 73.

13. Yalkut Shimoni, Proverbs 9:944.

14. Jerusalem Talmud, Megillah 70d.

15. Leviticus Rabbah 13:3, Midrash on Psalms 146.

16. Of the many books on this subject, the best is still Gershom Scholem, *Major Trends in Jewish Mysticism* (New York, 1995). See also Chapter 16 in this volume.

17. See Scholem, lectures 5–7.

18. This is the mystical understanding of Ecclesiastes 7:14. For a full discussion of evil in the Lurianic Kabbalah, see Isaiah Tishby, *Torat ha-Ra ve-ha-Kelipah be-Kabbalat ha-Ari* (Jerusalem, 1962). The description here is dramatically less complex than the actual Lurianic system.

19. This idea can serve as the basis for developing a Jewish environmental consciousness. See my "The Earth Is the Lord's," *Jewish Action*, Summer 1990, pp. 22–26.

20. This process is called *tikkun*.

21. A phrase made famous by President George Bush the elder and first used

by him in a speech on August 30, 1990.

22. Cf. Moses Hayyim Ephraim of Sudylkow, *Degel Mahaneh Efrayim* (Bene-Berak, 1969), Parashat Bo, s.v. *misharotam*.

23. Many sources can be cited for this fundamental Christian doctrine. One of the earliest and most complete is in the Christian Bible, II Corinthians 3:7–18.

24. There is a brief account of his life and thought in the *Encyclopaedia Judaica*, s.v. Shabbetai Zevi. For a fuller treatment, see Gershom Scholem, *Sabbatai Sevi, the Mystical Messiah* (Princeton, N.J., 1973).

25. The details can be found in the articles on Emden and Eybeshuetz in the *Encyclopaedia Judaica*. See also Sid Z. Leiman, "When a Rabbi Is Accused of Heresy: Rabbi Ezekiel Landau's Attitude Toward R. Jonathan Eibeschuetz in the Emden-Eibeschuetz Controversy," in *From Ancient Israel to Modern Judaism: Essays in Honor of Marvin Fox*, ed. Jacob Neusner, Ernest S. Frerichs, and Nahum M. Sarna, vol. 3 (Atlanta, 1989), pp. 179–194, and Mortimer J. Cohen, *Jacob Emden: A Man of Controversy* (Philadelphia, 1937).

26. The entire document can be found in the *Encyclopaedia Judaica*, s.v. Pittsburgh Platform.

27. See the discussion in Chapter 9.

28. Shemuel Almog, Jehuda Reinharz, and Anita Shapira, eds., *Zionism and Religion* (Waltham, Mass., 1998).

29. See Chapter 11, and Philip Birnbaum, ed., *Daily Prayer Book* (New York, 1949), p. 155.

Chapter 11
Dogmas, Beliefs, and Creeds

"Judaism does not focus on beliefs; it is much more concerned with actions."[1] Though one may read or hear many variations of this statement, the truth is not nearly that simple. Both historically and in the daily practice of Judaism, questions of proper belief and the personal expression of Jewish ideology come into play in an important way.[2]

In some faith systems, great synods have been convened to debate the creation or emendation of the religion's basic creed, which is, in many cases, then recited as part of worship or on ceremonial occasions.[3] No such synod has ever been convened under traditional Jewish auspices. This supports the idea that credo is not central to Judaism.

Nonetheless, twice each day, by biblical mandate, Jews recite the Shema, "Hear, O Israel, the Lord our God, the Lord is One."[4] This sentence and the paragraphs that it introduces demand one's fealty to many basic aspects of Jewish belief, such as God and His nature, the chosenness of Israel, and reward and punishment.

The Rabbis designated this recitation as *kabbalat ol malkhut shamayim* ("the acceptance of the yoke of heaven"),[5] and it is taught to children as one of the first two religious teachings they are to learn, the other being *torah tzivah lanu mosheh* ("The Torah was commanded to us by Moses").[6] It is also the last thing we are to say before we die.[7]

For a religion that supposedly does not center itself on beliefs, this all sounds suspiciously creed-like. Nonetheless, even the daily reading of the Torah passages that make up the Shema, which contain these elements of belief is structured and circumscribed by a significant number of rules, regulations, and requirements as to time, place, and manner of recitation.[8] Law and behavior remain in control of the expression of creed when it appears in Jewish liturgy.

The history of the efforts to create an authoritative list of principles of belief for Judaism is an intriguing one. Some argue that such principles were never formulated until the Middle Ages.[9] At that time, under the intellectual challenge of Islam and the resurgence of interest in Greek philosophy, which had become available in Arabic translation, much work of this sort was done.[10]

Many medieval scholars composed lists of what they regarded as the central elements of faith and belief required by Judaism. Their number include Hananel ben Hushiel (d. 1055/56) in North Africa, Moses Maimonides (1138–1204) in Egypt, [11] Moses ben Joseph of Lunel (12th cent.) in France,[12] Hasdai Crescas (d. 1412) in Spain,[13] and Joseph Albo (15th cent.), also in Spain.[14] We will now try to put these efforts into their historical context. While the Bible does not specifically list items of dogma, it provided some antecedents for this activity in that many areas of belief are implicit or explicit expectations of certain biblical passages, including the Shema mentioned above.

Obviously, belief in one God who is ethical, and who has expectations of how people in general, and Jews specifically, will behave, is critical to the biblical narrative.[15] Further, God's active rewarding of good behavior and punishing of bad behavior underscores virtually all of biblical history.[16] Finally, at the end of the biblical era, with the destruction of the Temple and the exile of the Jewish people from their land, emphasis is placed on the promise of a Messiah and a return and rebuilding of what once was.[17] However, nowhere in the

Bible are these ideas formulated into a listing of creeds or necessary doctrines.

In the talmudic era there was also no such formulation, but sources appeared that begin the process. Traditional Judaism had, by this time, experienced ideological challenges both from outside, in the form of Greco-Roman philosophy and culture, and from inside, as mounted by Sadducees, Essenes, and other sectarians offering fundamentally different explications of Judaism than those held by the Rabbis.

Often a faith community will feel a need to define what it truly stands for in the face of such pressure. The Mishnah tells us that those who have no share in the world-to-come include one who does not believe that the Torah comes from heaven, one who does not believe that the Torah speaks of the eventual resurrection of the dead, and the heretic (*apikoros*).[18] These appear to be three individuals whose credo is at odds with Judaism. The meaning of the last term is somewhat unclear, and a variety of definitions are offered in the Talmud to explain it.[19] The source that does so provides, in effect, an additional list of ideological beliefs, however small, that demarcate those who are acceptable in terms of their belief systems to God and the Jewish community from those who are not.

The philosopher Philo of Alexandria (20 B.C.E.–50 C.E.), also known as Philo Judaeus, is not generally accepted as belonging to the mainstream tradition, in part because he treated the biblical stories as allegories. Even he, however, felt constrained, in his encounter with Greek thought, to list eight principles of the Jewish faith.[20] Whatever else one might say about Philo, most, if not all, of his principles would be fully acceptable to traditional Judaism today. These include God's existence, His unity, His providence, and the revelation and eternity of the Torah.

Mention of divine providence brings us to one other issue of dogma that plays a role in rabbinic tradition. Rabbinic literature records a few instances of people consciously deciding to leave the Jewish community. (It is important to note that under Jewish law one who is born Jewish or who halakhically converts to Judaism always remains a Jew,[21] nonetheless human beings have the capacity to ideologically reject Judaism and live by another set of principles or beliefs.) Often their defection came as a result of a tragedy that was difficult to explain.[22] When such events led to disaffection with Judaism, it was the personal loss of belief in God's providing appropriate reward and punishment that led the person out of Judaism in the talmudic era. This is different than those who left Jewish belief after the Holocaust claiming that they could no longer accept that God existed at all. In the Talmudic era everyone believed in the existence of a Deity. It was His presence as an active caring force in this world that was questioned by some.

In some sources this disaffection comes with the declaration *let din ve-let dayyan* ("There is no judgment and no judge").[23] This was, as indicated, not a denial of God's existence, but rather, in keeping with classical Greek thought, a denial of God's involvement with mankind. Aristotle saw God as a necessary principle for the world to exist, but God, for Aristotle, is too sublime to be involved with mere physical and corrupt beings such as *homo sapiens*.[24] *Let din ve-let dayyan* may well be a declaration embracing such a view. Whatever its import, the individual who made this declaration was effectively removed from the Jewish community. This is another indication that creed had come to matter to the traditional Jewish community at least as early as the era of the Talmud.

When we reach the medieval period, defining the creed of Judaism becomes an even more important and central activity, especially for Jewish scholars in Spain and the eastern Mediterranean countries. Judaism in these societies was experiencing its second encounter with classic Greek philosophy. The first encounter with the Greco-Roman world had entailed not only ideological and theological challenges, but also physical threats. The Maccabean revolt and the celebration of Hanukkah, as well as the destruction of the Temple and many of the fasts and mourning periods of the Jewish year, commemorate important aspects of this earlier era.

This second encounter came in the medieval period by way of Islam. Muslim scholars translated classic Greek philosophical works into Arabic, and many important schools of Islam and their leading thinkers were significantly influenced by this material. Jewish scholars in Muslim countries read and studied these Arabic translations.[25] As Islam defined and refined its creed, it, too, presented theological and philosophical challenges to Judaism. These did not generally entail persecution and physical threats (where such took place, and they were relatively rare as compared to the Jewish experience with Christianity, they came from Islam, not from Greek philosophy), and so an intellectual response was called for.

The Kalam school of Islam (whose name means "the roots of religion") spent much time and effort in defining a philosophical exposition of the beliefs of its faith (what Jewish scholars would call *ikkarim*).[26] This school influenced many Jewish thinkers, including, most importantly, Saadiah Gaon (882–942), whose *Sefer ha-Emunot ve-ha-De'ot* was the first important medieval Jewish philosophical work, but also Samuel ben Hophni (d. 1013), the Gaon of Sura, and Bahya Ibn Paquda (11th cent.), the author of *Hovot ha-Levavot*, a major philosophical work written originally, as so many of these early philosophical texts were, in Arabic and then translated into Hebrew.

The earliest Jewish statement of fundamental principles in this era was made by Hananel b. Hushiel, mentioned earlier, who claimed that four beliefs were critical for any and every Jew: belief in God, the prophets, the world-to-come, and the Messiah.

The most famous list of essential beliefs, and the one that appears to have been more or less universally accepted in traditional circles, was compiled by Maimonides, who was also strongly influenced by Greek philosophy.[27] The thirteen principles of Maimonides constituted what the greatest Jewish sage of the Middle Ages regarded as a true philosophical summary of the faith, and for that reason went beyond being simply appropriate areas for inquiry and speculation, as were the principles of the Kalam school.

Maimonides held that one's relationship with God and ultimately one's place in the world-to-come were dependent on having correct beliefs in these areas. His formulation was designed, in part, to enable all Jews to develop the proper faith and avoid error.

Maimonides' list of the thirteen *ikkarim* is given below:

1. The existence of God, who is perfect and sufficient unto Himself, and who is the cause of the existence of all other beings.
2. God's unity, which is unlike all other kinds of unity.
3. God must not be conceived in bodily terms, and the anthropomorphic expressions applied to God in Scripture have to be understood metaphorically.
4. God is eternal.
5. God alone is to be worshipped and obeyed. There are no mediating powers able to grant man's petitions, and intermediaries must not be invoked.
6. God reveals prophecy to human beings.
7. Moses is unsurpassed by any other prophet.
8. The entire Torah was given to Moses.
9. Moses' Torah will not be abrogated or superseded by another divine law, nor will anything be added to or taken away from it.
10. God knows the actions of men.
11. God rewards those who fulfill the commandments of the Torah, and punishes those who transgress them.
12. The coming of the Messiah.
13. The resurrection of the dead.

Maimonides adds that a person who denies any of these principles has excluded himself from the community and is, therefore, a heretic.[28] In saying this, Maimonides raised these thirteen *ikkarim* to the level of a creed or fundamental dogma for Judaism.

Many authorities disagreed with Maimonides because of various theological problems that in their view were posed by the thirteen principles. For example, as pointed out by Abraham ben David of Posquières, also known as Ravad (ca. 1125–1198), a Jew who follows all the commandments and accepts almost all the principles of faith, but pictures God as an all-powerful, all-benevolent giant living in heaven, controlling matters down below, might well be mistaken, even seriously in error, but he hardly seems a candidate for exclusion from the Jewish people in this world and the next on this basis.[29] Yet this is the fate Maimonides claims awaits anyone who holds such a belief.

Building on criticisms of this kind, many other Jewish scholars formulated different lists of *ikkarim*. Among them were David b. Samuel Kokhavi (ca. 1300),[30] Abba Mari Astruc b. Moses b. Joseph of Lunel (ca. 1300),[31] Hasdai Crescas (d. 1412),[32] Simeon b. Zemah Duran (1361–1444), also known as Rashbatz,[33] Joseph Albo (15th cent.),[34] Isaac Arama (ca. 1420–1494),[35] Joseph Jabez (d. 1507),[36] Isaac Abrabanel (1437–1508),[37] and even Baruch Spinoza (1632–1677),[38] who was excommunicated from Judaism for his philosophical beliefs but not for his *ikkarim*.[39] Some of the formulations compiled by these thinkers are relatively simple expositions of a few principles of faith, while others are more complex presentations involving primary *ikkarim* and secondary or subsidiary important beliefs.[40] Often the most interesting aspect of these positions is the criteria used by the respective scholars for exclusion from or inclusion on their respective list of principles.

Despite all the debate, Maimonides' *ikkarim* seem to have captured the popular and rabbinic mind, to the extent that any list of principles has ever been given formal halakhic imprimatur. Aiding or perhaps reflecting this reality are the popular versions of the thirteen principles found in the Ani Ma'amin formula, which first appeared in the Venice Haggadah (1556), and in Yigdal, a song recited in davening (prayer), that first appeared in the 1300's. The careful reader will notice nuanced differences between these two versions and between the two of them and Maimonides' own words on the subject, which may be found in his commentary to the Mishnah in his introduction to Perek Helek, the tenth chapter of Tractate Sanhedrin.

Nonetheless, in one form or another, this list of thirteen principles is as close as we come to a creed of Judaism. It is important to note, however, that the judgment of a person's place in the community today remains far more dependent on his or her fealty to halakhically acceptable behavior than on the espousal of specific beliefs. One will often hear a person assessed by the criteria of whether or not he or she is Sabbath-observant. One will virtually never hear, unless the person discussed has made public statements to the contrary, an assessment based on whether he or she does or does not believe that Moses was the greatest prophet.

Finally, even failure to observe the Sabbath or other serious halakhic violations will not remove an individual from the community in a legal sense.[41] The final test of connection to the community is purely halakhic. Was one's mother Jewish or was one converted halakhically? If so, one is part of the community on some level. The rest, while interesting and important in understanding Judaism, is not finally the factor that determines who is and who is not included.

1. Cf. Michael Wyschogrod, "Some Reflections on Jewish Biblical Ethics in the Contemporary Context," in *Reverence, Righteousness and Rahamanut: Essays in Memory of Rabbi Dr. Leo Jung*, ed. Jacob J. Schacter (New Jersey, 1992), p. 316.

2. For further discussion and sources, see Menachem Marc Kellner, "Dogma in Medieval Jewish Thought: A Bibliographical Survey," *Studies in Bibliography and Booklore* 15 (Cincinnati, 1984), pp. 5–21.

3. The Catholic catechism and the Islamic profession of faith come to mind.

4. One of our most central prayers, the Shema consists of three paragraphs: Deuteronomy 6:4–9, Deuteronomy 11:13–21, and Numbers 15:37–41. For discussion of the proper times to recite the Shema, see Mishnah Berakhot 1:1–2.

5. Cf. Rashi, Berakhot 14b, s.v. *keri'ah keri'ah,* and *Shulhan Arukh*, Orah Hayyim 63:6.

6. Sukkah 42a.

7. In all likelihood this practice comes originally from the story of Rabbi Akiva's martyrdom, Berakhot 61b. See also Midrash on Lamentations 1:1. My esteemed friend and congregant Herman Wouk, a Pulitzer-Prize–winning author, tells a marvelous story of nearly being swept from the deck of a U.S. Navy ship during a typhoon at sea and reminding himself to recite the Shema should he actually enter the water. All of this occurred in the moments before he managed to grab a lifeline while his survival was in doubt. See Herman Wouk, *This Is My God* (Boston, 1988), p. 100.

8. See the first two chapters of Tractate Berakhot; Maimonides, *Mishneh Torah*, Hilkhot Keriat Shema; and *Shulhan Arukh*, Orah Hayyim 58–88.

9. Menachem Marc Kellner, "Dogma in Judaism," *Reconstructionist* 49:3 (1983), pp. 25–28.

10. Julius Guttmann, *Philosophies of Judaism* (New York, 1973), pp. 53–68.

11. Maimonides' list can be found in his introduction to his discussion of the tenth chapter of Sanhedrin in his *Mishnah Commentary*. It is also well known from the fourteenth-century poem Yigdal, which was written either by Daniel ben Judah, a dayyan in Rome or by Immanuel ben Solomon of Rome, and from the Ani Ma'amin statement of the "creed" by an unknown author, which appears for the first time in a sixteenth-century manuscript. These two versions differ from each other and from Maimonides' original in some important nuances.

12. His Talmud commentary is no longer in existence, but his views are quoted extensively by other scholars, especially Nachmanides.

13. See his *Or Ado-Nai.*

14. See his *Sefer ha-Ikkarim.*

15. Many verses attest to these principles; e.g., Deuteronomy 30:15–20.

16. The biblical books of Judges and Kings provide many examples.

17. Cf. Ezekiel 33–48.

18. Sanhedrin 90a.

19. Ibid. 99a–b. The term is obviously associated with the school of Greek philosophy known as Epicureanism, whose slogan is said to have been, "Eat, drink, and be merry, for tomorrow we die." But see *Routledge Encyclopedia of Philosophy* (New York, 1998), s.v. "Epicureanism," for discussion of what was in reality a significantly more sophisticated set of ideas, though still antithetical to Judaism. Both the hedonism and the fatalism of the slogan and the doctrine go against Jewish belief. However, the greatest objection is probably to the lack of consequences for one's actions which implies lack of God's justice, and, therefore, of reward and punishment, and even of God's involvement or awareness of the things that occur in this world.

20. Harry Austryn Wolfson, *Philo: Foundations of Religious Philosophy* (Cambridge, 1948), vol. 1, pp. 164 ff.

21. See Chapter 24.

22. Cf. Kiddushin 39b.

23. See Genesis Rabbah 26:6, Leviticus Rabbah 28:1, and the story of the tanna Elisha ben Avuyah (also known as Aher), Kiddushin 39b. The text clearly indicates that this was the reason for Elisha's apostasy even though it does not use the phrase.

24. *Encyclopaedia Britannica,* s.v. Aristotle.

25. Guttmann, loc. cit.

26. Ibid., pp. 69–94.

27. See n. 11 above.

28. This is his definition of *apikoros* in the introduction to the tenth chapter of Sanhedrin in his Mishnah Commentary.

29. See Ravad's comment to *Mishneh Torah,* Hilkhot Teshuvah 3:7. In fact, followers of early Jewish mysticism known as Heikhalot or Merkavah mysticism speculated on the immense dimensions of God's "body" that the mystics might under certain circumstances come to perceive, in works such as *Shiur Komah.* Ravad references these scholars and suggests that they may be greater even than Maimonides.

30. His philosophical work can be found in his *Migdal David;* his halakhic work, which is based on the *Mishneh Torah,* can be found in his *Kiryat Sefer.*

31. See his *Sefer ha-Yare'ah.*

32. See above, n. 14.

33. See the introduction to his *Ohev Mishpat.*

34. See above, n. 15.

35. See his *Akedat Yitzhak.*

36. See his *Yesod ha-Emunah.*

37. See his commentary to the *Guide for the Perplexed* and his *Rosh Amanah.*

38. See his *Tractatus Theologico-Politicus.*

39. See *Encyclopaedia Judaica,* s.v. Spinoza.

40. Cf. David ben Samuel Kokhavi's *Migdal David.*

41. See Chapter 24.

Chapter 12
Shabbat and Kashrut

T he two subjects that make up this chapter represent the ritual elements of Judaism that most visibly define[1] and distinguish the traditional Jew.[2]

Those who follow the laws of the Sabbath and the kosher dietary laws simply function in different ways than those who do not observe these rituals. While the two practices are distinct and important enough to deserve individual treatment, which we will provide below, we will begin by discussing elements that they share.

First, they both require structure and discipline. Taking twenty-five hours out of every week in order to avoid constructive work[3]—particularly when most of us lead such busy lives that we can hardly get done the things we need to do— requires great discipline. Refraining from driving, television, CDs, computers, pursuing one's livelihood and career, answering the telephone,[4] are certainly counter-cultural actions (or "non-actions") in modern society. They are difficult steps to take, particularly when pressures begin to grow, during college, graduate school, or professional life, to increase productivity or meet deadlines, all of which are, at least potentially, negatively affected by taking this complete and total day off.

The discipline comes, then, in the need to organize one's time to mitigate the impact on productivity and deadlines while at the same time preparing for the needs of the day, which include festive meals, fancy clothes, frequent guests, and attendance at fairly lengthy services and perhaps Torah classes.[5]

So, too, kashrut means, in a very food-oriented society,[6] that the vast majority of commercial places to eat as well as the largest proportion of the food produced in the world are off-limits to the Jew. The discipline here comes in the planning that must go into food-shopping, travel, and how to handle the critically important business lunch at the wonderful five-star (but not kosher) restaurant.

Is it all worth it?

A story will hopefully provide an answer. When I was a child, my family was not completely observant. Specifically, we would turn electricity on and off and, in particular, watch TV on the Sabbath. Toward the end of first grade, when I was six, my father (of blessed memory) told me that once I started second grade, I would begin studying Humash (Bible), and we would no longer be watching television on the Sabbath. We would be following the Sabbath "electricity" rules, as Jewish law required of us.[7]

Though I agreed at the time, several months after the TV went silent on Saturdays, a preview appeared that told me that on the next Saturday, *The Origin of the Lone Ranger* would be shown on one of the local stations. To a six-year-old, that announcement was like honey to a bee. So I went to my father and begged him and bargained with him in every way that I knew in order to be allowed to watch.

To his credit, my father did not give in, and to this day I have never seen that show. As upset as I was, I had learned a critical lesson. Being so caught up in a TV Western to the point that I wanted to renege on an important agreement was an indication that my priorities were not in order. My experience with my father taught me what was truly important in my life.

The lesson has continued to this day for me, and as I look at the world it seems to be one that others should learn as well.

What is truly important? What are the right priorities?

Are spiritual matters more important, or is fun more important? Is doing what one wants to do the way to go, or is keeping one's word the way to live?

Even if there had been no agreement with my father, keeping Shabbat and kashrut are both visible symbols of my commitment to my covenant, my contractual agreement with God.[8] Following a divine regimen helps give me a spiritual identity. This too is a far more significant commitment than my pursuing a special episode of my favorite TV show.

The second element that Shabbat and kashrut share is that they both restrict our access to the natural resources of this world. Kashrut restricts physical access. There are some delicious foods to consume "out there," but many of them are off limits to me. Shabbat is restrictive of time. Saturday is a non-work day on which there are many things I might want to do—but I can't do a good number of them.

In an era in which environmental consciousness is part of our culture, a training ground for our understanding that we must not simply take anything and everything that we can from this planet is both valuable and important. Everyone now recognizes that reasonable restrictions on our use of the world's resources are essential to the continued quality of human life on earth. Judaism provides just such a training ground in requiring these two ritual life-style components.[9]

Of course, there are also differences between the requirements of Shabbat and those of Kashrut. We begin with Shabbat. Speaking from their own outside perspective, non-Jews have often told me that they envy me my Sabbath. The idea of putting down life's burdens and creating a spiritual space in time where the concerns of career and business do not reach sounds like heaven to many people, regardless of religious affiliation.

On a non-Sabbath day, if I am standing outside my front door and the phone rings inside, the adrenaline starts to pump as I fumble for my keys. If opening the door doesn't go smoothly enough, I start to feel as if I want to tear the door off its hinges. If this same experience happens on Shabbat, the phone ringing is simply an event with no consequence. I don't get tense. I don't fumble for the keys. There is no adrenaline rush. I am not going to answer the phone anyway, so getting there simply isn't important.

When I was young, there was a fellow in my synagogue who was a terrible chain-smoker.[10] He would smoke on the way to synagogue on Friday night when Sabbath begins, and leave his matches and cigarettes in a secure, hidden place where he could light up the instant Sabbath was over Saturday night. Once the holy day ended he needed to give in to his cravings.

Amazingly he had absolutely no cravings during the Sabbath. Many observant Jews have told me similar stories. The desire for tobacco would leave as the Friday night prayer began, and return as we recited Maariv, the first post-Sabbath prayer, Saturday night. This prayer lasts some seven to ten minutes, after which my friend couldn't even wait to get home before the nicotine need had to satisfied. Again, Shabbat provided a healthy break.

But Shabbat is far more than a tension reliever or a temporary cure for addiction. It is the first call to *imitatio Dei* (the imitation of God) in the Bible.[11] The origin of our rest on Sabbath lies in God's resting on the first Shabbat after his six days of work in creating the world.[12] When we rest we are acting in divine fashion on the holy day.

It seems to me that there is a profound sense of mastery, whether divine or human, in not working at certain times, in letting go of the need to be in control of things every moment of every day. It is a modern Western cliché, embodied in the phrase "Don't just sit there, do something," that activity indicates mastery of a situation, or at least an attempt at mastery.

The opposite may very well be the case.[13]

Frenetic activity is often a sign that everything is falling apart. When we do so much that we become absolutely essential to everything that goes on, even to the point that it can't go on without us, we are not the masters of the situation but its slaves.

True mastery comes in the serenity of knowing that one is making a contribution, but also that things can proceed with others carrying the load and contributing as well, at least occasionally.[14] As God was confident that the world He had created was well constructed enough so that natural law could function on its own on the first Shabbat,[15] and in this way as Lord He could serenely sit back (as it were) and enjoy the Sabbath of Creation, we, too, can and should experience the same thing. It is an exercise in inner mastery and peace, a very Eastern concept, that comes with Shabbat.

The laws of Shabbat are quite extensive and complex.[16] In brief, they revolve around the idea that on the Sabbath we may not cause a "violent change in nature."[17] By definition the types of work that are prohibited are specifically the types of labor done in building the Mishkan,[18] the sanctuary that the Israelites carried with them in the desert.[19]

The sanctuary represented a holy place. Shabbat is holy time. Ultimately, sacred time is more important in this conceptual structure, which calls for cessation of the work that builds the sanctuary on the Sabbath.[20] In truth, no matter how holy an institution may be, it can become corrupted and defiled. However, the cycle of time, the passage of weeks, months, and years, eventually and inevitably brings healing, purification, and truth.[21]

Moreover, the sanctity of time is eternal and continuous. Shabbat comes each and every week no matter what.[22] While sanctity may adhere to a place, such as the site of the Temple in Jerusalem,[23] the site may cease to function as a holy location,[24] at least for some period of time, as when the Temple was destroyed. For this reason the sanctity of time has been made the dominant motif in the Shabbat structure. Sanctity must always be a part of a Jew's life.[25] In this way Shabbat becomes a true eternal covenant between the Jewish people and God.[26]

Finally, our description of Shabbat has so far focused on the negative—the restrictions. They are often what one encounters first when one looks at Shabbat from the outside.

From the inside, on the other hand, there are strong positive aspects called the joy of Shabbat or *oneg Shabbat*.[27] The largesse of the Shabbat meals,[28] the special songs of the prayer services, the fellowship of guests and time with friends, the closeness of family, the "mitzvah night" aspect of Friday night which encourages husband and wife to marital intimacy,[29] the Shabbat afternoon nap,[30] the study of Torah in classes, sermons, and informal study groups,[31] and simply the opportunity for quiet contemplation and thought, all make Shabbat special in a highly positive way.

An interesting debate reflecting the Jewish approach to these "creative" aspects of Sabbath rest plays out on the pages of the Bibles published by the Koren Press in Jerusalem. In these texts, chapter 2 of the book of Genesis begins as it does in all Bibles, after the description of God's creation on the sixth day and before the description of God's rest on Shabbat. However, in the opposite margin from where the chapter designation normally appears, there is a second designation for chapter 2, but this time at the end of the seventh-day-Shabbat-of-God's-rest description.[32] This dual designation represents a classic Jewish-Christian debate.

Christians controlled printing in the era of the development of the printing press. In the first printed Bibles, they divided the text into chapters in accordance with Christian interpretation.[33] The Koren texts conform to this because these chapter breaks have become standard over the more than five hundred years of Bible printing,[34] and citations in books that quote the Bible use this system. But Koren also provides an indication of where the "Jewish" chapters would be.[35]

The difference here is not just cosmetic. It reflects a debate on the question of whether Shabbat is to be considered one of the days of creation. For Christians, creation ends after six days. For Jews, Shabbat is also part of creation. It is a day of creative spiritual rest. Physical work may be prohibited; spiritual work, however, is the essence of the day.

Like Shabbat Kashrut involves restrictions. The general structure of the dietary laws involves prohibitions on meat from certain animals,[36] on mixing meat and dairy,[37] and on the way that animals which may be eaten must be killed.[38] In addition, there are requirements about removing insects from vegetables,[39] about not violating various agricultural laws that apply to Israeli produce,[40] about the utensils that are used,[41] and about other elements of the preparation process, such as the removal of blood by salting meat before it is cooked and eaten.[42] In short, it is a fairly pervasive regimen.

Our most primal and basic need is the need to eat. When we are first born, there is little if anything else for which we express need other than to eat and drink. In bringing that need into a strong spiritual structure, Judaism works to get our acquisitive actions under proper control, hopefully preventing us from descending into excess, hedonism, and perhaps even violence in pursuit of things we desire.

Further, although some deny that there is any specific symbolism associated with what is kosher as opposed to what is not kosher,[43] many do see at least pedagogic meaning in the structure of kashrut. For example, the separation of milk, the life-giving and sustaining liquid, from meat, which comes to us through the taking of an animal's life, teaches an important object lesson that we all must learn, i.e. that life, even of an animal we are are permitted to eat must be treated with respect.[44]

So, too, the fact that birds of prey and those that eat carrion are not considered kosher[45] may represent symbolically controlling our blood-lust by setting up restrictions on what we eat. Thus we do not consume birds that find their sustenance through aggressive behavior. A popular slogan in the 1960s, often seen on bumper stickers, declared, "You are what you eat."[46] At least symbolically, some of the kashrut laws may be related to this concept.

Further, it is interesting that the one law given explicitly by God to Adam and Eve in the Bible was a kashrut law, or at least a dietary law. Adam and Eve were told not to eat from the Tree of Knowledge of good and evil. In fairly short order, however, as told by the Bible, the first couple couldn't resist the temptation, especially given the snake's encouragement. This caused us to be exiled from the Garden of Eden, and made our existence far more difficult than it needed to be.[47] The struggle to control our appetite has been around for as long as human beings have existed. Kashrut has helped and continues to help in that struggle.

You will have noticed that no suggestion is made here that kashrut was designed for health reasons.[48] This is a common claim that some people make, often as a reason not to keep kosher. They argue that because of modern techniques of cleanliness we need no longer fear the diseases that kashrut once helped prevent. Aside from being factually incorrect (kosher meat can also carry diseases),[49] there are virtually no traditional sources that see kashrut as health legislation.

Instead, the suggested reasons speak to developing a sense of sanctity[50] and control of the aggressive pursuit of human needs, as described here.[51]

Finally, kashrut helps build Jewish communities in two ways. First, to support kosher stores so that kosher food is available, a critical mass of observant individuals must live in reasonable proximity. In fact, one of the signs of a maturing traditional Jewish community is the growth of kosher food outlets and restaurants.

Second, placing restrictions on eating the food that is generally eaten by Gentiles leads directly to limitations in socialization. This second limitation helps prevent intermarriage.[52] For a small minority such as the Jewish community, which sees itself threatened by assimilation and intermarriage, this, too, is a desirable outcome.

1. Some works on these subjects are Isaiah Grunfeld, *The Sabbath: A Guide to its Understanding and Observance* (New York, 1954); Abraham Joshua Heschel, *The Sabbath: Its Meaning for Modern Man* (Boston, 2003); Y. Neuwirth, *Shemirath Shabbat Kehilkhata: A Guide to the Practical Observance of the Sabbath* (New York, 1989); Adin Steinsaltz, *Miracle of the Seventh Day: A Guide to the Spiritual Meaning, Significance and Weekly Practice of the Jewish Sabbath* (San Francisco, 2003); Isaiah Grunfeld, *The Jewish Dietary Laws* (London, 1972); Y. Lipschutz, *Kashruth: A Comprehensive Background and Reference Guide to the Principles of Kashruth* (Brooklyn, 1988).

2. Along with the laws of family purity, these are the institutional bottom lines of the observant Jew and the traditional Jewish community.

3. Because of doubt concerning when the day actually begins and ends, the Sabbath may be said to commence at sunset, and concludes when three medium-brightness stars become visible in the sky, which is a good deal later than sunset. In addition, because of its importance, we add time to the Sabbath both at its beginning and at its end. (For discussion, see *Encyclopedia Talmudit*, s.v. *bein hashmashot*; *Shulhan Arukh*, Orah Hayyim 261:2–3 and 293:1.

4. See generally Neuwirth, *Shemirath Shabbat Kehilkhata*.

5. Preparation for Sabbath is an important part of the experience, see *Avodah Zarah* 3a and *Shulhan Arukh*, Orah Hayyim 242–267.

6. Note the number of food-related commercials on television and the prevalence of restaurants in commercial areas.

7. See Halperin and Oratz, *Shabbat and Electricity* (Jerusalem, 1993).

8. Exodus 31:17; Leviticus 11:44–45.

9. See my "The Earth Is the Lord's," *Jewish Action* 50, no. 3 (Summer 1990).

10. See chapter 27 for discussion of traditional Judaism's position on tobacco use.

11. See the discussion of ethics in chapter 21.

12. See Genesis 2:1–3.

13. See R. Joshua's opinion in Eruvin 100a, "Sitting and not doing anything is greater." The principle appears in many later sources as well.

14. Cf. Mishnah Avot 2:16.

15. See below, Chapter 17.

16. See the sources in n. 1.

17. A phrase that my sainted teacher Rabbi Joseph Soloveitchik used in this context.

18. Cf. Rashi, Shabbat 5a, s.v. *lediglei midbar*.

19. See Exodus 25–31 and 35–40.

20. Leviticus 19:30, 26:2; Yevamot 6a.

21. See Genesis Rabbah 8:5; Isaiah 40:27ff.; Hosea 14:2ff.

22. This is implied in the law that if one is, for example, in a desert and does not know what day it is and cannot find out, one counts seven days and then makes Shabbat for himself (*Shulhan Arukh*, Orah Hayyim 344:1).

23. Cf. Maimonides, Hilkhot Bi'at Hamikdash and Hilkhot Beit Habekhirah.

24. It retains its holiness, in any case, which is why traditional Jews avoid visiting it to this day.

25. Leviticus 19:2.

26. Exodus 31:16–17.

27. The phrase derives from Isaiah 58:13; see Radak ad loc., Shabbat 118a–b.

28. Cf. Shabbat 118a, 118b; Maimonides Hilkhot Shabbat 30:9, Hilkhot Ishut 12:10.

29. See chapter 30.

30. Sha'arei Teshuva, Orah Hayyim 4:17.

31. Shulhan Arukh, Orah Hayyim 290:2.

32. Genesis 2:3.

33. The chapter designations were created by a thirteenth-century British priest.

34. The first printed Bible (in Latin) was finished in 1465. The first Hebrew printed Bible that we know of was finished in 1488, though there may be ear-

lier printings. Most of our hebrew Biblical texts are based on early-sixteenth-century printings by Bomberg. The first English Bible was printed in 1535.

35. See *Koren Tanakh* (Jerusalem, 1986) third page of the introduction (the pages are not numbered.)

36. See Leviticus 11, Deuteronomy 14.

37. Based on the three times that the verse prohibiting cooking a kid in its mother's milk appears in the Bible: Exodus 23:19, Exodus 34:26, Deuteronomy 14:21. See Rashi to Exodus 34:26, Hullin 115b.

38. Cf. Hullin 28a.

39. See *Shulhan Arukh*, Yoreh De'ah 84.

40. See J. M. Epstein, *Arukh ha-Shulhan He'atid* (Jerusalem, 1969).

41. See Lipschutz, *Kashruth*.

42. See *Shulhan Arukh*, Yoreh De'ah 69 ff.

43. Cf. Maimonides, *Guide for the Perplexed* 3:26.

44. See the commentaries of Samson Raphael Hirsch and Elimelech of Lyzhansk, *Noam Elimelech*, Exodus 23:19, for a similar approach.

45. See Leviticus 11:13–20 and Deuteronomy 14:11–20.

46. See Isaac b. Moses Arama, *Akedat Yitzhak*, gate 64, n. 6, for similar sentiments.

47. Genesis 2–3.

48. See *Sefer ha-Hinnukh* 92.

49. For example, mad-cow disease.

50. See the biblical sources cited above and Arama, *Akedat Yitzhak*, gate 64.

51. See Hirsch's commentary to the full range of the dietary laws, particularly to Leviticus 17:10–12, and *Sefer ha-Hinnukh* 148.

52. Cf. Avodah Zarah 31b, 35b; *Shulhan Arukh*, Yoreh De'ah 112–114.

Chapter 13
The Experience of Prayer

The original version of this essay was published in my local Jewish newspaper and then was picked up by a Jewish website on the Internet. I don't believe I have ever received as much positive feedback from any piece of writing, and so I include it here as part of my discussion of the subject of prayer:

My father, of blessed memory, though an observant man, was not the most knowledgeable in terms of Jewish sources. Nonetheless, he found many important ways to express his belief in God and in Judaism. Most prominent among them was his dedication to prayer.

Professionally he was a traveling salesman, selling plumbing and heating supplies throughout New Jersey. I remember him getting up at four o'clock in the morning so that he could leave our home in Brooklyn and make it to services in a synagogue somewhere near a building site that was the location of his first appointment for the day. He could easily have gotten up at six or seven and prayed at home, but for him it was necessary to attend synagogue services as often as humanly possible.

Even in his seventies, my father would walk the eight blocks to the synagogue in rain and snow on the premise that "perhaps some old man won't show up and we won't get a minyan." In that regard, he was not so much unique as he was

131

a member of a generation for whom prayer was far more essential than it is for us today.

Our generation expresses its religiosity in dialogue. Study, analysis, lectures, reading, commentary, debate: these are the stock in trade of our religious experiences. For his generation, prayer was much more essential.

One dramatic indicator of the generational change: over the years, my father went to synagogue a half-hour before the regular time for services. He did this to recite psalms with other members of the congregation. My synagogue has recently begun an early morning activity some forty-five minutes before services, but in our case, it is study of Talmud, not the recitation of additional prayers, that brings people together at the crack of dawn.

There are many reasons for the decline of prayer as the central mode of expression of our religious identity, but I want to focus on only one of them in this discussion. I do so particularly because it is one that those who live in the modern era, with its emphasis on productivity and excessively long workdays, will recognize.

One of the truisms of prayer is that it is a nonexpedient activity. By this I mean that praying as long and as intensely as one likes accomplishes nothing practical, at least as far as is immediately obvious to the one involved in prayer. In essence then, perhaps God will respond affirmatively to my prayer,[1] perhaps not,[2] but at the time that I pray, any response is almost always unseen. Even over time it is rare to see a direct correlation between a specific prayer and God's response.[3] I can spend an hour and a half in the synagogue praying with all my heart, and at the end of that time, not one thing has moved from my in-box to my out-box. Further, much of our liturgy consists of praise of God or thanks to Him,[4] not requests.

We live in a world that very much measures all activities by their productivity. It may be professional productivity, it may be personal-satisfaction productivity, it may be financial-gain productivity, but our standard of value is measured by what we have accomplished with the time we have spent. This is a uniquely Western and materialistic view of the world and of the way that we decide whether or not things are important.

Proper prayer cannot occur against this backdrop and this measuring rod. Proper prayer is a suspension of other activity and a diminishing of one's focus on material things for the sake of the spiritual and the connection with God.[5]

The Talmud says that of our three daily prayers, the one that may be most effective in gaining a response is Minhah, recited in the afternoon.[6] Minhah is, in fact, an invention of the Jews.

Many societies pray early in the morning when they first wake up to thank God for having gotten them through the dangers of the dark and of sleep. For us, this is the prayer that we call Shaharit.

So, too, many cultures pray at night as protection against these dangers. For us this is Ma'ariv.

But Judaism invented the idea of midday prayer, or Minhah. When one prays in the middle of the day, one is required to put down one's work and say that one's relationship with God is simply more important.

This is a spiritual, anti-materialistic stance. It is also anti-expedient. It is no wonder then that the Talmud suggests that this is a prayer that may be well responded to by God.

For those who wish to develop the capacity to pray and to create a relationship with God through the act of speaking to Him, it is this mindset which must be developed. Prayer means the cessation of worldly activities. It requires the realization that they are in so many ways less important than more spiritual things. It demands the ability to focus elsewhere than only on the most immediate and most expedient.

The rewards are the act itself. In the sense and to the extent that I feel that I do not have to be a slave to my work and to my worldly pursuits, I have had an experience of empowerment and freedom that most moderns never encounter. Sadly, those who cannot experience this freedom are lacking something important in their lives.

I am not talking here about down-time or vacation-time. I'm talking about something that goes far beyond that. For us, down-time and vacation-time tend to mean filling our days with other types of expedient activities that are different in behavioral content from our professional activities, but that are not different in spiritual content. The individual who, having some brief time alone in his automobile, cannot drive without the sound of the radio or the CD player, the individual who, on vacation, over-programs every minute with golf or tours, has not achieved the transcendence of the physical implicit in the nonexpedient prayer experience.

For most of us, the constant need to surround ourselves with stimulation and input means that we do not allow ourselves this transcendent state of being. Hopefully, more people will try the nonexpedient prayer experience and learn to put aside all the small concerns that torment us and fill our days, minute by minute, so that a more spiritual connection with our existence can be made. It does not matter whether one is Jewish or not, observant or not, religiously connected or not. If one utters a truly heartfelt prayer, the closeness to God is real. This is explicitly stated in the Book of Psalms[7] and is recited three times a day as part of our prayers.[8] Certainly, it is easier to pray properly when one worships frequently and is used to the experience of prayer, but the possibility of real prayer exists for everyone at any and every moment.

For those who need a more expedient reason, I will close by telling the following story. Years ago, I worked in the garment center in Manhattan. My job was the strenuous task of carrying goods and clothing through the hot city streets of the July and August when I worked that job. I was the only person of the many whom I encountered in such a position who was wearing a kippah (skullcap).

One of the people I often spoke to in my work was a fellow who sold zippers. I would be sent to him whenever the order for five thousand zippers for the five thousand dresses being made by my company showed up two or three zippers short. In fact, this happened almost every day, which is itself a sad commentary on the business ethics of some zipper manufacturers of that time. Inevitably, I would make my way to this fellow's shop to make up the shortfall.

The owner was Jewish, and noticed my head-covering. He told me that although he had never before been observant, when his father died, he began to go to synagogue to recite Kaddish, the mourner's prayer recited for one day short of eleven months after the death of a parent.[9] In that context, he had discovered the experience of prayer. It was his belief that because he was now coming to work a little bit later each day and taking some time off in the middle of the day to pray, his stress level had gone down. As a result, his ulcers had gone away and he was much calmer and nicer in his interactions with people. Although he was making a little less money than he had previously made, he was saving that money and more in reduced medical costs.

Some would say that I have now provided a purely expedient reason to pray. But I would say that all I have done is indicate that living a more spiritual lifestyle and finding some time where one is able to see beyond the petty burdens of one's day-to-day existence, is by its very nature a healthier way to function.

There are those who may need to hear about this physical manifestation of improved health in order to be motivated to give prayer a try, while others will understand or come to understand that the very spirituality of the experience is why it promotes health. The well-being that prayer brings is not just physical health, but mental and spiritual harmony as well.

1. A classic example of a very brief but successful prayer can be found in Numbers 12:13 (see Rashi ad loc., s.v. *refah nah*) and Berakhot 34a. See also Nachmanides, commentary to Exodus 33:7.

2. For an example of a prayer that received a negative response, see Deuteronomy 3:23–27.

3. We generally leave our prayers at the point described by the words from the Prayer for the New Month, recited on the Sabbath before the renewal of the lunar cycle, that "the wishes of our hearts be fulfilled for happiness." In other words, that God take our prayers and fulfill them in His way and in His time. Philip Birnbaum, *Daily Prayer Book* (New York, 1949), p. 381.

4. All prayers are to begin with praise and end with thanks, Berakhot 34a. This is true of the Amidah, our central prayer, and it is also true of the general structure of the morning prayers, which begin with verses of praise (Pesukei de-Zimra) and end with Aleinu.

5. See the discussion of kavvanah and *devekut* in the next chapter.

6. Berakhot 6b.

7. Psalm 145:18.

8. In the Ashrei prayer. Birnbaum, *Daily Prayer Book*, pp. 57, 127, and 157.

9. Maurice Lamm, *The Jewish Way in Death and Mourning* (New York, 1969), pp. 149–175; Leon Wieseltier, *Kaddish* (New York, 1998).

Chapter 14

Some Additional Thoughts on Prayer

In the movie *Oh, God!*, George Burns, playing the deity as an octogenarian vaudevillian, appears several times to John Denver, a supermarket manager, with prophetic messages. At the end of the movie Denver bemoans the fact that he may never be in communication with God again. Burns/God responds, "For now, you talk and I'll listen."

Profundity can often be expressed through humor, and Burns's one-liner reminds us that prayer is the reverse of prophecy.[1] It is, at base, communication between the human being and God.[2] To say this is to provide prayer with a gravitas that belies the casual way in which it is often treated. For those who ignore prayer and do not communicate directly with God, other pursuits seem far more significant. Sadly, even among those who pray regularly the act is often done in the most casual and non-thoughtful manner, carrying none of the seriousness implicit in thinking about prayer as the reverse of prophecy.

Part of the problem is that we pray to an unseen Being. Forming a true connection can, therefore, be extremely difficult. Our literature expounds two concepts that aid the process by helping to structure this part of our relationship with the Creator. These constructs are kavannah[3] and *devekut*.[4]

The Hebrew word *kavannah* means "inclination" or "intent" and asks us to find mechanisms and spiritual energy to focus our hearts and minds on the words of prayer and through them on God. To do this, many different approaches can be tried. One is to use the meaning of the words as a source of inspiration. Often people are unaware of what the prayers say and therefore are forced to recite them by rote. Obviously, prayer would be a considerably more positive experience if people understood the meaning of what they were communicating to God.

Not only can the direct meaning of the prayers inspire one to spiritual heights, but free association is allowed here, and virtually any thought important to the individual that is evoked in any fashion by the words ought to be encouraged. For this reason alone, study of the prayers should be given priority in Jewish educational settings.

These comments invite the question of why traditional Jews insist on retaining the Hebrew liturgy even in eras when most Jews do not speak the language. First, no translation can possibly capture the nuances of another language. Hebrew terminology is simply best suited to express the Jewish cultural values implicit in our prayers from which both the language and the prayers emerge.[5] Second, it is an ultimately unifying experience to walk into any Orthodox synagogue, anywhere in the world, and find that the central prayers are essentially the same. For traditional Jews, this means that they are truly part of a worldwide community at prayer.

Thankfully, objections to Hebrew as the language in which we speak to God have diminished with the re-establishment of the State of Israel and its adoption and reinvigoration of Hebrew as its national tongue. Pride in Israel makes questioning of the language of prayer difficult if not impossible.[6]

One other neglected area of study can help us in prayer as well. Most Jews are remarkably unaware of the history of the prayers they recite.[7] Every six weeks or so for many years I have replaced the usual sermon on Saturday morning in my synagogue with a discussion of liturgy. I have used this time to talk about the history of one or another prayer or of some other important liturgical element, such as the prescribed melody for chanting the prayers. This series, which I call "Connections in the Prayer Book," has taught me and, hopefully, my congregants about the important array of forces—historical events, philosophical challenges, censorship and the reaction to it, schisms within the community, theological expressions and concerns—that have shaped our religious life both in prayer and in other areas of religious practice. This type of study can also provide inspiration for kavannah.

Mentioning the *nusah*, or liturgical chant, offers another avenue for kavannah. Generations of cantors and other talented experts on Jewish liturgical music created chants and songs to fit, not only the words of the prayers, but also the days or even the time of day when various prayers are recited. You might find the same words on a weekday as on the Sabbath or a holiday, you might find the same prayer on a Friday night as on a Sabbath morning, but you would not recite the same text in the same way on the different occasions. The spiritual moods are different, and the musical modes are not, and should not be, the same.[8]

Some prayer leaders have begun to use more modern tunes in their presentation of the liturgy.[9] Sometimes this is inspiring and helpful. Unfortunately, in many cases the music is simply wrong. It can be inappropriate as to time and place and distortive of the words and their purpose. Often, it causes inappropriate spacing of the words and wreaks havoc with the meaning by separating words that belong together and joining those that should remain apart.[10] The use of tunes in one service that belong in a different service at a different time has also become an all-too-frequent occurrence.[11]

The opportunity to lead the prayers, at least on an occasional basis,[12] is often readily available to anyone obligated to take part in communal prayer.[13] Any man over the age of thirteen and one day may fill that role.[14] One need not be a Rabbi or a cantor. While having many possible participants is desirable, the need for better training of those who want to serve in this capacity is clear.[15]

Beyond the formal aspects of the liturgy, almost anything can be used to enhance kavannah if it works. The shapes of the letters, the light coming through the windows, the smudges on the pages of my prayer book, can all be called on, if effective, to carry my heart and soul heavenward.

What we are talking about, ultimately, is creating an appropriate mood for prayer. The mood can vary. At times we approach God with emotions and words that tend toward fear, anxiety, and a sense that in the presence of the Almighty we are nothing.[16] In other parts of the liturgy these "powerless" prayers give way to powerful expressions of celebration, joy, and confidence in our relationship with our Creator.[17] There are also moments when we are to feel gratitude,[18] pride,[19] and a range of other emotions.

To create such moods takes work, but it can be done. Jewish thought assumes that human beings are capable of structuring their emotional state through their intellect. In fact, directing one's feelings to the appropriate emotional posture is a requirement in a number of halakhic contexts. We are, for example, to be joyous on a holiday[20] and sad in the house of mourning.[21] It is the assumption of Jewish law that we can direct and control our emotions in these settings as well as in prayer.

However, as with any mood, the emotional environment appropriate for prayer can easily be shattered. For this reason idle chatter and socializing during services are seen as extremely negative.[22] Sadly, far too many people give in to the desire to communicate with their friends rather than their God while at services.

Devekut (or cleaving to God) is the end product of all of these attempts at proper mood and kavannah. At a certain point one can lose oneself in prayer and feel truly connected to the divine.[23] This spiritual, at least partially meditative state is called *devekut*. To use a mundane sports analogy, it is like being in "the zone" for an athlete. Basketball players will report seeing the basket as a gaping cavern that they cannot miss, and baseball players will speak of the pitch as if it were as easy to hit as a beach ball at certain moments of peak performance in their careers. In a spiritual sense, an altered state of consciousness of this type can and does come to someone who is actively focused on his or her prayer life. When it comes, one has achieved *devekut*.

Underlying the search for kavannah and *devekut* is the individual person praying. The Hebrew word *le-hitpallel* ("to pray") is in the reflexive mode. It requires one to look deeply inside oneself and present oneself to God honestly and completely. Only if one is willing to do this can prayer work. As the Rabbis say, *rahmana leba ba'ei* ("God requires the heart").[24]

Herein lies an answer to one of the frequent complaints about Jewish prayer—that it is repetitive, with essentially the same texts being recited every day or every Sabbath. While this is true, the reality is, also, that I am a different person every day. When I come to pray I can find today's new reality in the siddur, and it may well lie in different words or in a different nuance of the service than the place where I found it yesterday. This makes the prayers continuously meaningful.

In addition, several points in the prayer service are recommended as places to add one's own personal prayers. First, one can use the blessings of the Amidah,[25] Judaism's prayer par excellence, especially its central thirteen supplications, in this way. If you wish to add a personal plea that parallels the subject of any individual blessing, you are free to do so.[26] For example, if someone is ill it would be entirely appropriate to add a prayer for that person to the blessing known as Refa'einu,[27] which deals with God's power to heal. Similarly, a financial problem can be raised in the blessing of Barekh Aleinu,[28] which is understood to be a supplication for one's livelihood. In the same vein, praying for help with a test in school could be accomplished in the first of these thirteen blessings (Atah Honen), which deals with wisdom.[29] However, it is extremely doubtful that a prayer of this type would work without appropriate studying.

The last of the thirteen, known as Shema Koleinu, is a catchall blessing.[30] In it we ask God to hear and respond to all of our prayers. As such, any personal prayer can be added at this point.

A similar moment for expressing whatever one wants to say comes immediately after the Amidah. One can recite "even the full confessional of the day of Yom Kippur" at this point.[31] Interestingly, the Talmud records a series of personal post-Amidah prayers in both the Babylonian[32] and the Jerusalem Talmuds,[33] one of which can be found in our prayer books as our post-Amidah prayer,[34] while some of the others are used in other parts of the liturgy where they were found to be appropriate.[35]

Tahanun, the prayer of supplication recited after the Amidah on weekdays that have no festive character, may also originally have been a nonstructured opportunity for post-Amidah prayers.[36] Again, over time a set text was established.

This pattern of options for individual supplication being filled by set texts may simply reflect eras in history when ordinary Jews were unable, because of lack of education or sophistication, to compose prayers of their own.[37] Liturgical custom filled the vacuum with what we find in our prayer books at these points in the prayer service. Nonetheless, the option for individual prayer remains open, and many people make use of these opportunities. Moreover, God is available for personal communication at any time.

Some recent scientific studies have shown a statistical correlation between recovery from illness and prayer in that those for whom prayer is recited have a better prognosis than those for whom no supplication is made. These results are quite intriguing.[38]

On the other end of the spectrum, when a person is terminally and painfully ill, prayer for a quick and easy death is permitted.[39] Underlying it all is our faith that "God will fulfill the requests of our heart *for good*."[40] God is not a puppet who must simply do as we ask. He is, instead, a loving father who can be influenced by what His children request. Whatever his answer,[41] when we talk, He will be listening.

1. There are many books on Jewish prayer, written from a variety of perspectives and focusing on different aspects ranging from history to interpretation to the laws and methodologies of successful prayer. One work does a good job with all of these and more: Bernhard S. Jacobson, *Netiv Binah* (Tel Aviv, 1964. Three volumes of Jacobson's work are available in English: *The Weekday Siddur* (Tel Aviv, 1973), *Meditations on the Siddur* (Tel Aviv, 1966), and *The Sabbath Service* (Tel Aviv, 1981).

2. A prophet is not a fortune teller but rather someone who serves as God's spokesman. If God speaks to someone and gives him a message to be shared, he is a prophet. The English word implies "fortune-telling," but the Hebrew

navi relates to *niv sefatayim*, meaning "expression of the mouth." The prophet is God's spokesman, not a spiritual reader of the future. See *Encyclopaedia Judaica*, s.v. Prophets and Prophecy; Abraham Joshua Heschel, *The Prophets*, introduction; and above, Chapter 4.

3. There are many important discussions of these concepts in hasidic literature, e.g., the ethical will of Israel ben Eliezer, the Ba'al Shem Tov (ca. 1700–1760), the founder of Hasidism; see *Hanhagot Yesharot* 59–62.

4. The word *devekut* means "cleaving," or becoming intimately subsumed and attached to something or someone else, See Even-Shoshan, *Milon Hadash*, s.v. *devekut*. Interestingly, the intimacy of the husband-wife relationship is expressed in these terms in Genesis 2:24.

5. For example, the word *shalom* is appropriately translated into English as "peace." However "peace" can mean simply the absence of conflict, whereas *shalom* comes with the implication of the related word *shalem*, which means "complete" or "whole." This is a far more powerful concept than is implied by the term "peace."

6. The issue of the use of English in services was a seriously debated question even in Orthodox circles in the immediate post-World War II era, when the modern State of Israel either did not exist or had not yet made its influence felt. See Yaakov Yehiel Weinberg, *Responsa Seridei Aish* 2:9.

7. Some important sources regarding this history are the Jacobson volumes cited in n. 1, E. Levi, *Yesodot Hatefilah* (Tel Aviv, 1967) and Ismar Elbogen, *Jewish Liturgy: A Comprehensive Guide* (New York, 1993).

8. A major figure in the standardization of liturgical music was Rabbi Jacob ben Moses Moellin (1360?–1427), also known as Maharil, the foremost talmudist of his generation and head of the communities of Germany, Austria, and Bohemia. He defined appropriate liturgical chants not just by day and time, but by local communal variation. In other words, he describes the way the same prayer was chanted with different nuances or completely different modes in different communities in Europe in his time. This helped establish these local variations as local customs that could not be violated. See *Sefer Maharil (Minhagim)*, Hillhot Yom Kippur 11.

9. This in itself raises questions. See Eliezer Waldenberg, *Responsa Tzitz Eliezer* 13:12. For similar concerns much earlier in halakhic history, see Maimonides *Responsa Rambam* 254, and for varying opinions, Ovadiah Yosef, *Responsa Yabbia Omer* 6:7 and *Yehave Da'at* 2:5.

10. I recall a prayer leader who began the U-va le-Tziyyon prayer of the morning service in a way that could only be translated as "A redeemer shall come to Zion and to those who return. There is sin in Jacob." The correct diction would have had him saying, "A redeemer shall come to Zion and to those who return from sin in Jacob." His version, while more creative, was clearly inappropriate. Proper spacing of the words would have avoided the problem. His improper division of the words into incorrect phrases made the prayer into something its author never intended.

11. Moellin required proper use of liturgical tunes. See *Sefer Maharil* (Minhagim), Order of Prayers for Passover 12. See also Joseph Caro , *Shulhan Arukh,* Orah Hayyim, 128:21; Solomon ben Joseph Ganzfried, *Kitzur Shulhan Arukh* 100:12.

12. A permanent hazzan or cantor must meet a list of criteria; see *Shulhan Arukh*, Orah Hayyim 53.

13. Women and minors are exempt; *Shulhan Aruch*, Orah Hayyim 55:1. For further discussion, see below, Chapter 29.

14. *Shulhan Arukh*, Orah Hayyim 53:6.

15. Some Orthodox communities now require prospective prayer leaders to go through an audition before being allowed to lead services. This is done to detect and correct problems such as those described here before they show up in the synagogue in the middle of a prayer service.

16. For example, the words in the daily Tahanun, or penitential prayer, read: "We know not what to do, but our eyes are upon Thee," while the Yom Kippur Viddui, or confessional, says, "What are we? What is our life? What is our goodness? What is our virtue? What our help? What our strength? What our might? What can we say to You, Lord our God and God of our fathers? Indeed, all the heroes are as nothing in your sight, the men of renown as though they never existed, the wise as though they were without knowledge, the intelligent as though they lacked insight; most of their actions are worthless in your sight, their entire life is a fleeting breath; man is not far above beast, for all is vanity."

17. The Sabbath afternoon Amidah contains the words "You are One and Your Name is One; and who is like thy people Israel unique on earth? You gave your people a crown of distinction, a crown of triumph—a day of rest and holiness."

18. See the Psalm of Thanksgiving (Mizmor le-Todah), psalm 100.

19. Many sections of the Hallel prayer.

20. Deuteronomy 16:14.

21. Maimonides, *Mishneh Torah*, Hilkhot Avel 13:9; *Shulhan Aruch*, Yoreh De'ah 378:7.

22. *Shulhan Arukh*, Orah Hayyim 124:7, 146:2; *Responsa Yechave Da'at* 3:16.

23. See Gershon Scholem, "Devekuth or Communion with God," in *The Messianic Idea in Judaism* (New York, 1971), pp. 203–227. As a talmudic precursor to this, see the description of Rabbi Akiva's private versus public prayer, Berakhot 31a.

24. This is the usual formulation of the phrase (Rashi, Sanhedrin 106b, s.v. *rabuta*), but the talmudic formulation is *ha-kodesh barukh hu libah ba'ei* (Sanhedrin, loc. cit.).

25. The prayer called Shmone Esrei, the eighteen, though the current version has nineteen blessings.

26. Avodah Zarah 8a; *Shulhan Arukh*, Orah Hayyim 119:1.

27. The eighth blessing (the fifth of the thirteen).

28. The ninth blessing.

29. The fourth blessing (the first of the middle thirteen).

30. *Shulhan Arukh*, Orah Hayyim 119:1. See also Avodah Zarah 7b.

31. Maimonides, Hilkhot Tefillah 6:2.

32. Berakhot 16b–17a.

33. Berachot 4:7 (7d).

34. The paragraph that begins *elokai nezor*, which was the prayer of Mar berei De-Ravina, a fourth-century Babylonian amora famous for his saintly character; see Berakhot 17a.

35. For example, the first paragraph of our Birkhat ha-Hodesh recited on the Sabbath before the New Moon, is the daily personal prayer of Rav, the third-century amora who founded the academy at Sura; Berakhot 16b.

36. See *Encyclopaedia Judaica*, s.v. Tahanun.

37. See Jacobson, *Meditations on the Siddur*, chap. 4., pp. 28–36.

38. See the chapter on miracles, Chapter 17.

39. See the story of the death of Rabbi Judah the Prince and the prayers of his maid; Ketubot 103b–104a, and the commentary of Rabbenu Nissim of Gerona to Nedarim 40a. But see Waldenberg, *Responsa Tzitz Eliezer* 5, Ramat Rahel 5.

40. From the end of the first paragraph of Birkhat ha-Hodesh; see n. 35 above.

41. The answer can sometimes be no; e.g., Moses' beseeching God to be allowed to enter the Promised Land, and God's negative response, Deuteronomy 3:23–26.

Chapter 15
Tzedakah and Gemilut Hasadim

It is a well-known truism of Judaism that the Hebrew term *tzedakah* bears a very different connotation than "charity," its English counterpart.[1] Charity is giving by one in a superior position to one in an inferior position. It carries the sense of a gift given out of concern and compassion. However, it also brings with it the implication of some degree of degradation for the recipient.[2]

Tzedakah is entirely different. Because it is derived from the same root as *tzedek*, meaning "righteousness," it conveys the idea that the transfer of money to those in need is not fully volitional, but rather is something that is required. This is often explained as deriving from Judaism's underlying assumption that money and wealth are ultimately not the property of the one in whose care they are found. In the final analysis, all affluence comes from God, and it is He who has determined that a part of it must be given to those who are in need.[3]

This is not to say that Judaism is against private property. Quite the opposite is true. Many laws are based on the assumption of private property as an important reality. In fact, some laws assume an excessive preoccupation with protecting one's property to be part of human nature.[4] On occasion this can even lead to leniency in the law.[5] However, in ultimate terms, from the perspective of heaven and eternity, property, like everything else, is in God's final control.[6] From this perspective comes the imperative to give tzedakah, because God wants His assets to be shared in this way.

Nonetheless, even within the tzedakah structure the importance of maintaining an individual's private property appears. It is embodied in the limit placed on charitable giving. While one is required to give at least ten percent of one's annual earnings to tzedakah, one may not give more than twenty percent.[7] Our tradition was concerned that overly gracious contributors could themselves become dependent on others.[8] Further, excessive giving involves denial of reasonable self-interest and that is not appropriate. Hillel's famous comment, "If I am not for myself, who will be for me? But if I am only for myself, what am I?"[9] is also embodied in this law.

A number of sources urge people to go to great lengths to avoid becoming dependent on the community.[10] This appears to suggest that charity has a degrading quality. The seeming contradiction between this point and what we said at the beginning of our discussion in this chapter may reflect an important pedagogic aspect of our tradition. Occasionally Judaism will speak differently to those on opposite sides of an issue. For example one who borrows money is required to repay as he or she has promised.[11] On the other hand, the lender is required not to oppress or shame the borrower in pursuit of his or her money.[12] Often, the lender will demand of the borrower that he or she return the money, and the borrower will challenge the lender for being too aggressive. Jewish law words their respective imperatives in a way that requires the borrower to focus on the obligation to repay the debt, and tells the lender that he or she must go easy in pursuit of that repayment.

Similarly, in the charity situation the prospective giver is never to see superiority in possessing relative wealth. At the same time, the potential recipient is encouraged to avoid being in the position of needing charity even if fairly heroic measures are the only means available to prevent getting to that point.

The limit for the poor person is reached when refusal to take charity creates actual danger for the impoverished individual; at that stage taking tzedakah becomes an obligation, and if the poor person won't accept it, we are bound to get it to him or her by subterfuge if necessary.[13]

Further, the comments directed at the donor calling for compassionate empathy challenge us to reach for the optimum of a society where being poor is not a shameful situation. Reminding the prospective recipient that we have not fully succeeded in this regard provides a focus on the cold reality of this world for all of us and on the tasks and burdens that we all face that we should meet if at all possible.

In this connection, it is important to note that Judaism sees work as a positive value.[14] In fact, we first encounter God in the Bible, in the story of creation, as worker and builder.[15] Encouragement of those in poverty to be part of the labor force if at all possible, is consistent with this value.[16] Productive labor is, for us, a positive expression of man's place in the universe.[17]

We have touched on the concerns about human dignity and the value placed on employment within Jewish thought. These ideas find a central place in Judaism's presentation of the proper way to engage in the giving of tzedakah as a "righteous" activity. In one way or another, a premium is put on work and on making sure that no one feels either superior or degraded by the process. This comes through most clearly in the classic eight levels of charitable giving formulated by the great medieval philosopher Moses Maimonides (1138–1204):

> There are eight degrees of charity, one higher than the other. The highest degree, exceeded by none, is that of the person who assists a poor Jew by providing him with a gift or a loan or by accepting him into a business partnership or by helping him find employment—in a word, putting him where he can dispense with other people's aid. With reference to such aid, it is said, "You shall strengthen him; be he a stranger or a settler, he

shall live with you" (Leviticus 25:35), which means strengthen him in such a manner that his falling into want is prevented.

A step below this stands the one who gives alms to the needy in such manner that the giver knows not to whom he gives and the recipient knows not from whom it is that he takes. Such exemplifies performing the meritorious act for its own sake. An illustration would be the Hall of Secrecy in the ancient sanctuary, where the righteous would place their gifts clandestinely, and where poor people of high lineage would come and secretly help themselves to succor.

The rank next to this is of him who drops money in the charity box. One should not drop money in the charity box unless one is sure that the person in charge is trustworthy, wise, and competent to handle the funds properly, as was Rabbi Hananiah ben Teradyon.[18]

One step lower is that in which the giver knows to whom he gives, but the poor person knows not from whom he receives. Examples of this were the great sages who would go forth and throw coins covertly into poor people's doorways. This method becomes fitting and exalted, should it happen that those in charge of the charity fund do not conduct its affairs properly.

A step lower is that in which the poor person knows from whom he is taking, but the giver knows not to whom he is giving. Examples of this were the great sages who would tie coins in their scarves which they would fling over their shoulders so that the poor might help themselves without suffering shame.[19]

The next degree lower is that of him who, with his own hand, bestows a gift before the poor person asks.

The next degree lower is that of him who gives only after the poor person asks.

The next degree lower is that of him who gives less than is fitting but gives with a gracious mien.

The next degree lower is that of him who gives morosely.[20]

As indicated, providing employment—helping the individual find self-sufficiency—is the most cherished value of all. In addition, one should take note of the fact that from beginning to end, the difference between the levels has little to do with the amount of the gift. In almost all cases, it is the emotional impact on the recipient, and at times even on the donor, that determines the hierarchy. Sensitivity to people's feelings is at the heart of tzedakah.

This is in keeping with the Torah's emphasis that the needy be given *dei mahsoro* (lit. "sufficient for his need," i.e., whatever is necessary to satisfy his particular needs).[21] The Talmud, based on this verse, recounts a number of instances of charitable giving tailored to the specific needs of the recipient.[22] One of these tells us of the famous Hillel serving as a runner before the horse (which he also provided) of a poor man. He did this because the fellow had once been rich and thus had been accustomed to this degree of honor, and having now become poor, was suffering psychologically from its lack.[23]

It is in part for this reason that personal acts of kindness, or gemilut hasadim, are considered to be superior in an ultimate sense to acts of tzedakah.[24] Personal acts of kindness are easier to shape according to individual needs than tzedakah. The Talmud cites other reasons as well.[25] Kindness has no limit, unlike what we have seen in the case of charity. So, too, gemilut hasadim can be performed both with and without money and to both poor and rich alike. Obviously, tzedakah is more limited in all these respects.

Further, acts of kindness, as specified in rabbinic literature,[26] include dramatic events, such as visiting the sick, comforting the mourner, and helping the bride and groom to rejoice, as well as simple acts, such as offering a kind word or giving a timely piece of advice.[27] All through our lives there are many opportunities for gemilut hasadim; one only needs to be open to the opportunities and possibilities.

The greatest kindness one can engage in is kindness to the dead.[28] Since such acts can never, in principle, be repaid by the one to whom the kindness is done,[29] they must, by the realities of nature, be a purely altruistic kindness. Such things as serving on a hevra kaddisha, the "sacred society" that prepares the dead for burial,[30] or completing a task for one who has passed away would fall into this category.

Many of the named acts of kindness mentioned in rabbinic literature are derived talmudically from actions that God performs in the biblical narrative. God buries Moses,[31] visits Abraham while he is recovering from his circumcision,[32] and provides a marriage for Adam and Eve.[33] Based on a principle often called by its Latin name, *imitatio dei*, or the imitation of God, we are required to do the same.[34] Deriving acts of kindness in this way reminds us that when we perform them we are truly doing Gods work.

Most see these requirements as emerging from the biblical verses that speak of us as "walking in God's path."[35] Obviously, that is not something we can do in a literal sense.[36] Instead, we are to imitate God's actions.[37] Maimonides, on the other hand, sees these altruistic behaviors as coming from the commandment to "love your neighbor as yourself."[38]

In any case, acts of kindness are the glue that link people into a community or society.[39] While laws are critical, an intensely law-based society will produce far too many individuals demanding their just due at every turn. This is not conducive to the well-being of society. Only the mutual goodwill engendered by reciprocal acts of kindness will enable people to neglect whatever minor slights will inevitably occur. It will also help draw people together into a community of concern and mutual regard.

1. A. Cohen, *Everyman's Talmud* (New York, 1949), p. 219.

2. Some worthwhile sources on these subjects are Jack Spiro, "An Exploration of Gemilut Hasadim," *Judaism* 33:4 (1984), pp. 448–457; A. Eisenberg, *Tzedakah: A Way of Life* (New York, 1963); Cyril Domb, *Ma'aser Kesafim* (New York, 1980) .

3. Cohen, *Everyman's Talmud*, loc. cit. See also J. D. Eisenstein, *Otzar Yisrael*, s.v. *tzedakah*.

4. The talmudic principle is *adam bahul al mamono* (a person is confused regarding his money); Shabbat 117b, 120b

5. Cf. Shabbat 153a–b.

6. Avot 3:7.

7. Ketubot 50a. See Domb, *Ma'aser Kesafim*, chap. 1.

8. Ketubot 50a, Maimonides, *Mishneh Torah*, Hilkhot Arkhin 8:13.

9. Avot 1:14. See also Bava Metzia 62a, and the famous case of two people traveling in the desert with only enough water for one of them.

10. Cf. Shabbat 118a, Pesahim 113a, Berakhot 48b.

11. Nachmanides, Commentary to Leviticus 19:17.

12. Exodus 22:24–26.

13. Bava Metzia 31b. See Menahem Meiri, Shekalim 5:3a.

14. Israel H. Weisfeld, *Labor Legislation in the Bible and Talmud* (New York, 1974), especially pp. 43–57.

15. Genesis 1–2.

16. For a discussion of the imperative to imitate God, see below, Chapter 21, and also see the end of this chapter.

17. See also Cohen, *Everyman's Talmud*, pp. 191–196.

18. Avodah Zarah 18a.

19. The last two paragraphs refer to incidents described in Ketubot 67b.

20. *Mishneh Torah*, Hilkhot Matnot Aniyyim 10:10.

21. Deuteronomy 15:8.

22. Ketubot 67b.

23. Ibid.

24. Sukkah 49b.

25. Ibid.

26. Cf. Ecclesiastes Rabbah 7:7:3.

27. Jonah ben Abraham Gerondi (Rabbenu Yonah), *Iggeret ha-Teshuvah*; Israel Meir ha-Kohen (Hafetz Hayyim), *Ahavat Hesed* 3:5. For further discussion, see *Encyclopedia Talmudit*, s.v. *gemilut hasadim*.

28. The term for such kindness is *hesed shel emet* ("kindness of truth"); its source appears to be Genesis 47:29.

29. Rashi, ad loc.

30. See Maurice Lamm, *The Jewish Way in Death and Mourning* (New York, 1969), pp. 5–7, 239–247.

31. Deuteronomy 34:6.

32. Genesis 18:1.

33. Ibid, 2:22.

34. Sotah 14a; see below, Chapter 21.

35. Deuteronomy 13:5, 28:9. Cf. Jacob ben Asher, *Tur*, Yoreh De'ah 335.

36. Sotah 14a.

37. Ibid., and see also below, Chapter 21.

38. Leviticus 19:18. See *Mishneh Torah*, Hilkhot Avel 14:1.

39. Jacob Emden, Commentary to Avot 1:18; and see Judah Loewe ben Bezalel of Prague (Maharal), *Netiv Gemilut Hasadim*, chap. 3, for a somewhat more mystical statement of this idea.

Chapter 16
Mysticism

A ll religions give rise to mysticism, and Judaism is no
exception.[1] Religious practitioners eventually find
themselves too tied to the ground, the earth, the mundane physicality of daily life, no matter how sanctified and
sacred, and yearn for more.[2] Of course, every system of mysticism will contain elements unique to its particular faith background, but it will share with all mysticisms transcendence of
the physical world for a focus on something beyond. Often different mysticisms share much more. This is true even if, as
some Jews do, one believes in a divinely revealed Jewish mysticism.[3] Nonetheless, similarities to other mysticisms remain.[4]
This is an indication that mysticism responds to a deep-seated
human need. For this reason many people, even those who are
not particularly observant, are more than receptive to these esoteric teachings.[5]

Outside the circle of those who believe in the divine origin of
the Kabbalah (the best known Jewish mysticism, which became
popular in the Middle Ages), which makes its acceptance and
implementation mandatory, mysticism thrives under one of
two circumstances. Times of great difficulty or persecution push
people to escape the cares of this world, and mysticism can help
provide such an outlet.[6] Conversely, times of great prosperity
and affluence are also often times of increased popularity for
mysticism.[7] People who pause in the rat-race of their lives for

even a moment may come to question the meaning of an existence given over almost entirely to the pursuit of material pos-
sessions.[8] Finding the wanting of material things much more
valuable than the having of them can cause a crisis of meaning
and bring some to challenge the very purpose of life. At some
point, one may begin to wonder whether that is really "all
there is." Particularly children of affluent people, raised in
opulence and engaged in continuous conspicuous consumption, may come to wonder whether life has meaning beyond
the materialism of their homes and the apparently money-cen-
tered values of their parents. In these circumstances as well,
mysticism offers a possible answer. Nonetheless, the path of
mysticism is not without its dangers,[9] about which, more later.

What is mysticism?[10] Simply put, it is the study of the spiritual content of the universe, and for Jews, it is the study of
God. It is not the study of what God wants us to do; that is religion. It is the study of what God "is" and how He functions.
Such questions are not asked by mystics as an intellectual exercise; they are pursued as a life quest, and meaningful answers
are more to be experienced and lived than thought about and
analyzed. When George Harrison yearned for "My sweet
Lord, I really want to know You, / I really want to be with
You,"[11] he was stating the mystic's desire with a rock-and-roll
beat. When Norman Greenbaum sang about "going up to the
Spirit in the sky,"[12] he was doing the same thing.

For Jewish mystics, this quest poses an obvious problem.
Lacking a body and form, being infinite and fundamentally
beyond human understanding, the Jewish God is not easily
accessible to the mystics.[13] In fact, Jewish mysticism labeled
this initial reality of God the Ein-Sof (the Incomprehensible
Infinite).[14]

However, in an act of unknowable and only dimly understood love called *zimzum* ("contraction"),[15] the Ein-Sof partially retreated in one area of its essence, allowing room for the

physical world as we know it to exist. The first to enter this area were God's ten sefirot ("numbers"), or garments.[16] As clothing conceals but also allows us to partially reveal ourselves to others, so, too, God's garments conceal His essence (which we could never endure seeing directly) while revealing something about Him. The garments that emanate from God include His kindness, His justice, His rule, and His wisdom. It is from the study of the sefirot that Jewish mystics can begin to gather some knowledge of God and His method of functioning.

At the very moment of the creation of these "garment" structures, ten sefirot of evil simultaneously appeared, to keep constant, as it were, the balance of spiritual charge in the universe.[17] (It is remarkable how many of the constructs of kabbalistic metaphysics have analogues in contemporary scientific understanding of the nature and origin of the universe. Some even see strong parallels between string theory, the most up-to-date understanding in contemporary physics of the origin of the universe, and the doctrine of the sefirot.[18] Of course, the sources describing the sefirot are hundreds, if not thousands, of years older than the first presentation of string theory.)

These spheres of evil, the "dark side of the force," as it were,[19] have no vitality of their own. However, for reasons debated in mystical texts, a break occurs, a shattering of the vessels between the ninth and tenth sefirot, that scatters sparks of God everywhere, including into the sefirot of darkness.[20]

This merging of the sparks of God with these husks of evil, as they are called, creates the reality that we know. Everything that exists—the book you are reading, the chair you are sitting on, you yourself—is ultimately made from sparks of God in husks of evil.

I will pause here in describing the mystical system to make two important points. First, while this all sounds awfully esoteric, it is expressed in ways that reflect the deepest of human experiences. As indicated, the Ein-Sof retreats to make room for us in an act of love.[21] So, too, all acts of love are acts of retreat. When I make room in my life for a spouse, I can no longer do things only my way. I raise my children, and almost every day, though it may be painful, I retreat a little bit so they can grow up and have their own lives.

Second, we have here a critical difference between mystical and nonmystical thought, with vast implications for how one sees the world and one's place in it. For those who are not mystics, God created the world, and though He is present in it, the world is not part of Him and does not stem from His essence. For the mystic, the precise opposite is true. The world we know is an illusion. At its root, everything we make contact with owes its existence to the spark of God that is present at its core.

Depending on which view I follow, the difference in how I perceive myself and my place and stake in the universe is dramatic. Specifically, the mystical worldview will yield an approach to the world that is significantly more passive, respectful, spiritualizing, and sanctifying (both in the holy and the taboo untouchable sense) than will emerge from a rationalist worldview.

Returning to our sparks of God embedded in the husks of evil, see chap. 10, this is obviously not a place where sparks of God want to be. They yearn to return to God. We help them to do so in the kabbalistic system by performing mitzvot, God's commandments, with their physical embodiments and in their presence.[22] For example, lighting Shabbat candles or waving a lulav helps the sparks of God embedded in these items and in the surroundings where the mitzvah is performed move upwards toward God. If we focus our intent on the right holy thoughts as we perform these acts, we affect and raise these sparks even more.[23]

The sparks of God can be thought of as being in exile when in the husks of evil yearning to be redeemed. Thus, the diaspora experience of the Jewish people parallels that of the divine sparks.[24]

When all the sparks return to their proper places, the world will be redeemed, the Messiah will come, and our human task will be complete.[25] In the meantime, every positive act no matter how small, is a step toward bringing the Messiah—and may even be the very last step that will bring final redemption to God's lost sparks and exiled people. As such, every mitzvah, every good deed, is of cosmic significance.

There is, of course, much more to Jewish mysticism, or Kabbalah, but that is beyond our scope. However, Kabbalah is not a basic belief of Judaism, and one can be a full and complete Jew while disbelieving all of it. Nonetheless, one must recognize its contribution. Many of our prayers, and especially a large segment of our Friday night rituals, emerge from this worldview.[26] So, too, many rituals and customs that are familiar to even the most nonmystical Jew originated in mystical teachings.[27]

There was an earlier mysticism in Jewish tradition that preceded Kabbalah. Kabbalah, the system described above, was first popularized in the thirteenth century, but the earlier one, known as Hekhalot or Merkavah mysticism, may date to the talmudic period, the Second Temple period, or even earlier.[28] Its literature features adepts such as Rabbi Akiva entering heaven (sometimes called Pardes) to stand before God's throne.[29] This experience involves many dangers and requires traversing many (usually seven) levels of heaven. However, the visions and experiences are worth the risk for those who succeeded. While there are no practitioners of this brand of mysticism around today, the visions of these early mystics found their way into many of our prayers.[30] In fact, were we to remove all the mystical influences from our siddur, very little would remain.

One word of caution. Jewish mysticism is "currently in vogue."[31] Many groups offer mysticism classes and experiences, often on a one-time basis and even to rank beginners. The people who lived and live the Jewish mystical tradition and make it work are deeply religiously committed people. Their fidelity to Halakhah and Jewish values acts as a check against mystical excess. Nonetheless, terrible tragedies, such as the historically shameful episodes involving the false messiah Shabbetai Zevi and the charlatan Jacob Frank, came out of these teachings.[32] How much more must one be concerned about fundamental errors and abuses if the practitioners are mere dabblers and dilettantes.

Spirituality must be lived and pursued constantly; it cannot be turned on and off like a light switch. Also, false momentary highs raise expectations and may leave a person with no place to go for follow up. That type of experience can "turn off" far more than it "turns on." Nonetheless, even for those who do not live mystically, it is clear that mysticism is a powerful force in Jewish life. As such it must be treated with respect.

1. Gershom Scholem, *Major Trends in Jewish Mysticism* (New York, 1995), p. 7. This is still the best of the many books on the subject of mysticism.

2. In addition to the songs cited in the text below, this sentence is most directly related to Simon and Garfunkel's "El Condor Pasa." I cite these titles and these lyrics from the popular music of my youth because many of them have made mystical themes part of the popular culture and are, therefore, relevant to the discussion in this chapter.

3. *Encyclopaedia Judaica*, s.v. Kabbalah; Scholem, *Major Trends*, p. 9. To cite one actual mystical source, see Elijah ben Solomon Zalman (the Vilna Gaon), commentary to Sifra de-Tzeniuta, chap. 1.

4. See Joseph Dan, *The Early Kabbalah* (New York, 1986), pp. 5–6, for a discussion of the similarities between Kabbalah and Oriental mysticism.

5. D. van Biema, "Pop Goes the Kabbalah," *Time* 150:22 (November 24, 1997), religion section.

6. The destruction of the Second Temple and the long night of exile in Europe are prime examples.

7. The counter-culture of the 1960s, the music cited above in n. 2, and the article cited in n. 5 all reflect this dynamic.

8. The many recent conferences on spirituality and the popularity of books and articles on the subject indicate that we are living through another era of this type.

9. As I write these words, Johnny Walker Lindh, son of affluent parents, is going on trial for being a member of the Taliban. The journey that led him to this point began as a search for meaning of the kind discussed here.

10. Scholem, *Major Trends*, pp. 3 ff., discusses several definitions. The one presented here is my own, but it draws on elements in his discussion.

11. The song is titled "My Sweet Lord."

12. The song is titled "Spirit in the Sky."

13. See above, Chapters 1 and 11.

14. Scholem, *Major Trends*, pp. 207 ff.

15. Ibid., pp. 160 ff. See chap. 6.

16. Ibid., pp. 205 ff.

17. This is the mystical understanding of Ecclesiastes 7:14. For a full discussion of evil in Lurianic Kabbalah, see Isaiah Tishby, *Torat ha-Ra ve-ha-Kelipah be-Kabbalat ha-Ari* (Jerusalem, 1962). The description here is dramatically less complex than the actual Lurianic system.

18. Cf. Michio Kaku, *Hyperspace: A Scientific Odyssey Through Parallel Universes, Time Warps, and the Tenth Dimension* (New York, 1994).

19. There are many parallels between the *Star Wars* movies and Jewish mysticism. For those with a sharp eye, there is also a reference to Star Trek in this chapter. Science fiction is often mystical in character.

20. See Scholem, *Major Trends*, lectures 6 and 7, and especially, Tishby, *Torat ha-Ra*.

21. Cf. Shemuel Toledano, *Sefer Mavo le-Hokhmat ha-Kabbalah* (n.d.), sec. 2, gate 6, chap. 7. It also allows for evil to come into the world; see Tishby, *Torat ha-Ra*, and Scholem, *Major Trends*, p. 263.

22. This is called *tikkun*. See Scholem, *Major Trends*, pp. 265 ff.

23. This is kavvanah in the mystical sense. Scholem, *Major Trends*, pp. 273 ff; Arthur Green, *Your Word Is Fire: The Hasidic Masters on Contemplative Prayer* (Brattleboro, Vt., 1993); Jacob Immanuel Schochet, *The Mystical Dimension* (Brooklyn, 1990).

24. Scholem, *Major Trends*, pp. 284 ff. Cf. Solomon ha-Kohen Rabinowich of Radomsko, *Tiferet Shelomoh al ha-Torah* (Jerusalem 1965), Likutim, II Samuel 1.

25. See the sources cited above in Chapter 10.

26. See Ismar Elbogen, *Jewish Liturgy: A Comprehensive History* (New York, 1993), esp. chap. 44.

27. See Abraham P. Bloch, *The Biblical and Historical Background of Jewish Customs and Ceremonies* (New York, 1980); Abraham Isaac Sperling, *Ta'amei ha-Minhagim* (New York, 1968).

28. Gershom Scholem, *Jewish Gnosticism, Merkabah Mysticism and Talmudic Tradition* (New York, 1960); Peter Schäfer, *The Hidden and Manifest God* (Albany, N.Y., 1992).

29. Hagigah 14b.

30. Elbogen, loc. cit.

31. This would seem to be a fulfillment of the prophecy of Amos (8:11–14) that there will come a time when there is a famine and thirst for God's word, but that those seeking it, while making great efforts, may not succeed in finding it.

32. See above, Chapter 10, and *Encyclopaedia Judaica*, s.v. Frank, Jacob, and the Frankists.

Chapter 17
Miracles

The power implicit in God's omnipotence includes the ability to supersede the natural order and create a miraculous reality that lies outside the normal rules of natural law.[1] The prototype of such miracles is the splitting of the Red Sea.[2] Despite a few attempts by traditional scholars such as Umberto Cassuto to offer a naturalistic explanation of this event,[3] the usual reading of the text, and certainly the midrashic picture of what occurred,[4] describe the behavior of the water in question in ways that defy the physical laws of how liquids function in this universe.

Three issues confront us in discussing this topic. First, the theological and scientific meaning of miracle. Second, the contemporary reality of miracles. Third, the effect of miracles on our relationship with God.

Classical Jewish sources take two completely divergent views of miracles. On the one hand, some thinkers, such as Hasdai Crescas and Nachmanides, see miracles as a sign of God's concern, involvement, and love.[5] For those who hold this position, the more miracles one discovers, the better. The passages in the Passover Haggadah that increase the number of plagues visited by God on the Egyptians from ten to forty or fifty and then find 200 or 250 plagues at the Red Sea, as well as those that recount the long list of God's miracles on behalf of our ancestors in our founding years, are part of this tradition.[6]

Maimonides and some others, however, see God's miracles as potentially an indication of failure.[7] If the CEO of a corporation needs to run down to the mailroom with some degree of frequency to see to the sorting of the mail, he has not set up a very efficient or well-run company. So, too, if God needs to step in and constantly adjust His universe, it can't be that good a piece of work. Some sources describe the miraculous "new entities" that appear occasionally in history as having been created by God on the first Friday afternoon at dusk as part of the seven days of Creation.[8] These entities include the rainbow, the tablets of the ten commandments, and the well that followed the Jews in the desert to provide water.[9] Such sources make these miracles an element of God's original plan for the world.[10] As such, they are not miraculous as they are not outside the rules of God's original creation.

This approach is also reflected in the sources that speak of God making the Red Sea's existence conditional on its opening to permit the Jews to pass through as they left Egypt or making the earth's coming into being dependent on its willingness to swallow Korah's band of rebels who challenged Moses, Aaron, and God.[11] In these sources, the miraculous events of history have again been made part of the creation. In effect, God's magnificent work in bringing order out of chaos was designed from the very first to deal with every possible eventuality. The CEO can, therefore, rest comfortably in His penthouse office in heaven, doing the things He needs to do while the mailroom takes care of itself.

A deeper philosophical debate underlies this difference concerning the nature of miracles. The approach that looks to minimize miracles sees God's creation as having brought natural scientific laws into being. These laws govern the functioning of the universe.[12]

It is interesting to note in this regard the first few sentences of Genesis. After the initial appearance of heaven and earth in the first verse, there appears to be a problem. The earth is "confused," and the presence of God is found on the face of the deep. In response God calls "light" into existence, which seems to solve the problem.[13]

Obviously, despite the emergence of light, these are very opaque verses. Nonetheless, ever since Einstein, science has understood the speed of light to be the fundamental constant in the universe. This essential reality of the universe mitigates between the energy state of existence and the matter state of existence (this is what the equation "energy equals matter times the speed of light squared," or $e = mc^2$, means). In other words, light brings order to the universe, and the verses in Genesis may describe God providing that order in the first moments after creation.

Scientists teach us today that after the mysterious "big bang" that brought our universe into existence, there were several moments when the physical constants of the universe had not been firmly established and matter/energy could not and did not maintain its discreet existence as we know it. After the universe settled down a bit and the necessary physical constants, the most important of which is the speed of light, settled in place, the universe, in a "physics" sense, became a place of order. It is intriguing how much of this theory one can read into the first few verses of Genesis.

In any case, the coming of natural law to the universe is a critical element for the minimalist theory of miracles. Scientific discovery of the physical laws of existence is a testimony to God's glorious creation. When these laws function well, God's wisdom is revealed. Miracles that violate these laws are challenges to that glory. For this reason two elements must always be part of one's understanding of miracles, according to this school of thought. First, any approach that minimizes the supernatural aspects of a miracle or offers a naturalistic explanation for it is a positive step.[14] Second, any true miracle must be traceable to a compelling motivation or a fundamental need.[15] Thus, the splitting of the Red Sea, which almost everyone sees as miraculous, will be explained, according to this school, by the fact that the nascent Jewish nation, recently freed from slavery and Pharaoh's claims of supreme authority, needed a display of God's true ultimate power in the universe in order to be able to begin its path in history appropriately.[16]

Supporting this overall approach[17] are statements like those of Maimonides that faith in Judaism is not based on miracles, but that the core events supporting our belief are revelation and God's direct communication with Moses, which were witnessed by the entire nation.[18]

On the other side of this discussion, some take the view that, in truth, no universe with constant natural law exists.[19] Rather, reality is a product of that which God holds in His mind from moment to moment.[20] This reality is "renewed, in His goodness, from day to day" or more precisely "from one period of time to another."

If this is the nature of existence, there is no a priori reason why God's next renewal of creation needs to produce the same set of physical laws as His last one did. It is just as easy for God's mind to create a world with split seas as one with seas that are whole. Out of kindness to our sanity and sensibility, the universe remains generally constant.[21] This allows us to discover what we see as natural law. But given need, or even the opportunity for God to show his love and concern, the next moment may well offer a reality radically different from the last. Such an approach tends to downplay the importance of the discovery of scientific laws. Still, the intricate interplay of nature remains a monument to God's creative genius through all the different realities He may choose to create.[22]

Are there miracles today?[23] A recent study, showing that people who were prayed for when ill had a higher survival rate than those for whom prayers were not offered, even if they were unaware that prayers were being said on their behalf, suggests that there are.[24] Certainly, the Jewish community's reaction to the Six-Day War and the recapture of Jerusalem seemed to deem it a miracle at the time. So, too, many happy or salutory events in people's lives evoke that reaction, at least immediately after they occur. Sadly, perhaps, such reactions tend to diminish over time. With familiarity, the miraculous, all too often, become familiar and unremarkable.

However, an important truth about miracles is that they can never be allowed to settle the question of God's existence completely.[25] If one did, if a neon sign appeared in the sky proclaiming God's reality, the human enterprise would be diminished to the point of insignificance. Under such circumstances, we would lose much of our free will. Further, our capacity to make commitments that transcended ourselves and the limited perception of our senses would be all but gone. As such, the quality of faith would suffer a crippling blow. Not only would our relationship with God suffer as a result, but our capacity to love one another, which requires trust in the unseen, would be undermined.

In a less scientific era, more spectacular miracles might occur because technology could not verify their supernatural nature. Today's miracles are, of necessity, more subtle. In the end it is here that miracles remain. That is just over the edge of probability, challenging our disbelief, hinting at an all-powerful loving God, but never getting us all the way there. Unprovability is the essence of their charm and their meaning.

George Burns, in Hollywood's humorous personification of God as an eighty-year-old in tennis shoes and baseball cap, is asked to do a miracle to prove that he is the Deity. He responds by saying that miracles increase the distance between man and God.[26] In part the preceding discussion supports that statement. Even for those who see miracles as a positive sign of God's hand in human affairs, and certainly for those who see miracles as a threat to God's perfect creation, the supernatural power of God is a manifestation of God's ultimate "otherness" as opposed to the human being. This increases the gulf between the human and the divine.

Perhaps for this reason we are always to see ourselves as controlled by natural law. While we can pray for miracles, relying on the supernatural is a losing proposition for us and prohibited by the Talmud's reminder, *ein somekhin al ha-nes* ("one does not rely on miracles").[27] Though they may be necessary or appropriate at times, and even may constitute a sign of love, a steady diet of wonders prevents us from connecting with God through the most important part of our relationship with Him. That is the image of God that is within us.[28] The similarities between man and the deity, and the challenge to sanctify those similarities are the elements that should truly animate our relationship with our Creator,[29] not our contemplation of how unalterably "other" God is from us.

Put another way, miracles are a sign of man's helplessness and powerlessness.[30] As discussed in Chapter 5, Judaism and Judaism's God are far happier and more comfortable with human beings who find themselves capable of meeting the challenges laid down by God and entering into a relationship with Him on that basis, than with a human creation incapable of functioning within the structure created for it and needing to be completely dependent on God's largess.

1. See Psalms 74:13–17. For a philosophic basis for this argument, see Saadiah Gaon, *Sefer ha-Emunot ve-ha-De'ot* 2:4, 3:4–5. An interesting compendium on the entire subject of miracles is Dan Cohn-Sherbok, ed., *Divine Intervention and Miracles in Jewish Theology* (New York, 1996). See also H. Kreisel, "Miracles in Medieval Jewish Theology," *Jewish Quarterly Review* 75:2 (1984), pp. 99–133.

2. Exodus 14–15. See *Sefer ha-Hinnukh* 132.

3. Umberto Cassuto, *A Commentary on the Book of Exodus* (Jerusalem, 1974), pp. 167–168.

4. Exodus Rabbah 21:10.

5. Hasdai Crescas, *Or Ado-Nai* 2, propositions 3:1–3 and 4:2; Nachmanides, "The Law of the Lord Is Perfect," in *Ramban: Writings and Discourses*, ed. Charles Chavel (New York, 1978), pp. 47 ff.

6. The paragraph popularly known as Dayeinu and the summary paragraph that follows directly after it.

7. Maimonides, *Guide for the Perplexed* 2:25.

8. Avot 5:6.

9. Genesis 9:12–14, Exodus 32:15–16, Rashi on Numbers 20:2, Ramban on Numbers 20:8.

10. Maimonides comes to the same conclusion on philosophical grounds, *Guide* 3:25.

11. Genesis Rabbah 5:45, Exodus Rabbah 21:6, and others.

12. This is the approach taken by Maimonides; see above, nn. 7, 10, and below n. 14.

13. Genesis 1:1–3.

14. See Maimonides, *Guide* 2:46–47; for an example of a biblical commentator who takes a minimalist approach to a miracle, see Radak to II Kings 4:4.

15. For Gersonides (Ralbag), a prophet or other righteous man must be present for a miracle to occur. See Robert Eisen, *Gersonides on Providence, Covenant, and the Chosen People* (Albany, N.Y., 1995).

16. This seems to be the implication of Exodus 14:31.

17. Though challenging the simplest reading of the verse cited in the last footnote.

18. Maimonides, *Mishneh Torah*, Hilkhot Yesodei ha-Torah 8:1.

19. In this regard we can cite the passage from the morning prayers that reads: *ha-mehadesh be-tuvo be-khal yom tamid ma'aseh bereshit* ("who renews each day, in His goodness, the work of creation"), Philip Birnbaum, ed., *Daily Prayer Book* (New York, 1949), p. 73. A rabbinic antecedent to this may be found in the claim that many unseen miracles, such as our digestive system, allow us to eat our daily bread; Exodus Rabbah 24:1.

20. Rabbenu Yeruham, *Da'at Torah*, Genesis, p. 40.

21. For an approach that makes miracles entirely a matter of human perception, see Elijah Eliezer Dessler, *Mikhtav me-Eliyahu* (Jerusalem, 1977), vol. 1, p. 177–183. See the Chapter on Evolution in this volume.

22. S. Bornstein, *Shem mi-Shemuel* (Tel Aviv, 1948), Genesis, Va-Yera 672–673.

23. See Niddah 31a for a comment that we would not recognize a miracle if we saw one.

24. See R. Byrd, "Positive Therapeutic Effects of Intercessory Prayer in a Coronary Care Unit Population," *Archives of Internal Medicine* 81:7 (July 1988), pp. 826–829.

25. See above, n. 9.

26. In the movie *Oh, God!*

27. For an early statement of this principle, see *Hiddushei ha-Ran*, Sanhedrin 65b. This is based on Pesahim 64b.

28. Genesis 1:26–27.

29. See above, Chapter 5.

30. And perhaps even of his sinfulness. Zadok ha-Kohen of Lublin, *Peri Tzaddik* (Jerusalem, 1965), Mi-Ketz 10.

Chapter 18
Afterlife

Perhaps no greater misconception about Jewish belief exists, even among Jews, than on the issue of the afterlife.[1] At least in my experience, the most widely held inaccurate idea about the faith structure of Judaism is the notion that Jews do not believe in life after the grave.

This notion is unquestionably false, and belief in an afterlife, usually referred to as the world-to-come, is well established.[2] Perhaps the perception that even traditional Jews do not believe in existence beyond this world comes from the relatively small degree of attention paid to this concept in Jewish religious discussions or teachings even among the most observant of our people.

This lack of focus has two important roots. First, while for some faith systems entry into heaven or its equivalent is a matter of some doubt and existential angst, for Judaism making the "cut" is relatively simple. The Mishnah begins what is, perhaps, its most philosophically important chapter with the words, "All Israel has a share in the World-to-Come."[3] Apparently, one is "in" as a matter of course.

In other rabbinic discussions of this issue, an opinion is advanced that gentiles who follow the basic Noahide code (see the discussion of gentiles in Chapter 8) also have a share in the World-to-Come.[4] This opinion was accepted by most authorities and implies a relatively easy entry for gentiles as well (see the discussion of conversion in Chapter 24).

The Mishnah and the Gemara mention exceptions to the rule that "all Israel has a share in the World-to-Come." For example, those who do not believe that the Torah came from heaven or who deny the resurrection of the dead at the end of days (see the discussion of dogmas in Chapter 11) are excluded from the final reward.[5] However, the Mishnah also makes the claim that in the roughly two thousand years from Abraham to the close of the Mishnah, only seven Jews out of the hundreds of thousands who lived during that period were denied a share in the coming world.[6] For most people, then, life in the World-to-Come is a pretty safe bet, and lots of energy need not be spent on worrying about whether or not one will get in.

Later Jewish writings envisioned a period of punishment intervening between death and entry into the next world. This period, however, was no longer than twelve months for all but the absolutely worst sinners,[7] after which one would find one's place in one's reward. Only for exceptional sinners, such as the Talmud's infamous seven, would denial of the World-to-Come be an eternal reality.

The second factor in downplaying discussions of heaven is Judaism's focus on granting value to this world and its challenges. The tractate known as Ethics of the Fathers includes the claim that an hour of bliss and lack of stress in the World-to-Come is equal to one's entire existence in this world.[8] This is not surprising, as it is a sentiment one can find in the ideology of many faiths. Ethics of the Fathers also states that "one hour of good deeds and repentance in this world is better than the entirety of the World-to-Come."[9] This is a much more remarkable claim.

I have often commented that the latter statement is the single most important talmudic teaching in defining Judaism's unique world-view. All faith perspectives understand the next life to be a place of joy and goodness devoid of moral failure, unfulfilled need, and suffering. For most this is an entirely welcome goal to strive for. Judaism, on the other hand, sees it as removing something very valuable from our lives—the ability to transform ourselves and our world in positive ways.[10] Though compensatory pleasures may exist in the World-to-Come, this element cannot be replaced and its lack is palpable.[11]

The last point embodies Judaism's focus on this world and its challenges. People like Elijah or Enoch, who abandon the concerns of this world for a holy life in a cave or on a mountaintop, are diminished in our tradition for doing so.[12] The tasks of this world, with all their moral ambiguities, and with the contact one must necessarily have with things that are far less than divine and pure in meeting these challenges, are to be borne by everyone.[13] For this reason a focus on the World-to-Come is counterproductive. Too much contemplation of what will be removes our desire and ability to focus on what is.[14]

Instead, we are given hints and a promise. The hints serve as a sign that if we do our job in this world, then when our time is done a reward awaits, and that reward is guaranteed by God's promise.

Hints about an afterlife appear in early biblical literature from Genesis on. The word *sheol,* found with some frequency in the Bible,[15] was traditionally translated into English as "the grave." It is now known to have been the name for the realm of the dead throughout the ancient Near East,[16] just as "heaven" is a generic term for a similar concept across many cultures and religions today.

Understanding this word in this way changes the meaning of many biblical passages. Particularly intriguing is the story in the Book of Samuel in which the prophet Samuel, himself is raised from Sheol after his death by Saul.[17] We now can understand this to mean that he brought him from the afterlife. So, too, the story of Elijah being taken into heaven in a fiery chariot takes on a new dimension, as there is a place beyond this world where people continue to exist.[18] Nonetheless it is true that the Bible is very inexplicit about the nature of the afterlife.

The Talmud provides many more details, but they are often contradictory. Are the souls of the dead aware of what happens in this world?[19] Does one retain one's physical body and the capacity to do physical things, such as eating?[20] Is purgatory hot or perhaps unbearably cold?[21] On these and many other questions, rabbinic tradition is divided.

This division not only remains but grows wider as embellishments and more elaborate pictures of heaven are drawn in the literature of the Middle Ages and into the modern period. In fact, the debate on corporeality in the afterlife may be considered a linchpin in the philosophical speculation of Maimonides (who denied any physicality in the afterlife)[22] that was in opposition to the views of many other medieval scholars, most notably Saadiah Gaon (882–942), perhaps the foremost Jewish thinker of the geonic period.[23]

The definitive Jewish statement about the afterlife may well be the Talmud's comment, *ayin lo ra'atah* ("no eye has seen it").[24] At least no eye belonging to someone of this world has visited there in a way that would allow its owner to report to us what it is like. Nonetheless, armed with our hints and our promise, we take up our tasks in this world and believe that our honest, good efforts here will end in eternal reward from a living and compassionate God.

1. See Simcha Paull Raphael, *Jewish Views of the Afterlife* (Northvale, N.J., 1994).
2. See generally J. D. Eisenstein, *Otzar Yisrael*, s.v. *olam*.
3. Mishnah Sanhedrin 10:1, Sanhedrin 90a.

4. Tosefta Sanhedrin 13:2. Maimonides codifies this opinion in *Mishneh Torah*, Hilkhot Teshuvah 3:5.

5. Continuation of the mishnah cited above in n. 3.

6. Ibid. Three kings, Jeroboam (primarily I Kings 11–16), Ahab (primarily I Kings 16–22), and Manasseh (primarily II Kings 21), and four commoners, Balaam (primarily Numbers 22–24), Doeg (primarily I Samuel 21), Ahithophel (primarily II Samuel 15–17), and Gehazi (II Kings 4–5, 8). Even these are in dispute; see Sanhedrin 90a ff.

7. See Eduyyot 2:20, Genesis Rabbah 28:9, Rosh Hashanah 16b–17a. Some of the sources are contradictory on this point, and the last one cited here seems to suggest that the end result of the twelve months of punishment is oblivion, and not entry into the World-to-Come.

8. Mishnah Avot 4:17.

9. Ibid.

10. This becomes even stronger in Jewish mystical doctrine, wherein the mission of people in this life is *tikkun olam* (i.e., healing or fixing the world), while the next world presents no such challenge. See Gershom Scholem, *Major Trends in Jewish Mysticism* (New York, 1995).

11. Maimonides, in his lengthy introduction to the tenth chapter of Tractate Sanhedrin in his Mishnah Commentary, presents a different and unique view of life in the World-to-Come. Given what he says, it is difficult to see how this world is better in any way than the World-to-Come.

12. Elijah: I Kings 19; Enoch: Midrash Aggadah Bereshit 5:18; *Sefer ha-Yashar* (Jerusalem, 1986), Genesis 11a–13a.

13. See Ta'anit 11a.

14. The Talmud, in Bava Batra 17a, tells of four persons who died simply because the snake in the Garden of Eden brought death into the world (Genesis 3) and not because of any sin on their part. These four, Benjamin the son of Jacob, Amram the father of Moses, Jesse the father of David, and Caleb the son of David, may have been fully righteous, but their accomplishments fade into insignificance when compared to what their famous relatives achieved. The involved life seems to be much more significant than the pure life.

15. The Mandelkern Concordance records sixty-five occurrences.

16. Brown, Driver, and Briggs, *A Hebrew and English Lexicon of the Old Testament* (Oxford, 1980), s.v. *sheol*.

17. I Samuel 28. Though the word Sheol does not appear, the "raising" of Samuel conforms with the general picture of Sheol as a realm below; cf. Genesis 37:35.

18. II Kings 2.

19. Compare Shabbat 152b with Berakhot 18b–19a.

20. Compare Berakhot 17a with Bava Batra 75a.

21. Compare Sanhedrin 29b with Berakhot 57b.

22. See his *Mishnah Commentary*, introduction to the tenth chapter of Sanhedrin, and his *Treatise on Resurrection*.

23. Saadiah Gaon, *Sefer ha-Emunot ve-ha-De'ot* 9:5.

24. Berakhot 34b.

Chapter 19
Astrology

The place of astrology and the supposed influence of the stars or other occult phenomena on our lives should, in our self-proclaimed scientific age, be a settled matter; but it is not.[1] Despite complete and total scientific denial of the validity of these things, somehow they remain part of the popular imagination. A brief review of history is in order here. At one time, astrology was virtually the only way mankind studied the stars. With the coming of the scientific revolution, and people like Newton, Galileo, Kepler, Copernicus, and Brahe, astronomy, the scientific study of the stars severed its ties with astrology, the study of the influence of the stars and planets on our lives.

By the mid-twentieth century, this divorce seemed to be complete. Astrology was referred to, generally, as pseudo-science, meaning false and faulty study masquerading as science, while astronomy, especially with the coming of the space age, was held in very high esteem. However, and perhaps a bit surprisingly, towards the end of the last century and on into the new millennium, with the rise of new-ageism and the diminished certainty about whether anything is or is not true, and even whether truth exists, astrology and the occult have made something of a comeback—at least in popular culture.

Judaism's relationship to the subject has in recent years followed much the same path as that of secular society. This despite the fact that in its origins Judaism differed very dramatically from the surrounding cultures in its attitude to such matters. The Bible tells of cultures for which astrology was fundamental to how they did business.[2] The peoples of Egypt, Babylon, Persia, and the other lands of the early Middle East saw astrology and the occult as providing essential guidance for the way in which they led their lives.[3] Nonetheless, astrology does not play a role in the biblical narrative.[4] When Abraham confronts a famine in the land, he does not ask an astrologer whether he should go down to Egypt.[5] When Jacob is not given the wife he anticipated,[6] he doesn't ask for a star chart reading. When Rebecca's twins struggle within her, she goes only to seek God,[7] not an earlier version of Jean Dixon or the Psychic Hotline. And that is precisely the point.

Situations are handled in one of two ways in the Bible; either God speaks and is then obeyed or disobeyed,[8] or God is silent and people make their own decisions.[9] Astrologers are not heard from, and thus a literary blow is struck for free will and against stellar influence. In fact, the only direct mention of astrologers in the Bible is a description of their being wrong when, at the time of the Babylonian invasion, they predicted that the Temple would be saved and the people not be exiled.[10]

When we move to the Rabbis of the Talmud and their biblical commentary, we note two things. First, the Rabbis found astrology playing a role in many stories where it is not mentioned in the Bible.

For example, Potiphar's wife was interested in seducing Joseph because an astrologer told her that she would have a son by him.[11] Of course she never did, but the astrologer was only off by a little bit, because she had a grandson by him. Joseph is described as marrying Asenath, daughter of Potiphera (Mrs. Potiphar, according to the Midrash), who bore him Manasseh and Ephraim.[12]

So, too, the Pharaoh of the Egyptian exile drowned the male children of the Jews in the Nile because his astrologers had told him that the Jewish savior would meet his fate through water.[13] Their error, of course, was that it was the water Moses brought forth from the rock by beating it and not speaking to it that caused him to lose favor with God,[14] not the waters of the Nile.

Even Abraham is seen as a great astrologer in rabbinic literature.[15] His complaint to God that he had no children is understood by the Rabbis as an astrological forecast by our first patriarch that the stars mandated that he would have no offspring.[16] It was in response to this astrological prediction that God took him out of his tent to show him that while the stars foretold that Abram would have no children, they forecast that Abraham would.[17] God then changed Abram's name to Abraham and made him the founder of the Jewish people.[18]

These three sources all make the second point. In the Rabbis' analysis of the biblical narrative, almost always when astrologers are present, they are wrong in some small detail. However, that detail makes the information they present faulty and brings grief, failure, and unexpected consequences to those who rely on it.[19]

The Rabbis of the Talmud are intriguingly, themselves pictured as consulting astrologers whose words sometimes come true. Nonetheless, they refer to these practitioners as Chaldeans[20] or Casdians,[21] thereby equating them with the people of Ur of the Chaldees, from whom Abraham broke away to begin his journey to God's promised land.[22]

Further, the Rabbis often find a way, through Jewish belief and practice, to defeat dire predictions by astrologers. For example, Rabbi Akiva (ca. 50–135), one of the foremost of the tannaim (the scholars of the Mishnah), had been told by an astrologer that his daughter would die on her wedding day, but she survived because she acted charitably to a poor person at that time,[23] thus teaching us that *tzedakah tatzil mi-mavet* ("charity saves from death").[24] Similarly, when R. Nahman (d. ca. 365), a Babylonian amora, was a child, an astrologer predicted that he would grow up to be a thief, but he became a great teacher instead because his head was always kept covered, first by his mother and then by himself. On one occasion, when his head covering accidentally came off, his natural desires took over. He took some fruit that did not belong to him, thus fulfilling the prediction in a way not expected when the astrologer made it.[25]

Some rabbinic sources see the stars as affecting one's personality, not the future course of events. For example, being born under the influence of Mars, the red planet, will give one an interest in blood. But whether that will cause someone to be a thief, a butcher, a doctor, or a mohel (ritual circumciser) is entirely one's own choice.[26]

Finally, one talmudic source, citing the verse "You shall be complete (*tamim tehiyeh*) with the Lord your God,"[27] prohibits reliance on astrology,[28] and according to other sources, *ein mazal le-yisrael* ("There is no astrological influence on Israel").[29] Nevertheless, we all say *mazal tov*, meaning "good planet" or "good constellation," on appropriate occasions.[30]

Come the Middle Ages and a great debate ensues among traditional authorities on the subject of astrology. Maimonides (Rambam), the great medieval philosopher, physician, and rabbinic authority, building on the *tamim tehiyeh* verse, claims that the many sources evoking astrology in the Talmud and Midrash are to be understood as individual opinions and therefore are not binding.[31] He insists that astrology is false, idolatrous, and prohibited, for one cannot believe in an operative superhuman power in the universe other than God.[32] He even blames the destruction of the First Temple on Jewish involvement with astrology.[33]

Roughly contemporary with Maimonides was the famous biblical exegete Abraham Ibn Ezra (1089–1164). Although Ibn Ezra was probably familiar with Maimonides' views on the subject, he nonetheless wrote books on astrology,[34] calling it a noble and sublime science, and he included astrological teachings in his biblical commentary.[35] However, even he accepted the idea that Jews could on occasion escape astrological influences, particularly negative influences, on the premise that *ein mazal le-yisrael*.[36]

Joseph Caro (1488–1575), the author of the Code of Jewish Law (*Shulhan Arukh*), moderated this view somewhat. In his *Bet Yosef*, he held that while astrology has its place and influence, one must be careful because astrologers can make errors, and therefore one should never rely on them completely.[37] In the *Shulhan Arukh* Caro includes Rambam's prohibition against seeking advice from astrologers but also treats some astrological considerations seriously.[38] For example, he says that we ought not begin new ventures on Mondays or Wednesdays, for these days are controlled, respectively, by the moon and Mars, both of which are unlucky.[39] So, too, we should only get married while the moon is growing during the first half of the lunar month and not while it is getting smaller.[40] Interestingly, these halakhot are not generally followed by even the most observant members of the contemporary Jewish community.

Significantly closer to the Maimonidean position is the fifteenth-century philosopher Joseph Albo, who conceded that astrology might have some influence but felt it was so fraught with errors and theological problems that it was best avoided.[41] Clearly medieval thinkers were split on the matter.

Jewish mysticism of the medieval period, like all mysticisms, gravitated toward the acceptance of astrological influences. In Jewish mystical teaching, all parts of the created universe, including celestial phenomena, emerge, in some way, from God and contain a spark of His essence.[42] As such, the theological problems of astrological influence diminish somewhat. After all, if the stars are made from God's essence, if a spark of Him, as it were, is there in the celestial bodies, it is ultimately God, embodied in the stars, who is influencing our lives in this worldview.

Moving finally to the modern period, a popular book of the 1940s and 1950s was *The Jewish Woman and Her Home* by Hyman Goldin. Though a good number of its characterizations would be out of touch with many traditional homes today, the book's section on astrology is very interesting. Goldin warns his presumably female readers, in the strongest terms, against bringing such pseudo-science and false idolatrous beliefs into their homes[43]—an authentically Maimonidean position.

I doubt that anyone openly disagreed with Goldin's stricture at that time, and for myself, I would have been content to leave it there. However, intellectual honesty demands one last stage to our story.

Recently, an article appeared in a major halakhic journal on the subject of alternative medical treatments.[44] The author, a well-known Jewish medical ethicist, joins in condemning these types of beliefs. The editors of the journal, however, felt constrained to add a footnote indicating that some believe these things to be legitimate.[45]

With the growth in the Jewish community of groups that do not value secular knowledge as much as other groups do, and with the emphasis these groups place on mysticism and their belief that mystical structures are extremely important operative factors in human affairs, it is no surprise to find astrology and the occult making a reappearance.

Nonetheless, it is important to note two things. First, astrology is not a fundamental Jewish belief, and complete disbelief and even opposition is the mainstream view. Second, even those who accept astrology as part of mysticism prohibit reliance on the newspaper's horoscopes or on the Psychic Hotline or its ideological associates. Perhaps astrology somehow finds a legitimate place for those who are experts in Kabbalah (mysticism). Until one reaches that point and then sees its validity, pseudo-science is pseudo-science.

1. Some literature on the subject: Y. Schwartz, "Jewish Implications of Astrology," *Journal of Halachah and Contemporary Society* 16, (1988), pp. 6–23; L. Stitskin, Maimonides' Unbending Opposition to Astrology," in *Studies in Judaica in Honor of Dr. Samuel Belkin*, ed. L. Stitskin (New York, 1972).

2. Jeremiah 10:2.

3. Egypt: Pesikta de-Rab Kahane 4:7. Babylon: Daniel 2:2, 4, 5, 10, and 5:7, 11. Persia: Nachmanides, on Leviticus 18:25. For a discussion of the Near Eastern background, see the *Anchor Bible Dictionary*, s.v. Astrology.

4. See *Encyclopaedia Judaica*, s.v. Astrology.

5. Genesis 12:10.

6. Genesis 29:25.

7. Ibid. 29:22.

8. Deuteronomy 28:1, 28:15.

9. This is true in many biblical sources. Eventually this silence can become truly painful, Amos 8:11.

10. Isaiah 47:13.

11. Genesis 39.7, Genesis Rabbah 85:5.

12. Genesis 41:45, 50. See Rashi to Genesis 34:1.

13. Exodus Rabbah 1:24.

14. Numbers 20: 1–13.

15. Bava Batra 16b. The apocryphal Book of Jubilees 12:16–18, describes Abraham as overcoming the beliefs of the astrologers, while Tosefta Kiddushin 5:17 explains God's blessing to Abraham (Genesis 24:1) as giving him the gift of astrology.

16. Shabbat 156a.

17. Rashi, Genesis 15:5.

8. Genesis 17:5.

19. Exodus Rabbah 1:24.

20. Cf. Shabbat 119a, Pesahim 113b,. The Talmud also refers to them by a Greek term, *itztagninim* (Shabbat 156a). Both designations indicate that this is a foreign phenomenon.

21. The term actually appears in the Bible, in Daniel, one of its latest books, in reference to the court astrologers of Babylon. See above, n. 3.

22. Genesis 11:28.

23. Shabbat 156b.

24. Proverbs 10:2.

25. Shabbat 156b

26. Shabbat 156a. See also Pesahim 113b. Some in this source see this as connected to the day on which one is born while for some it is dependent on the hour of the day that one comes into this world.

27. Deuteronomy 18:13.

28. Pesahim 113b. Note that one common term for "idolatry" in Jewish thought, *avodat kokhavim u-mazalot*, literally means "worship of stars and planets."

29. Shabbat 156a–b, Sukkah 29a, and Genesis Rabbah 44:12.

30. There is a belief that every individual has a personal patron star; Shabbat 53b, Bava Kama 2b.

31. Maimonides, *Mishneh Torah*, Hilkhot Avodat Kokhavim 1:16.

32. Maimonides, "Epistle to the Scholars of Montpellier Concerning the Decrees of the Stars," in *Iggerot ha-Rambam*, ed. Shilait (Jerusalem, 1987), pp. 474–490.

33. Ibid., p. 480.

34. For example, Raphael Levy and Francisco Cantera, eds., *The Beginning of Wisdom: An Astrological Treatise by Abraham Ibn Ezra* (Baltimore, 1939). See also *Encyclopaedia Judaica*, s.v. Astrology.

35. See his commentary to Exodus 23:28. Another supporter was Saadiah Gaon, whose commentary to *Sefer Yetzirah* contains astrological material.

36. See his commentary to Deuteronomy 4:19. For him, escape from stellar influence requires that the individual perfect himself.

37. *Bet Yosef*, Yoreh De'ah 179. This criticism appears in Talmud Sotah 12b and Exodus Rabbah 1:24 long before Caro expressed his concern.

38. Yoreh De'ah 179:1.

39. Ibid. 2. See his longer explanation in *Bet Yosef*, Yoreh De'ah 179.

40. Ibid.

41. *Sefer Ikkarim* 4:4. See also the skepticism of his teacher Hasdai Crescas, *Or Ado-Nai* 4:4.

42. See Gershom Scholem, *Major Trends in Jewish Mysticism* (New York, 1995).

43. Goldin, *The Jewish Woman* (Brooklyn, 1941), p. 127.

44. Fred Rosner, "Unconventional Therapies and Judaism," *Journal of Halachah and Contemporary Society* 19 (Spring 1990), pp. 81–102.

45. The editor's note appears on pp. 93–94.

Chapter 20
Authority vs. Autonomy

The central philosophical debate of our society, as we begin the twenty-first century, is the issue of authority versus autonomy.[1]

For those who believe in the former, morality derives from an objective outside source. For those who believe in the latter, right and wrong are a matter of personal choice and decision.

Autonomy has the advantage of elevating the status of the human being and, if practiced correctly, of emphasizing individual responsibility. All too often, however, it is used as an excuse for the loosest type of behavior for which no responsibility is ever accepted. Most frequently, it is reminiscent of the response given to Moses by one of the two Jews whom he encountered when they were fighting with each other. Moses was raised in Pharaoh's palace. When he first emerged into the world outside the royal court, he encountered an Egyptian beating a Jew. Moses killed the Egyptian. In this way he indicated that one is morally responsible for the actions that he performs. The next day he came upon two Jews fighting. When Moses demanded, "Wicked one, why are you striking your friend?" The reply was, "Who has made you personage and overlord or judge over us?"[2] In modern parlance, "Who made you the boss?" All too often, autonomy devolves into just this claim in response to moral challenge.

Further, as a philosophical matter autonomy is reminiscent of a character one finds in the nineteenth-century philosophical/mathematical work called *Flatland* by Edwin A. Abbott.[3] The book tells the story of scientists from the third dimension visiting scholars in the second dimension. The description of the world they encounter is meant as social satire.

At one point both sets of scientists visit a one-dimensional creature, meaning an infinitesimal dot. The dot, which cannot see beyond itself, fills its own universe—as least as far as it can perceive that universe. In fact it continuously sings its own praises, speaking passionately of how wonderful it is, since all existence is within its body.

When the two- and three-dimensional scientists approach the dot, they tell it in no uncertain terms that it is a wretched, infinitesimal creature which cannot even imagine the glory of what actually fills the universe around it. The dot rejects their comments, praising itself for its ability to both raise questions about its own glory and then to dismiss them as internal challenges meant to heighten its awareness of its own greatness. The dot cannot and does not even realize where the questions originate.

To my mind, the philosophy of autonomy as presently practiced sounds very much the same. Each person is a self-enclosed ethical universe. Each person is taught to sing his or her own praises as an autonomous source of moral authority. Each person is taught not to see an outside ethical universe. When a challenge is raised, either to a particular action performed by the autonomous individual or to the system of autonomy, the believer rejects it in almost the same terms as the Jews fighting in Egypt rejected Moses' words: "Who made you the boss?" This happens because the believer in autonomy can see no outside voice of morality that has any validity. Ultimately, however, the human being, when stripped of any presence outside himself, is an infinitesimal dot as against the eternity of space and time that makes up the universe in which we live.

Authority, on the other hand, creates a structure and a patch of ground on which to stand and from which to take in and make sense of the universe. Situations that arise and moral questions that one confronts can find answers in objective sources. This guidance is critical to finding an appropriate direction for oneself in a very complex world. It also frees one to make decisions in areas that are not morally controlled, meaning regarding questions where the choices are morally neutral or morally equivalent. In addition it gives one the opportunity to be individually creative in meeting one's ethical obligations. Finally, it gives one a sense of transcendence. Being part of something much larger than I am, taking my place in a relationship with God, which for the Jew means living according to His authority as centered in Torah and Halakhah, allows me to become much more than the handful of chemicals that make up my body.

It is in this way that we give meaning to the rabbinic claim that "there is no one who is free other than one who is involved in Torah."[4]

1. The issue discussed in this chapter provides a subtext to many of the other chapters in this book. For that reason no bibliographical list is provided here.
2. Exodus 2:11–14.
3. Edwin Abbott, *Flatland: A Romance of Many Dimensions* (New York, 1998).
4. Mishnah Avot 6:2.

Chapter 21
Ethics

The question of the place of ethics, that is, of objective standards of moral behavior other than those articulated in Torah and other classical texts, within Judaism is a complicated one.[1] On the one hand, there is our core acceptance of the idea that the Torah was revealed by God. Our belief in that revelation includes the fundamental idea that what God communicated to us is whole and complete (*torat hashem temimah*).[2] Similarly, we assume that the Torah's laws are righteous, given that the God who gave them is ultimately and absolutely righteous.[3] In light of these beliefs, independent ethical constructs to guide behavior would seem to be unnecessary.

On the other hand, many sources in halakhic literature indicate that there is a dimension of proper behavior in Judaism beyond that which is codified. Most directly, a number of talmudic sources speak of people acting *lifnim mi-shurat ha-din* ("beyond the line of the law"),[4] in situations where doing so adds a dimension of concern or kindness not present if one were only to follow the requirements that are halakhically defined. For example, returning a lost object to its original owner in circumstances where Halakhah would allow someone to keep what he has found can be described as acting *lifnim mi-shurat ha-din*.[5]

One medieval thinker attempted to find a way to integrate these meta-halakhic acts into the halakhic legal system. In his

Sefer Mitzvot Katan, Rabbi Isaac ben Joseph of Corbeil in northern France (d. 1280), included the obligation to go beyond the letter of the law in his list of the 613 commandments.[6] This suggestion that the Jewish legal system requires one to go beyond the legal system is truly thought provoking.

Commenting on the Torah's imperative that we "be holy,"[7] the great Spanish sage Nachmanides (1194–1270) speaks of the individual who follows the letter of every halakhah and is still a reprobate.[8] As with any legal system, even the most punctiliously observant person can find leeway or loopholes for inappropriate activities. A truly ethically sensitive individual will avoid such behavior. Nachmanides offers gluttony as an example of behavior that should be avoided even though it is technically legal.

Further, Rabbinic literature contains many examples of what philosophers would define as the call to *imitatio dei* or the imitation of God. These sources entail examination of God's activities as they are described in the biblical narrative in order to discover ethical imperatives that one should strive to imitate.[9] These divine behaviors include virtually the entire range of the personal-service acts of kindness found so frequently in our religious literature.[10] God visits Abraham after his circumcision,[11] from which we learn that we, too, are to visit and care for someone who is ill.[12] God comforts Isaac after the death of Abraham;[13] so, too, we are to make our presence felt to those in mourning.[14] The Almighty provides clothes for Adam and Eve,[15] and we are also to help those lacking these basic necessities.[16]

The impetus to imitate God goes further. The fact that God unveiled His Torah on Mount Sinai and not on one of the taller and more impressive mountains, the fact that God revealed Himself to Moses in a burning bush and not in a mighty oak, both challenge us to imitate His modesty in our own actions.[17]

A note of caution: There is concern that we not learn from God's anger. While it is true that God is often portrayed as wrathful,[18] He controls His anger. In our case our anger controls us.[19] As such, we not only do not emulate God when we get angry, but we alienate ourselves from God by allowing our anger rather than God to rule over us. For this reason the Rabbis say that anger can be tantamount to idolatry.[20]

We are also told by the Torah that we are to "be blameless before the Lord and before Israel."[21] In modern parlance this is God's call to avoid impropriety, about which only "God" may be in possession of the complete truth, and also to avoid the appearance of impropriety about which "Israel" may draw a negative conclusion even if it is incorrect. As a moral people and as ethical individuals, we are to be guiltless not only in fact (in God's eyes), but even in appearance (in Israel's eyes).[22]

Keeping an appropriate state of mind can help produce ethical behavior. For this reason it is suggested that we continuously view ourselves, in fact, that we view the entire world, as equally balanced between good and bad deeds.[23] Thus, our next action will tip the scales one way or the other. As we approach that action, we will come to see our fate, the fate of every human being, and, in fact, the fate of the entire world, as dependent on that next act. Perceiving our lives and our actions in this way should influence us to act in a more ethically appropriate manner in everything we do.

The call to ethical behavior is often seen as part of the prophetic tradition. We frequently find our prophets reminding the people or the king that God has no interest in rituals or sacrifices if those performing such acts are uncaringly involved in oppressing the poor, the widow, and the orphan.[24]

A more modern manifestation of the same tradition appears in the Musar movement of the nineteenth century.[25] Founded by Rabbi Israel ben Ze'ev Wolf Salanter (1810–1883) in Eastern

Europe, it focused on training people to react ethically to every situation that life brings. In many yeshivot (schools of Jewish learning), under the influence of his teachings, ethical instruction became part of the basic curriculum. These yeshivot featured a functionary known as a *mashgiah ruhani,* or spiritual adviser. He was responsible both for teaching ethical principles to the students of the yeshiva and for providing them with personal ethical guidance. The faculties of many yeshivot today continue to include just such an individual.

Most important, Israel Salanter taught by example how one can use oneself as a tool to raise ethical sensibility. A simple story provides an important example of how, with two brief interactions, he was able, at a distance, to show his own moral sensibility and thereby teach others an important and difficult ethical lesson.[26]

One Friday afternoon a poor woman came to the Rabbi of a small town with a chicken for him to examine concerning a potential kashrut (kosher dietary law) problem. The Rabbi examined the chicken and told the woman not to worry, as it was fine.

The woman left to return to her Sabbath preparations when the Rabbi realized he had been mistaken. He ran through the street to the woman's home, and by banging on her door and shouting at the top of his lungs, he managed to stop the woman just before she put the chicken in with the water, vegetables, and other ingredients already present in her soup pot.

Apparently, the Rabbi had some enemies among the people in his town. They decided to use this incident to try to remove him from his post. They claimed that he was an ignoramus for not having known the law immediately. They worried loudly that he had nearly caused the woman and others to eat nonkosher chicken. They complained that it was undignified for the Rabbi to have run through the streets in this way. They even expressed concern that the poor woman's pot had almost lost its kosher status, which would have occurred had the chicken been put into it.

The Rabbi and his followers battled back. The fight was long and hard, but eventually the Rabbi won. Unfortunately for him, it was a hollow victory. His position as Rabbi became more secure. However, he was broken in spirit by the fight.

In his anguish he wrote a letter to the great Rabbi Israel Salanter describing what had occurred. He asked for nothing. He simply was looking for an ear that would listen and an eye that would read.

The town had recently been blessed with its first telegraph wire connecting it to the rest of the world. A few days after the Rabbi sent the letter, a telegram arrived for him from Rabbi Israel Salanter that read, "On the matter that you asked me about, the answer is 'permitted'."

The Rabbi was mystified. He hadn't asked a question. He didn't know what was being permitted. He couldn't figure out what was going on. He began to put pen to paper to ask for clarification when two days later a second telegram came from Rabbi Salanter that read, "On second thought, concerning the matter about which you asked me, the answer is 'prohibited'."

Salanter's actions did the trick. By showing the Rabbi and the townspeople that even he, the great Rabbi Israel Salanter, could rethink a question and come to a more restrictive conclusion, he helped to fully restore the relationship of the Rabbi to himself and his townspeople. It also shamed those who had acted inappropriately into realizing their mistake. Salanter had done this by using himself as the tool and the catalyst.

Salanter displayed one other critical capacity in this story. One might well ask how the townspeople would have known of the telegrams, since the telegrapher would have been required to maintain confidentiality.

To do this type of ethical educating requires a good deal of insight into human nature. Hopefully, with a little effort we can all improve our intuitive sense of how others operate and of what is truly important to them so that we can respond appropriately in all our interpersonal relationships.

Salanter knew that despite any regulations concerning confidentiality, a telegram from him, the leading Rabbi of his day, to a small town newly wired for telegraphy would remain a secret for about as long as it took the telegrapher to read the message. Frankly, even if no one else was present in the office when the message arrived, the telegrapher would have run to find the nearest available living soul in whom he could confide.

Sure enough, this insight into human nature provided the key to the appropriate reconciliation of the Rabbi and his flock. True to Rabbi Salanter's expectations, the whole town knew of the telegrams and their content probably before the town Rabbi had a chance to read them himself. Happily, they understood the message being directed at them. As a result, the town's Rabbi was strengthened in his sacred calling. To accomplish these things, Salanter used who he was to do what needed to be done.

Finally, it is important to understand that for traditional Jews, the law of the Torah and normative Halakhah cannot be altered in response to the demands of contemporary ethics.[27] In any conflict Torah law will hold sway. However, when used to supplement the specifics of Torah law, ethics can enhance Torah's quest for justice, proper behavior, and a world that is healed of its pain, its strife, and its unethical conduct.[28]

1. There are many important books and articles on this subject and they cannot all be listed here. One of the most significant is: Aaron Lichtenstein,

"Does Jewish Law Recognize an Ethic Independent of Halakhah?" in *Modern Jewish Ethics: Theory and Practice*, ed. Marvin Fox (Ohio State University, 1975).

2. Psalms 19:8, Cf. Ramban, Leviticus 4:25.

3. Cf. Deuteronomy 4:7–8.

4. Bava Metzia 30b et passim.

5. Ibid. 24b.

6. *Sefer Mitzvot Katan* 49.

7. Leviticus 19:2.

8. See his commentary on the Torah, ibid.

9. Many sources discuss this concept; see *Encyclopaedia Judaica*, s.v. Imitation of God. An important treatment of the concept appears in Martin Buber, *Israel and the World: Essays in a Time of Crises* (Syracuse, N.Y., 1997), pp. 67–78.

10. Sotah 14a, et passim.

11. Genesis 18:1.

12. Sotah 14a, Genesis Rabbah 8:13.

13. Genesis 25:11.

14. Sotah, loc. cit.; the Midrash cites a different source for the same idea.

15. Genesis 3:21.

16. Sotah, loc. cit.

17. Sotah 5a.

18. Cf. the passages known as the Tokhehah ("admonition"), Leviticus 26:15–46 and Deuteronomy 28:15–65.

19. Genesis Rabbah 49:8.

20. Maimonides, *Mishneh Torah*, Hilkhot De'ot 2:3, citing "the early sages."

21. Numbers 32:22.

22. Cf. Pesahim 13a, Yoma 38a.

23. Ecclesiastes Rabbah 10:1; Maimonides, *Mishneh Torah*, Hilkhot Teshuvah 3:4.

24. Cf. Isaiah 1:10–17.

25. There are a number of works on the subject. See, for instance, Immanuel Etkes, *Rabbi Israel Salanter and the Mussar Movement* (Philadelphia, 1993) and Zalman Ury, "Salanter and the Musar Movement," in *Studies in Judaica in Honor of Dr. Samuel Belkin as Scholar and Educator*, ed. Leon Stitskin (New York, 1972).

26. I heard the story from Rabbi Dr. Norman Lamm, my esteemed teacher, chancellor of Yeshiva University.

27. It is on this point that many of the differences between Orthodox and Reform Judaism, and more recently between Orthodox and Conservative Judaism, have developed.

28. A critical thinker who espoused this type of approach was Rabbi Abraham Isaac Kook (1865–1935), first Ashkenazi chief Rabbi of modern Israel. See his essay "Fragments of Light: A View as to the Reasons for the Commandments," in *Abraham Isaac Kook*, ed. Ben-Zion Bokser (New York, 1978), pp. 303–323.

Chapter 22
Beginning of Life: The New Ethical Frontier

aving a baby![1] For a married couple, nothing compares to the joys and trepidation of the moment when a baby —hopefully healthy—is born to them. I have often joked that at that instant our identities change automatically. Parents, without being asked, begin to lose their own names and become Mommy and Daddy, Abba and Imah, and there is nothing anyone can do about it. Psychologically, one's stake in the world, the way one lives one's life, the options one can pursue—or is prevented from pursuing—are all changed in significant ways.

From a Jewish perspective, in having a baby one has added the next link to the golden covenantal chain that stretches from Abraham to the coming of the Messiah.[2] Further, since we see salvation as a national phenomenon, not as an individual coming to redemption,[3] keeping that chain strong and healthy is important from the vantage point of the Jewish people, and not just as a fulfillment of my own desire to produce offspring who will carry my memory and family name beyond my limited lifetime.

Reflecting the importance of procreation are the four different halakhic and Midrashic imperatives that require a Jewish man to have children.[4] Number one is a pentateuchal or biblical requirement embodied in the first mitzvah (law) commanded by the Bible.[5] Second is a prophetic verse that teaches us that God created the world to be settled and not to be barren.[6] Having children is the way we ensure that this will be realized.[7] Third, in the section of the Bible called the Writings, or Ketuvim, we find a verse that recommends "planting one's seed in the morning and not holding back one's hand in the evening."[8] According to the Rabbis, this verse calls upon people to have children both when they are young and when they are old.[9]

Fourth and finally there is a messianic side to all this. The Talmud claims that all the souls that will ever find their way to this earth were created at the beginning of time. Each of these souls must get its chance to live, and the Messiah will not appear until all of them have come into this world. Thus every child born is a step toward the ultimate redemption.[10]

It is for these reasons that men, who, as we said are required to procreate, may not choose to refrain from having children.[11]

Add to all of this the fact that we live in a post-Holocaust era in which one-third of our people, including a million of our children, were murdered during the Second World War, and you can understand why having children is considered so important an act in the Jewish community.

Nonetheless, and despite the strong push to procreate, birth control is not necessarily prohibited.[12] Once one has fulfilled the basic requirement for procreation, which is to bring both a male and a female child into the world[13] more allowance for family planning may apply. However, preventing pregnancy is a serious business, and one's reasons for doing so should parallel the breadth and depth of the seriousness with which procreation is encouraged in the sources cited above. For this reason it is appropriate to seek rabbinic counsel before using birth control to determine whether that course is appropriate, for how long it should continue, and what method should be used.

Concerning this last point, the less the method chosen impedes contact between husband and wife, the better in terms of Jewish law.[14] Sexual intimacy helps vitiate the prohibition of wasting seed.[15] It is this prohibition that is Jewish law's greatest concern in seeking a halakhically acceptable way to accomplish birth control.

Because of this, absent a medical contraindication, the birth-control pill is the best mechanism currently available.[16] It parallels the "cup of roots" mentioned in rabbinic literature[17] as a permitted birth control method for women who have reason to avoid conception.[18] A word of caution is worth repeating here: whether one is using the "pill" or any other preventative to procreation, there are halakhic issues involved that should be discussed with a Rabbi.

The Talmud tells us that there are three partners in the creation of a human being: father, mother, and God.[19] Nonetheless, modern technology has allowed us to make great progress in fixing things that were once entirely in God's hands when they go wrong. In other words, when physical, physiological, or biochemical problems prevent pregnancy, medical interventions have been developed that can often solve the problem. Perhaps, more dramatically, even when one or both partners cannot conceive, and current science is unable to change that fact, mechanisms exist that may allow a couple to have a child anyway. We will discuss these procedures below.

Catholicism takes the position that human beings are generally prohibited from intervening in this area, which is viewed as God's realm in His capacity as Creator.[20] For Judaism, no such "in principle" hesitation exists. The natural resources and techniques that we find or discover in this world are all raw material for our developing this earth in ways that serve God and God's purposes.[21] They are not ruled out of bounds simply because we are using them to conceive a child.

Therefore, given all that has been said thus far about the importance of having children, it is not surprising that support can be found within the halakhic community for almost all infertility-management techniques. This support does not come without opposition, but over time it has grown as each technological development becomes more familiar and produces more babies.

Whether we are talking about artificial insemination,[22] test-tube babies,[23] surrogate motherhood,[24] donor eggs,[25] or even cloning,[26] lenient voices can be heard. Many observant people rely on these voices to help bring a child into the world.

Each of these methods comes with its own set of halakhic concerns, however. We will present a brief overview to get the flavor of the discussion and debate.

Artificial insemination raises questions about how best to collect the sperm even when it comes from the woman's husband. As a general rule, since the purpose is ultimately for procreation the prohibition of wasting seed does not arise.[27] In addition, the more the wife is involved in the collection process, the better, at least according to many halakhic authorities.[28]

If the donor is someone other than the husband, some thinkers raise concerns that this may constitute adultery or simply be unseemly and inappropriate given that it touches on areas of intimacy.[29] Others maintain that there is no prohibition against creating a child in this way.[30] However, should one accept the lenient position and conceive a child through this method genetic counseling should be part of the process to help resolve the many psychological and personal issues that following this path may awaken.[31]

Test-tube babies, or *in-vitro* fertilization, also raise the question of sperm collection in much the same way as artificial insemination. It is further complicated by the fact that after fertilization in the laboratory, not all the embryos may be implanted in the mother. Some hold that disposing of the remaining fetuses is a form of abortion.[32] Generally, freezing the embryos and allowing them to pass the point of appropriate viability (five years) is considered acceptable.[33]

Finally, this process can produce a pregnant woman who is carrying as many as five or six or even more embryos. This may be dangerous to all of them and to the mother. Fetal reduction surgery would, therefore, be permissible, down to the number that would both best ensure a healthy outcome for all concerned and retain appropriate incorporation of Judaism's strictures on abortion.[34]

When we move to surrogate motherhood, concerns that are more societal than medical enter the picture. Are we engaged in selling children, a form of slavery, in allowing this process to go forward? What does it say about our attitude toward women if we allow a woman to effectively rent out her uterus as an incubator?[35] Moreover, this too raises questions about sperm collection,[36] as well as the issues of adoption discussed below.

On the other hand, a new life may be brought to a loving family that might otherwise have no way to accomplish this goal. The Bible relates several stories about concubines or subsidiary wives who served in something like a surrogate-mother role.[37]

The major additional issue when it comes to donor eggs, our next subject, is the question of whether the genetic mother or the birth mother is to be considered the child's parent, or whether the child may in fact have either no mother or two mothers. All of these possibilities have been suggested by Torah scholars.[38]

A donor egg situation came before the Bet Din (rabbinical court) in Washington. The donor of the eggs was a non-Jew, and the birth mother a Jew. The question raised was whether the baby needed conversion (see chapter 24). We decided, after considerable research and consultation, that the birth mother was the halakhic mother. Nonetheless, we took the baby (a girl) through the mikvah experience just in case someone might have a different opinion as to her status. However, we did not write standard conversion papers for her. Instead we composed a letter indicating what we had done, why we had done it, and our belief that this girl was, in fact, a naturally born Jew.

On the cutting edge of science and societal concern is the issue of cloning. Despite the fact that as I write these words this procedure is on the verge of significant governmental restriction by U.S. law,[39] I can think of no conceptual reason to prohibit it from a Jewish perspective as long as it can be made safe. At present, however, some of the medical problems developed by cloned animals and detailed in the press preclude its use by humans.[40]

Assuming this can be overcome, there will be concern, as with donor eggs, about the issue of who is the mother. As presently conceived (pun intended), in order to clone someone an egg cell will have its DNA removed. Donor DNA material will then be inserted and stimulated to reproduce. When it begins to grow, the egg cell will be implanted in a host mother. The rest of its growth will take place *in utero* until the clone is born.

Maternity should, therefore, follow the same pattern as with donor eggs. Paternity is the more intriguing question. If the DNA donor is a woman, there simply may be no father. Even if it is a man, this procedure is obviously not the usual path to paternity. Nonetheless, it is likely that the genetic father would be considered the biological father, since the father's contribution, even in normal procreation, is essentially that of donating genetic material.[41]

There is also concern that cloning may be done for exploitive or inappropriate purposes. That too will need to be controlled if this technology moves forward and becomes available.

On the other hand, I am profoundly concerned by the U.S. government's attempt to prevent this technology from being implemented under any circumstances. If prohibited here, it will be done in less civilized countries under far less regulation and control. This may well open the door to many immoral types of exploitation.

Further, if, as I believe it will, cloning becomes possible. I worry about the civil rights of those who are born through this process.

In Jewish law they are fully human, but will they be treated that way by society? Won't prohibitive laws concerning their creation make them even more likely to encounter discrimination? Would it not be better to regulate cloning instead of prohibiting and criminalizing it?[42]

Of course there is always the low-tech solution to infertility: adoption.[43] Taking a child into one's home and raising it as one's own is considered to be an act of perpetual charity,[44] and puts one in the category of biblical heroes like Moses and Naomi.[45] Many halakhic accommodations are allowed in order to both prevent embarrassment and to make the adoptive child and parents feel themselves to be more of a family unit. For example, the child may be called to the Torah using his name and the name of his adoptive father.[46] Similarly, a ketubah (Jewish marriage document) can include the name of the adoptive father.[47] In addition, when the adoptive parent passes away, the adoptive child can and often does observe the same mourning rites as for a biological parent.[48]

The Talmud tells us that when we die, we are challenged by God concerning procreation. But the question we are asked is not *ha-parita ve-ravita?* ("did you procreate?"); it is *asakta be-firya ve-rivyah?* ("were you involved in procreation?").[49]

The blessing of the new technologies described above along with the continuing possibility of adoption is that they offer many more opportunities for our answer to God's question to be yes regardless of the outcome in our pursuit of bearing children.[50]

The new technologies have also made the instances of success in that pursuit that come with the actual birth of a baby ever so much more frequent. As such they are a true Godsend.

1. For sources on the subjects covered in this chapter, see Christopher J. De Jonge and Christopher L. R. Barratt, eds., *Assisted Reproductive Technology: Accomplishments and New Horizons* (Cambridge, 2002); E. Westreich, "Medicine and Jewish Law in the Rabbinical Courts of Israel; Matters of Infertility," *Jewish Law Annual* 12 (1997), pp. 45–64; Immanuel Jakobovits, "Male Infertility: Halachic Issues in Investigation and Management," *Tradition* 27:2 (1993), pp. 4–21; M. Halperin, "Erectile Dysfunction and Male Infertility: Medical Background and Halachic Aspects," *Medicine, Ethics and Jewish Law* 1 (1993), pp. 171–182; idem, Halakhah Survey: Artificial Insemination, *Tradition* 8:2 (1966); Noam J. Zohar, "Artificial Insemination And Surrogate Motherhood: A Halakhic Perspective," *S'vara* 2:1 (1991), pp. 13–19; Fred Rosner, "Artificial Insemination in Jewish Law," *Judaism* 19 (1970), pp. 452–464; J. David Bleich, "Survey of Recent Halakhic Periodical Literature: Surrogate Motherhood," *Tradition* 32:2 (1998), pp. 146–167; Eli D. Clark, "Surrogate Motherhood in the Case of High-Risk Pregnancy," *Journal of Halachah and Contemporary Society*, 38 (1999), pp. 5–38; J. David Bleich, "Surrogate Motherhood," Jerusalem: *City of Law and Justice* (1998), pp. 389–413; M. Halperin, "*In-vitro* Fertilization (IF), Insemination and Egg-Donation in Medicine," *Ethics and Jewish Law* 2 (1996), pp. 27–33; idem, "Applying the Principles of Halakhah to Modern Medicine: *In-vitro* Fertilization, Embryo Transfer and Frozen Embryos," *Proceedings of the Association of Orthodox Jewish Scientists* 8–9 (1987), pp. 197–212; idem, "*In-vitro* Fertilization, Embryo Transfer, and Embryo Freezing," *Assia: Jewish Medical Ethics* 1:1 (1988), pp. 25–30; Bleich J. David, "*In-vitro* Fertilization:

Questions of Maternal Identity and Conversion," *Tradition* 25:4, (1991), pp. 82–102; Ezra Bick, "Ovum Donations: A Rabbinic Conceptual Model of Maternity," *Tradition* 28:1 (1993), pp. 28–45; Edward Reichman, "The Halakhic Chapter of Ovarian Transplantation," *Tradition* 33:1 (1998), pp. 31–70; Fred Rosner, "Test Tube Babies, Host Mothers and Genetic Engineering in Judaism," *Tradition* 19:2 (1981), pp. 141–148; Daniel B. Sinclair, "Surrogacy and Cloning," *Le'ela* 44 (1997), pp. 24–29; J. David Bleich, "Survey of Recent Halakhic Periodical Literature: Cloning, Homologous Reproduction, and Jewish Law," *Tradition* 32:3 (1998), pp. 47–86; Avraham Steinberg, "Human Cloning: Scientific, Ethical and Jewish Perspectives: *Assia: Jewish Medical Ethics* 3:2 (1998), pp. 11–19; John D. Loike, "Human Cloning and Halakhic Perspectives," *Tradition* 32:3 (1998), pp. 31–46; Michael J. Broyde, "Cloning People and Jewish Law: A Preliminary Analysis," *Journal of Halacha and Contemporary Society* 34 (1997), pp. 27–65; "Forum: Judaism, Genetic Engineering, and the Cloning of Humans," *Torah U-Madda Journal* 9 (2000); Melech Schachter, "Various Aspects of Adoption," *Journal of Halacha and Contemporary Society* 4 (1982), pp. 93–115. We present this long list because of the sensitivity of the issues involved.

2. See chapter10.

3. In Christianity, salvation involves an individual "coming to God" (cf. John 3:16). In Judaism, it is a national return from exile (cf. Isaiah 27:13).

4. See the discussion of women and Judaism in chapter 29.

5. There is a debate in the Talmud as to which verse the obligation is derived from, Genesis 1:28 or Genesis 35:11. See Yevamot 65b.

6. Isaiah 45:18.

7. Yevamot 62a.

8. Ecclesiastes 11:6.

9. Yevamot 62b.

10. Yevamot 62a.

11. See chapter 29 and Yevamot 63b.

12. For extensive discussion of these issues, see David Feldman, *Marital Relations, Birth Control and Abortion in Jewish Law* (New York, 1968).

13.Yevamot 61b, *Shulhan Arukh* 1:5.

14. See Feldman, *Marital Relations*, chaps. 4–6; *Responsa Mahaneh Hayyim* (Pressburg, 1862), no. 53.

15. There are several different suggestions in halakhic literature as to where

this prohibition can be found in the Bible. See Feldman, *Marital Relations*, chap. 6.

16. Women should always have a gynecological examination before taking the "pill." In a very small number of cases the pill can have serious negative effects on the person taking it. The doctor should decide whether this is a concern before the woman begins using it.

17. Shabbat 110a; Maimonides, *Mishneh Torah*, Issurei Biah 16:12; *Shulhan Arukh*, Even ha-Ezer 5:12.

18. A birth control pill for men might well be a violation of the biblical prohibition against castration, Deuteronomy 23:2, Shabbat 110b, Kiddushin 25a, and Maimonides and *Shulhan Arukh* ad loc.

19. Kiddushin 30b.

20. See the *Instruction on Respect for Human Life in Its Origin and on the Dignity of Procreation (Donum Vitae)* (Washington: United States, Catholic Conference, 1987). And see above, chapter 5.

21. This is the implication of God's charge to the first human beings that they are to control the world and rule over it. See Genesis 1:28, and cf. Judah Aryeh Leib of Gur, *Sefat Emet*, Vayikra, Behar, 1893.

22. See Jakobovits, loc. cit.; Zohar, loc. cit.; Rosner, loc. cit. The famous lenient responsa of R. Moshe Feinstein on this subject appear in his *Iggerot Mosheh*, Even ha-Ezer 1:71, 2:11, and 18. In Even ha-Ezer 4:32 he raises a concern that artificial insemination from a donor might evoke feelings of jealousy in the infertile husband. Though occasionally read as a prohibitive concern, it sounds to me like an argument for genetic counseling. Such counseling should, in my opinion, always be part of infertility cases because of the often-devastating effect that not being able to have children has on the self-image of the couple and particularly on the one who has the biological or physical problem.

23. See the articles by Halperin cited in n. 1. Since the sperm donor is the husband and the egg cells come from the wife in this procedure, many of the issues that are concerns in the other procedures are not relevant here. The major item of discussion is how the sperm is collected. There are concerns in Jewish law about "wasting seed" that may be violated if one is not careful. See below.

24. See the articles by Zohar, Bleich, and Clark cited in n. 1. Personally, I remain troubled by this procedure for some of the reasons suggested by the

authors cited, in addition to one I have not seen discussed elsewhere. The Talmud describes the parent-child relationship as based on responsibilities that the parent has to the child (the reverse is also true, but that is not relevant here), Kiddushin 29a ff. In a surrogate situation, a biological relationship is created by the surrogate mother with a child, which is then legally severed through a contract entered into by the adoptive and biological parents. To me this smacks of the biological mother shirking her responsibilities. The surrogacy situation differs from the usual adoption case where, under the duress of difficult circumstances, a baby is given up to a better home. In the case of surrogacy the adoption transfer is premeditated and calculated. I find this reality troubling. Nonetheless, lenient opinions exist in the traditional community, and I know someone who received a permissive response when he asked a well-known halakhic authority whether he and his wife could enter into a surrogacy arrangement. They then proceeded to build their family in this way under rabbinic sanction.

25. See the articles by Bick, Bleich, Reichman, and Rosner in n. 1.

26. See the articles by Sinclair, Bleich, Steinberg, Loike, and Broyde, and the forum in *Torah U-Madda Journal* cited in n. 1.There is real concern about whether this procedure produces healthy offspring. Until that is resolved, the method should be prohibited. See above, chapter 5.

27. Cf. Shalom Mordecai Schwadron, *Teshuvot Maharsham* 3:268; Simchah Bunim Sofer, *Teshuvot Shevet Sofer*, Even ha-Ezer 1; Hayyim Ozer Grodzinski, *Teshuvot Ahi'ezer* 3:24; Abraham Bornstein of Sochachev, *Avnei Nezer*, Even ha-Ezer 63; Aaron Walkin, *Teshuvot Zekan Aharon* 1:66–67 and 2:97; Zevi Pesach Frank, *Teshuvot Har*, Even ha-Ezer 1; Moshe Feinstein, *Iggerot Mosheh*, Even ha-Ezer 1:70–71, 2 :16, 18, and 3 :14; Ovadiah Yosef, *Yabi'a Omer*, Even ha-Ezer 2:1; Joshua Baumol, *Teshuvot Emek Halakhah* 1:68; Ya'akov Yitzchak Weisz, *Teshuvot Minhat Yizhak* 1:10, 3:47, and 4:5; Shelomoh Zalman Auerbach, *No'am*, 1:145–166; Eliezer Waldenberg, *Tzitz Eliezer* 3:27, 9:51, sha'ar 4, chap. 6; R. Yisra'el Zev Mintzberg, *No'am*, 1: 129; and others. There are those who disagree.

28. Rabbi Moshe Feinstein, *Iggerot Moshe*, Even ha-Ezer 1:70, There are those who disagree, cf. R. Shlomoh Luria, *Yam shell Shelomoh*, Yevamot 8:15.

29. See the sources in the articles cited on the subject.

30. Some sources suggesting leniency are Hagigah 15a, Bach and Taz, Yoreh De'ah 195, citing *Haggahot Semak*; Maimonides, Mishnah Commentary, Sanhedrin 7:4 and Horayot, 2:4.

31. See Rabbi Moshe Feinstein's comment cited in n. 22.

32. See chapter 28.

33. The lack of direct action that negatively affects the frozen fetus combined with the early stage in conception with which we are dealing and the fact that the embryo has never been implanted inside a mother and therefore has little if any standing in Jewish law all allow for this conclusion.

34. J. David Bleich, "Survey of Recent Halakhic Periodical Literature: Pregnancy Reduction," *Tradition* 29:3 (1995), pp. 55–68.

35. See the articles on this subject cited here and my comment in n. 24.

36. There would be no license to do this other than by artificial insemination.

37. Cf. Genesis 16 and 29–30. The biblical institution is significantly different than the modern surrogacy structure. Most significantly, the biological mother retained a parental relationship with her child.

38. See the articles cited on this topic above.

39. The House of Representatives passed a ban on February 27, 2003; the Senate and the President are expected to make this proposed ban into law.

40. See n. 26. Dolly, the first cloned sheep, was euthanized on February 15, 2003, because of medical problems that were highly unusual in a sheep of her relatively young age.

41. See the cited articles on this subject.

42. I testified to this effect before Congress. The testimony had some effect at the time, but that is long gone and I have not been invited back to discuss the subject again.

43. For a general discussion of the laws of adoption, see the article by Schachter cited in n. 1; also see Rabbi Moshe Feinstein, *Iggerot Mosheh*, Yoreh De'ah 1:162.

44. Ketubot 50a.

45. Sanhedrin 19a.

46. Feinstein, loc. cit.

47. See the marvelous midrash on this in Exodus Rabbah 46:5. Our custom is to add the word *ha-migadlo* ("who raised him") or the feminine form, *ha-migadla* ("who raised her"), after the adoptive father's name. This word is skipped when the ketubah is read out loud at the marriage ceremony so as to avoid embarrassing anyone. I am told that this was a suggestion of the Rabbinic Court of London dating from the end of the nineteenth century, based on *Shulhan Arukh*, Hoshen Mishpat 42:15.

48. Moshe Isserles. See Rema, Yoreh De'ah 374:6 (Hatam Sofer, Orah Hayyim 1:64). See the ethical will of Judah the Pious. For general discussion of laws of adoption, see R. Moshe Feinstein, *Iggerot Mosheh*, Yoreh De'ah 1:162.
49. Shabbat 31a.
50. For a halakhic discussion of whether adoption fulfills the obligation to procreate, not just to be involved in procreation, see *Hakhmat Shelomoh*, Even ha-Ezer 1:1. See also Moses Alshikh, Commentary to Avot 6:1, for a more mystical and, perhaps, more emotionally satisfying resolution to the question.

Chapter 23

End of Life Issues: Transplantation, Definition of Death, Right to Die

In the preceding chapter we discussed the importance that Jewish thought invests in the act of creating life. That sense of the preciousness of existence carries over to and is expanded by the value Judaism places on every single human being.[1]

If one were to create a philosophical paradigm for the ontological worth of the individual in American culture, one would likely begin with the ringing words of the Declaration of Independence: ". . . all men [people] are created equal." To my knowledge no such principle can be found in Jewish sources. Rather, Judaism would make the claim that all human beings are infinitely valuable.

In mathematics, infinity can be defined as "a number, some of whose sub-sets are equal to the whole."[2] In arithmatic terms, infinity minus five equals infinity. The subset "infinity minus five" is equal to the whole: infinity.

Judaism says the same thing about each individual soul in the famous comment, "One who saves a single life, it is as if he saved an entire universe."[3] The subset "a single human being" is equal to the whole: the universe. As such, every life is infinitely valuable, and our intuition therefore, tells us that we must go to great lengths to preserve each and every person's existence whenever possible. After all, every human being is singular, unique, irreplaceable, and will never come again.[4]

To that end, organ transplantation, which can often save a life, or at least dramatically enhance its quality, is something that should be encouraged, not just for needy recipients, but also for all of us as potential donors subject to the Halakhic issues discussed below. Thus we should make it known that if a tragedy were to occur, our organs, where halkhically allowable, will be available to save someone else. By the same token, donation of organs that can be transplanted from a living donor, such as a single kidney or bone marrow, while not an act that Judaism mandates, is encouraged as praiseworthy and even as heroic.[5]

Despite the fact that there are prohibitions against defiling the dead[6] and delayed burial,[7] as well as concerns that injuring a living donor and putting a donor at some risk through surgery violate Jewish law, the imperative to save a life simply is more important.[8]

In fact, this hierarchy of relative importance is true for all the laws of Judaism except three. In the case of murder, idolatry, and sexual immorality, one must die rather than violate either the sanctity of someone else's life, the covenant between God and us, His chosen people, or the prohibition against incest, adultery, or other similar serious sexual violations.[9] In these three cases, one would also be required to die rather than receive medical treatment that entailed violation of one of these three fundamental strictures.[10]

Many people are under the impression that traditional Judaism is opposed to organ transplants, particularly those involving parts of the body that are harvested after the death of the donor. To a certain degree, this traces back to the strong restriction on autopsy in Jewish law, and to our cultural abhorrence of damaging the body after death.[11] We mentioned these concerns above. As indicated, when saving a life they are not the determining factor.

However, the concern is relevant in that it precludes us from signing the donor cards that come with a driver's license.[12] Signing that document allows one's body to be used for medical research, not just for transplantation of organs into someone who is ill. Although the prohibitions that we mentioned are suspended in cases of immediate need, they remain in force and preclude use of a Jew's deceased body for research that ultimately may not help someone who is ill.[13] Only when there is a clear and present instance of a seriously compromised patient in need may organs be removed from a Jew's body after death for direct medical use.[14]

When it comes to non-Jews who wish to donate their organs to science, Judaism does not set rules for them. As discussed in the chapter on gentiles, for the most part we allow non-Jews to make their own decisions.[15]

The driver's license form, as indicated, is usually, problematic. Other mechanisms must, therefore, be employed if someone wishes to donate his or her organs. Along with informing one's relatives and others who might be involved in making decisions at a critical juncture of one's wishes in this regard, a living will or advance directive is an important tool. This document indicates what should be done and who should be consulted if one becomes incapacitated. It also can indicate one's willingness to donate one's organs under halakhically appropriate circumstances. The Rabbinical Council of America will provide anyone interested with an appropriate form. I have modified it somewhat for my congregants, and the modified form is available from my synagogue.

One further concern is sometimes raised as a challenge to a permissive attitude on organ transplantation on the part of Judaism. Since traditional Judaism includes a fundamental belief in bodily resurrection in the messianic era,[16] there is some anxiety about the question of whether the donor of a transplant and the beneficiary will both be able to share the organ that was transplanted when their bodies are reconstituted at the end of days. To this concern my only response is that a God who can resurrect the dead will certainly be able to figure out how two resurrected persons will each be able to have the organs they need for bodily existence even if they both had the same organ at different times during their lives.

Finally, some people remember an ad that appeared in the *New York Times* and other newspapers when the first human heart transplants became a reality. The ads were signed by leading orthodox Rabbis of the day, condemning these procedures. Thus they inadvertently conveyed the impression that Orthodox Jews were opposed to transplants. In fact, what the ads opposed were only those first transplants. The Rabbis objected because no definition of death then existed which allowed a heart to be removed from a donor with any assurance that he or she was truly no longer using it. There were also no anti-rejection drugs that presented any reasonable possibility of success in the procedure. Everyone knew that the recipient's body would reject the new organ within a matter of weeks, and that the patient would, without any doubt, die. For this reason the process was called "the murder of two people" in these ads.

Since then things have changed dramatically. There are now many anti-rejection drugs, and the five-year success rate of heart transplants is nearly 70 percent.[17] As such, the implantation aspect of the procedure is clearly permissible.

It is the other side of the process that remains at least debatable. Rabbi Moshe Tendler, rosh yeshiva and professor of biology at Yeshiva University and a congregational Rabbi in Monsey, New York, argues forcefully for acceptance of a definition of brain death that he believes meets halachik criteria and that would make vital organs, such as heart, lungs, kidneys, and liver, viable for transplant even if taken from the donor after the conditions he describes have been met. In his opinion, if one can show that the entire brain has died down to and including the breathing centers in the medulla or lower brain, the person is halakhically dead, even though machines may be keeping the lungs breathing, the blood pumping, and the organs healthy.[18] This position is supported by many halakhic sources,[19] by the Chief Rabbinate of Israel,[20] and serves as the basis for both versions of living wills and advance directives mentioned above.

In opposition stand Rabbi J. David Bleich, professor of Jewish law and ethics and professor of law at Yeshiva University, and Rabbi Hershel Schachter, rosh yeshiva and rosh kollel at Yeshiva University. Rabbi Bleich holds that a person is alive until breathing ceases,[21] and Rabbi Schachter makes the presence or absence of blood circulation the critical criterion.[22] For both, the patient is still alive even if the designated physiological process is being performed by machine. If we wait until these processes stop completely, most of if not all the deceased's organs are unlikely to be of any use for transplant, for they too will die.

Nonetheless, these latter scholars believe that organs that have been obtained inappropriately may be used to save a life if someone who needs one or more of them to survive is present. The living will/advance directive of Agudas Harabonim of America takes their position into consideration and simply requires consultation with a Rabbi before any significant action is taken if one becomes incapacitated.[23]

Moving beyond the issue of transplant, this debate about the definition of death incorporates a profound difference of opinion as to the proper treatment of people at the end-stage of life. If one accepts Rabbi Tendler's definition, then a halakhically brain-dead person on life-support should be unhooked from the respirator and buried. To not do so is to violate the Torah's prohibition of delayed burial, which is tantamount to disrespecting the dead.[24] On the other hand, according to Rabbis Bleich and Schachter, doing so would be an act of murder.[25]

This leads us, finally, to the question of whether and when euthanasia might be permitted. Without question, active euthanasia, a Dr. Kervorkian–style death, is universally prohibited.[26] The human soul was given by God, belongs to God, and can be taken only by God.[27] Life is too precious and unique, too infinitely valuable for a human being to become the instrument of terminating someone's existence. From a Jewish perspective, Kervorkian is simply a serial murderer.[28]

The situation is dramatically more complex when it comes to passive euthanasia. May care be withheld from someone who is terminally ill, thus allowing the patient to die? There are some voices who claim that care must be given in any way possible, for as long as possible,[29] but many sources suggest that this is not so.

To cite some of them:

On the day when Rabbi Judah Hanasi died, the Rabbis decreed a public fast and offered prayers for heavenly mercy. . . .

Rabbi's handmaid ascended the roof and prayed: "The immortals desire Rabbi [to join them], and the mortals desire Rabbi [to remain with them]; may it be the will [of God] that the mortals overpower the immortals." When, however, she saw how often he resorted to the privy, painfully taking off his tefillin [the black leather boxes containing Torah passages that are worn on the arm and the head] and putting them on again, she prayed: "May it be the will [of the Almighty] that the immortals overpower the mortals." As the Rabbis incessantly continued their prayers for [heavenly] mercy, she took up a jar and threw it down from the roof to the ground. [For a moment] they ceased praying and the soul of Rabbi departed to its eternal rest.[30]

They found R. Hanina b. Teradion sitting and occupying himself with the Torah, publicly gathering assemblies, and keeping a Scroll of the Law in his bosom. Straightaway they took hold of him, wrapped him in the Scroll of the Law, placed bundles of branches round him, and set them on fire. They then brought tufts of wool, which they had soaked in water, and placed them over his heart, so that he should not expire quickly. . . . "Open your mouth" [said his students] "so that the fire enter into you [and you die quickly]." He replied, "Let Him who gave me [my soul] take it away, but no one should injure him- or herself." The executioner then said to him, "Rabbi, if I raise the flame and take away the tufts of wool from over your heart, will you cause me to enter into the life to come?" "Yes," he replied. "Swear to me." He swore unto him. He thereupon raised the flame and removed the tufts of wool from over his heart, and his soul departed speedily. The executioner then jumped and threw himself into the fire. And a *bat kol* [voice from heaven] exclaimed: R. "Hanina b. Teradion and the executioner have been assigned to the World-to-Come."[31]

If there is something that is causing the soul to delay its departure, for example if there is, close to the house [where the terminally ill patient may be found], the sound of knocking, such as a woodchopper [chopping wood], or if he has salt on his tongue, as these delay the soul's departure,[32] one is permitted to remove them as there is no action taken here at all. Rather he has removed the impediment.[33]

In each of these cases action was taken that hastened death, or, more correctly, something that was preventing the person's death was removed. This is the crucial difference. Surrendering to the illness that has struck a human being without continuing the fight may be permissible if the only way to prevent or slow the dying process is to employ heroic measures that have, at best, a limited chance of success. For example, chemotherapy for advanced liver cancer would not be required according to this approach, if the patient did not wish to go through the extremely difficult side- effects of that experience with its limited effectiveness in curing the disease.

On the other hand, there are limits to the choice to refuse treatment. One who is otherwise healthy cannot refuse a necessary appendectomy because such refusal may result in a burst appendix and death. The surgery is so uncomplicated and the risk from the procedure so small that the option to refuse is simply inappropriate.[34] Certain types of medical intervention must be undertaken by those who are ill, because their lives, which belong to God, are infinitely valuable, as was discussed above.

Moreover, denial of food and hydration is inappropriate even in the case of the terminally ill patient.[35] A person deprived of nutrition and liquid will die of starvation or thirst, not of their underlying illness. This would entail introducing a new factor that took the person's life. It would be active, not passive, euthanasia.[36]

Finally, to reiterate, since many of these decisions concerning when or whether to institute or continue care, as well as whether one wishes to donate one's organs, are made at the point when the individual is incapacitated, a living will/advance directive that reflects one's wishes is extremely important. One is never too young to execute such a document. Once written it should be reviewed periodically to ensure that one's choices have not changed, so that the document remains a true reflection of what one actually wants should the need arise.

We all strive to live ethical lives. It would be truly sad if our last act in this world did not reflect the same commitment to ethics.

1. There are many articles and books on the subjects dealt with in this chapter. A representative sample includes: "Heart and Other Organ Transplantation and Jewish Law," in Fred Rosner, *Modern Medicine and Jewish Law* (New York, 1972); Nachum L. Rabinovitch, " What Is the Halakha for Organ Transplants?" *Tradition* 9:4 (1968), pp. 20–27; Immanuel Jakobovits, "Halakhic Debate On Brain Death," *Le'ela* 41 (1996), pp. 29–30; Fred Rosner, "Rabbi Moshe Feinstein and Brain Stem Death," ibid., pp. 30–35; J. David Bleich, "Brain Death: Medical Myth and Semantic Sleight of Hand," ibid., pp. 35–39; Moshe D. Tendler, "Care of the Critically Ill," *Responsa of Rav Moshe Feinstein*, vol. 1 (New Jersey, 1966); idem, "Halakhic Death Means Brain Death," *"Jewish Review*, January–February 1990; J. David, Bleich, *Time of Death in Jewish Law* (New York, 1991); Herschel Schachter, *Bedinei Met ve-Gavra Keteila in be'Ikvei ha-Tzon* (Jerusalem, 1997); Symposium, "Determining Death According to Halacha," *Journal of Halacha and Contemporary Society*, 17 (1989): Marshall J. Keilson, "Medical Aspects of Brain Death," pp. 7–13; Moshe David Tendler, "Definition of Death in Judaism," pp. 14–31; Herschel Schachter, "Determining Death," pp. 32–40; Aharon Soloveitchik, " Death According to the Halacha," pp. 41–48; Chaim Dovid Zwiebel, "Accommodating Religious Objections to Brain Death: Legal Considerations," pp. 49–68; Fred Rosner, *Jewish Attitude Toward Euthanasia, in Modern Medicine and Jewish Law* (New York, 1972); Reuven P. Bulka, "Kevorkianism: Judaic and Logotherapeutic Reactions," *Journal of Psychology and Judaism* 19:2 (1995), pp. 127–140; J. David Bleich, "Survey of Recent

Halakhic Periodical Literature: Treatment of the Terminally Ill," *Tradition* 30:3 (1996): pp. 51–87; C. D. Halevi, "Disconnecting a Terminal Patient from an Artificial Respirator, *Crossroads* (*Alon Shvut*) 1 (1987), pp. 147–155.

2. Cf. "Russell, Infinity, and the Tristram Shandy Paradox," by Shandon Guthrie. Available online at http://sguthrie.net/infinity.htm

3. Mishnah, Sanhedrin 4:5. The reading here follows the Mishnah in the Jerusalem Talmud. MSS. Kaufmann, an important and complete manuscript of the Mishnah, also reads this way. There are other reasons to see this as the correct reading and not to accept the current text, which limits this only to Jewish souls.

4. See Chapter 28 for a similar argument concerning abortion.

5. See discussion in Rosner, "Heart and Other Organ Transplantation and Jewish Law," (see n. 1) and J. David Bleich, "Compelling Tissue Donations," *Tradition* 27:3 (1993), pp. 59–89.

6. Deuteronomy 21:23. This is the basis of the Jewish prohibition against autopsy. See Ezekiel Landau, *Responsa Nodah Beyehudah*, Mahadurah Tinyanah, Yoreh De'ah 210; Fred Rosner, "Autopsy in Jewish Law and the Israeli Autopsy Controversy."

7. *Shulhan Arukh*, Yoreh De'ah 357.

8. See the articles cited in n. 5.

9. Sanhedrin 74a ff. See generally *Shulhan Arukh*, Yoreh De'ah 157. See also Maimonides, Hilkhot Yesodei ha-Torah, chap. 5, for a somewhat different formulation.

10. Pesahim 25a, Avodah Zarah 27b, Maimonides, loc. cit. Using idolatrous medicine may be worse than worshipping idols under physical duress. In the latter case, when the incident is over one is likely to hate the deity that one was forced to worship. On the other hand, if one is somehow healed by the medicine, one may be drawn to the idol it purported to represent. This suggestion appears to be implicit in Maimonides and is based on the comparison of R. Ishmael's opinion on Avodah Zarah 27b as opposed to his statement on Sanhedrin 74a.

11. See Rosner, op. cit.; Immanuel Jakobovits," Halakhah Survey: Autopsies," *Tradition* 7:1 (1964–65).

12. This is true in almost every state in the United States. Virginia is one exception. A signed card in Virginia means that the organ goes to a recipient. If the state wishes to do anything else, it must first contact a family member for permission, which according to Jewish law would almost always be denied.

13. This is the difference between what halakhah calls *be-faneinu* ("before us") and *lo be-faneinu* ("not before us"). In addition to Rosner, op. cit., see J. David Bleich, *Contemporary Halakhic Problems* (New York, 1983), p. 57.

14. In today's era of rapid communication and transportation, the pool of patients *be-faneinu* is quite large.

15. See above, Chapter 8.

16. See above, Chapter 11.

17. Information obtained from the National Institutes of Health.

18. See Rabbi Tendler's articles listed in n. 1 and his collection and translation of the relevant responsa by Rabbi Moshe Feinstein cited there as well.

19. Among them are Mishnah Ohalot 1:6 (see Maimonides' Mishnah Commentary ad loc.), Hullin 21a, and *Shulhan Arukh*, Yoreh De'ah 370.

20. In a widely publicized ruling. See Mordechai Halperin, "The Legal Significance of the Decision of the Chief Rabbinate Council on Heart Transplants In Israel," *Jewish Law Association Studies*, 6 (1992), pp. 59–63.

21. See his writings cited in n. 1. His primary source is Yoma 85a and its codification in Maimonides, *Mishneh Torah*, Hilkhot Shabbat 2:19 and *Shulhan Arukh*, Orah Hayyim 329:4.

22. He cites many sources, including Deuteronomy 12:23; Tosafot, Ketubot 5b, s.v. *dam*; and Sanhedrin 85b.

23. See the article by Zwebel cited in n. 1.

24. See sources cited above on delayed burial, defiling the dead, and autopsy.

25. See the articles by Bleich and Halevi on the subject cited in n. 1.

26. Cf. Maimonides, Hilkhot Evel 4:5; *Shulhan Arukh*, Yoreh De'ah 339:1.

27. See Maimonides, Hilkhot Rotze'ah u-Shemirat ha-Nefesh 1:4, and the morning prayer Elokai Neshama, which in English translation reads in part: "My God, the soul which you have given me . . . you will take it from me." Philip Birnbaum, *Daily Prayer Book* (New York, 1949).

28. See the articles on this subject cited in n. 1.

29. See Bleich's article on the subject cited in n. 1.

30. Ketubot 104a.

31. Avodah Zarah 18a.

32. Even if contemporary science disagrees on the medical realities, the moral and ethical position remains the same. See Chapter 27.

33. Rema, Yoreh De'ah 339:1.

34. This is a derivative of the requirement to preserve life which begins with the verse in Deuteronomy 4:15. See Chapter 27.

35. J. David Bleich, "Providing Nutrition and Hydration for Terminally Ill Patients," *Issues in Law and Medicine* 2:2 (1986), pp. 117–131. The Rabbinical Council of America's living will/advance directive as well as the one produced by my synagogue takes this position as well.

36. This appears to be the sense of the comments of the Shulhan Arukh and Rema, Yoreh De'ah 339:1.

Chapter 24
Conversion: Who Is a Jew?

N
o debate has more divided the Jewish world in recent years than the one over the issues that make up the title of this section.[1] It is important, therefore, to try and discuss these subjects as dispassionately as possible.

Traditional Judaism has two answers to the question of who is a Jew.[2] The first is, someone who is born of a Jewish mother.[2] The second, someone who converts to Judaism in a manner that conforms with Halakhah.[3] Both of these avenues to Judaism have become denominational flashpoints in today's Jewish world.[4]

While matrilineal descent was the universal norm for many centuries, in recent years Reform Judaism has accepted patrilineal descent (i.e., that one can be considered Jewish if one's father was Jewish), [5] a position which was then discussed and rejected by the Conservative movement.[6] Orthodox Judaism, not surprisingly, never entertained making the change at all. Obviously, this creates a tense and difficult situation in which one or more groups embrace people as Jewish who are rejected as Jews by others. Particularly when the question arises of whether someone is to be considered Jewish for purposes of marriage,[7] such differences in the way religious identity is defined by the various denominations within Judaism may well be a cause, however inadvertent, of great tension, conflict, and even of open confrontation.

Classically, the explanation for matrilineal descent as the determinant of Jewish identity was the virtual guarantee that one could always tell who was the mother of a child, whereas one had no such guarantee regarding the father.[8] Now that we can test for familial relationships genetically, it turns out, quite shockingly, that in more than ten percent of the cases in which patients and their claimed biological fathers are examined for their genetic makeup, the listed father turns out not to be the father after all. And this is in situations of medical testing due to illness, where there is no reason to suspect that the presumed fathers of the test subjects were not really their genetic parents.[9] This statistic seems to prove the validity of the matrilineal principle.

Others explain that in the traditional family the mother has a greater influence than the father on the child's religious identity.[10] Therefore her religion determines the child's affiliation.

Whatever the actual reason, the origin of the matrilineal principle has become part of the debate. Some scholars, particularly those arguing for Judaism to accept the children of a Jewish father and a non-Jewish mother, claim that the matrilineal principle developed under the influence of Roman law.[11] If true, the principle is "only" two thousand years old and therefore younger than the thirty-five-hundred-year-old Pentateuch.

Even if this is so, it should still be difficult to overturn a legal precedent with a pedigree of two millennia. Legal systems recognize that settled law leads to expectations on the part of the community, develops a history and life of its own, and spawns derivative effects throughout its entire structure.[12] For that reason, uprooting a law cannot be done lightly, and if splitting the community is the result, it generally is not worth it. Unfortunately, just that deleterious outcome has emerged from the patrilinearity debate.

Further, there may be good evidence that matrilinearity is far older than the claimed second century C.E. origin discussed above. Chapter 10 of the Book of Ezra, which is at least six hundred years older than the claimed Roman era decree mentioned previously, records Ezra as demanding that Jewish men divorce their gentile wives. Verse 4 of the chapter speaks of removing the children born to them as well. If patrilineal descent had been the standard at this time, these would obviously have been Jewish children, and they would not have been asked to leave. It seems, then, that matrilineal descent is biblical in origin, whatever its specific point of emergence and rationale.

From a traditional perspective, the matrilineal principle remains in place. So, too, the talmudic principle that "the burden of proof [literally, the weaker hand] is with the one who wishes to change."[13] Consider the following analogy to the present situation in Judaism: The United States has had a single standard for citizenship throughout its history. Imagine what would happen if New Jersey were now to change that standard in a way that it knew would not be acceptable to New York. Such an action would cause countless problems, especially if New Jersey, while not agreeing with New York on many things, saw New York as an important source of American history and culture, and so indicated to its newest citizens. A formula for crisis would have been set in place. When the newest New Jerseyans visit New York and are then told they are not really American citizens, the crisis would be complete. This is precisely what is occurring in Judaism. Sadly, the communal rupture in this area seriously damages our ability to maintain a Jewish community that can work together on behalf of our most pressing causes or needs.

Conversion presents similar problems.[14] To understand conversion, one must recognize that it consists of two distinct elements. The first is ideology, and the second, ceremony.

Taking them in reverse order,[15] the conversion ritual for a man begins with circumcision, the eternal sign of the covenant of Abraham. Should the prospective convert have been previously circumcised, a drop of blood is taken so that the context of the act becomes one of commitment and covenant, not simply of surgery.

The next step, common to both men and women, is immersion in a mikvah, or ritual bath. This complete immersion represents a rebirth experience[16] and is in keeping with the halakhic principle that "a convert is as one newly born."[17]

In Temple times a special sacrifice was required of the new Jew,[18] and for a short time after the destruction of the Temple, converts were told to set aside money for such a sacrifice in anticipation of the Temple being rebuilt. Although the sacrificial and monetary requirements have since been suspended,[19] I have often imagined that they will lead to a unique moment once our central sanctuary in Jerusalem is rebuilt. When the Third Temple is in place, hopefully soon and in our lifetimes, I assume there will come a point in time when all the many people who converted during the difficult centuries that passed between the Second and Third Temples will come forward to fulfill their sacrificial requirement.[20] At that moment they will receive appropriate recognition from their fellow Jews for their life-changing free-will acceptance of Judaism.

Obviously, conversion requires some type of intentional commitment (about which more below) on the part of the new Jew. An adult can speak for him- or herself, but what about a child adopted from gentiles whose new parents want their baby to be Jewish?[21] In such cases conversion requires the same ceremony, but the requisite intent has to be provided by the rabbinic court after it determines that conversion is truly in the child's best interest. Even a baby can be converted in this way, in which case the child's father or another adult enters the mikvah to help with the safe immersion of the child.[22] One visible difference in the ceremony for a child is that the blessing after the immersion, which is said by the convert in the case of an adult conversion, is said by the bet din or rabbinic court (at least in our practice) on behalf of the baby.[23] All conversions take place before a court of three judges.

The bridge to the ideology and commitment elements lies in the questions that the Talmud and *Shulhan Arukh* (Code of Jewish Law) require that the convert respond to before conversion.[24] The first challenge posed is to point out to the prospective convert the terrible persecution that Jews have experienced and continue to experience around the world. The question is then asked "why do you want to join a people that is treated in this way?" He or she must respond by indicating a willingness to bear such burdens if necessary. One tests, thereby, the desire of the individual to join with the historic destiny of the Jewish people for good or for bad.

Second, the prospective convert is reminded that from the moment of conversion, all of Halakhah (Jewish law) becomes obligatory. This legal structure is often quite restrictive, such as in the case of the dietary laws, which severely limit what one may eat. The question is raised "will you abide by the dietary laws and refrain from the consumption of prohibited foods?" This tests the convert's willingness to lead a life governed by Halakhah.

Writ large, the commitment to make Halakhah the determining guide in one's life is called *kabbalat ha-mitzvot* (acceptance of the commandments). Here in Washington, where I live, and where I am involved in many of the Orthodox conversions that occur in this city, we require all adult converts to make a formal declaration in their own words committing themselves to the God of Israel, to Torah and mitzvot, to Halakhah, and to both the Oral and the Written Law before the actual conversion takes place.[25] *Kabbalat ha-mitzvot* in some fashion before a Rabbinic court is essential to the process.

It is here that the real differences in conversion between Orthodox Judaism and the other movements occur. Some in the non-Orthodox world do the ceremony differently, but even among those who follow the precise ritual steps, differences will appear concerning *kabbalat ha-mitzvot*. As one of our converts here in Washington told me, "When I had my non-Orthodox conversion, the bet din was concerned with what I knew about Judaism. When I converted with you, your bet din was concerned with how I live my life."

It must be understood that a conversion ceremony without acceptance of the halakhic lifestyle is not traditionally viewed as an acceptable conversion.[26] Further, the halakhic requirement that the members of the bet din be male and committed to halakhic observance may also not be met in conversions performed outside the Orthodox community. For these reasons conversions performed according to standards other than those described here are not considered valid within the orthodox community. This, too, can and does lead to any number of painful and truly tragic events, particularly when someone who thought they were fully Jewish finds their identity questioned and rejected at least by some.

As discussed, in the case of a baby, the required statement of commitment cannot be made by the prospective convert. If the court determines that the child will benefit from conversion, then it may go ahead and complete the process, on the basis of the talmudic principle that one may act to the benefit of one's fellow even outside of his or her presence.[27] The child, being unable to consent is functionally absent, and therefore criteria for "benefit" must be clearly defined if the bet din is to proceed.

To do so, we must remind ourselves of Judaism's attitude to conversion. As discussed in Chapter 8, which deals with the subject of Jews and gentiles, a moral non-Jew who follows the seven Noahide laws is granted a share in the World-to-

Come.[28] Thus, conversion to Judaism does not, in any sense, save the gentile's immortal soul.

Becoming a Jew means taking on 613 biblical obligations and a far larger number of rabbinic laws and communal customs. Even the most expansive understanding of the seven Noahide laws does not in any way approach the magnitude of the number of obligations incumbent on the Jew.[29] To take someone who is fulfilling or close to fulfilling his or her obligations under the seven Noahide laws, and to then put this person in a position wherein he or she is not fulfilling many, many Jewish obligations, grants the gentile no advantage and, in fact, creates a terrible disadvantage for the convert.

Further, bringing people into the fold whose ideological framework is not Jewish may have a negative impact on our ability to maintain an ideology that is truly Jewish.[30] Finally, one can legitimately question whether someone who converts for purposes of marriage or for any other motive that is not purely commitment to a new faith will remain loyal to Judaism no matter what happens. While there is no mechanism in Judaism for converting out of the faith, one can certainly act as if one no longer belongs, or as if one belongs to another faith group. If the way in does not come with a profound commitment, the way out would seem to be that much easier.

Returning to our baby, the prospective convert, the court would need to be sure that this child will grow up in an environment where a commitment to Jewish peoplehood and observance is a real possibility. This means, at the very least, that the family is committed to Shabbat and kashrut in the home, and day school education for this child.[31] Supporting the last of these requirements are the many demographic studies showing that twelve years of day school education is by far the strongest positive corollary with continued Jewish identity into adulthood.[32] In short, if these elements are present, one can be reasonably confident that the child will grow up to identify with Judaism and observe its commandments. If so, childhood conversion advantages the child, because it allows the child to live in his or her family as a co-religionist and to benefit fully from living a Jewish lifestyle. On the other hand, if the child is unlikely to maintain a Jewish identity or commitment, conversion becomes a disadvantage to the child. In this regard it is always important to remember that conversion is for the convert and only for the convert, not for the parents or anyone else, no matter how closely related or how concerned they may be.

Finally, despite the act of conversion by the bet din on behalf of the child, Judaism recognizes that the will of the child has not spoken. On reaching maturity the child has an opportunity to accept Judaism or recant.[33] However, this need not be and is not done in a formal question-and-answer session. If the child, having now reached maturity (twelve years and one day for a girl, thirteen years and one day for a boy), continues to live as a Jew, we consider that to be sufficient indication that the conversion was real and heartfelt. The one caveat is that the child must know of his or her conversion at the point of reaching maturity. Thus, adopted children must be told of their origin before they reach Bar or Bat Mitzvah age.

As indicated, in recent years differences have emerged between the denominations on many of these issues. Tragically, individuals who have been told they are Jewish in one place may discover that they are not considered to be Jewish somewhere else. This can be a very painful experience. Moreover, when members of different denominations begin to question whether they can marry one another and still be within the faith, it will be very hard to remain one people. While we are not at that state today, it may not be too long before such a turning point is reached. History tells us of groups that were excluded from the community for just this reason.[34] It would be tragic for the same thing to happen again.

1. For some important historical and halakhic background to these issues, see Lawrence Schiffman, *Who Was a Jew?* (Hoboken, N.J., 1985). Schiffman details how the Christian/Jewish split began as a matter of theology and ideology within the Jewish community and ended with the creation of two separate faith groups as a result of differences in defining who was a Jew.

2. Kiddushin 66b; *Shulhan Arukh*, Even ha-Ezer 4:19.

3. Yevamot 46b–47a; cf. Maimonides, *Mishneh Torah*, Hilkhot Issurei Biah 13:7. For further discussion and sources, see J. David Bleich, "The Conversion Crisis: A Halakhic Analysis," *Tradition* 11:4 (Spring 1971); Aaron Lubling, "Conversion in Jewish Law," *Journal of Halachah and Contemporary Society* 11 (Spring 1985).

4. See generally the "Symposium on Patrilineal Descent" in *Judaism* 34:1 (Winter 1985); Elie Kedourie, "Who Is a Jew?" *Commentary* 85:6 (1988), pp. 25–30; Leonard Fein, "Who Is a Jew? Covenant and Contract," *Forum on the Jewish People, Zionism and Israel* 62 (1989), pp. 27–38; and the various articles on the subject in the *Jewish Law Annual* 2 (London, 1979).

5. Report of the Committee on Patrilinear Descent on the Status of Children of Mixed Marriages, CCAR, March 15, 1983.

6. Cf. letter from Elliot Dorff, *Commentary* 107:1 (January 1999). The maintenance of matrilineal descent as the rule is considered a "standard of rabbinic practice" by the Conservative movement pursuant to adoption of that position by its Committee on Law and Standards on May 1, 1985 and formal adoption by its 1986 convention. The vote was 235–92 for this position.

7. See Yevamot 14b, which speaks of Bet Hillel and Bet Shammai being willing to intermarry with one another despite disagreements on many issues of marriage and divorce law. Once one group refuses to marry another because of status questions that must first be resolved, possibly by conversion, a split has truly developed that may lead to the creation of separate communities. This is the danger we face today.

8. Cf. *Encyclopaedia Judaica*, s.v. *yuhasin*.

9. I served on the Theological Committee of the Human Genome Project and this shocking statistic was reported to us by one of the geneticists who served as a resource to our subcommittee.

10. Proverbs 14:1. See also Menahem Brayer, *The Jewish Woman in Rabbinic Literature: A Psychosocial Perspective* (Hoboken, N.J., 1986), p. 10, and Lawrence Schiffman in the *Judaism* symposium cited above in n. 4.

11. Cf. Shaye J. D. Cohen and others in the *Judaism* symposium, above n. 4.

12. In American law this is known as stare decisis. See *Duhaime's Law Dictionary*, s.v. Stare Decisis.

13. Mishnah Bava Metzia 6:2.

14. See generally Maurice Lamm, *Becoming a Jew* (New York, 1991).

15 For discussion of the ceremonial elements of conversion, see Yevamot 47b and *Shulhan Arukh*, Yoreh De'ah 268:2.

16. See Norman Lamm, *A Hedge of Roses* (New York, 1966).

17. Yevamot 22a et passim.

18. Maimonides, Hilkhot Issurei Biah 13:1.

19. Rosh Hashanah 31b, Keritot 9a.

20. This will happen if, as is generally assumed, the Third Temple is built when the Messiah comes. Since resurrection of the dead is also part of that era all the converts who joined Judaism in the era between the Second and Third Temples should be there to offer their sacrifices.

21. Ketubot 11a, Maimonides, Hilkhot Issurei Biah 13:7.

22. If the child is under one year old and is put in the water face down, the membranes that kept him or her from swallowing amniotic fluid *in utero* will close and no water will be swallowed during the brief second of immersion in the mikvah.

23. *Responsa Hatam Sofer*, Yoreh De'ah 253; *Pithei Teshuvah*, Yoreh De'ah 268:8.

24. The prototype for much of this is Ruth's declaration of loyalty to her mother-in-law on the road between Moab, where they had lived, and Israel, where they were going (Ruth 1:16–17), Yevamot 47a–b.

25. See David Klinghoffer, *The Lord Shall Gather Me In* (New York, 1965), for one convert's view of the experience.

26. Cf. *Piskei Din Rabbanim*, sec. 10, p. 293; *Responsa Minhat Yitzhak* 1:121.

27. Mishnah Eruvin 7:11, Gittin 1:6.

28. Tosefta Sanhedrin 13:1. Maimonides codifies this opinion in *Mishneh Torah*, Hilkhot Teshuvah 3:5.

29. For an expansive view, see A. Lichtenstein, *The Seven Laws of Noah* (New York, 1981).

30. The acceptance of many converts from the Roman Empire who came with their own values and beliefs added to the ideological break between Judaism and Christianity in respect to "who is a Jew?" issues and made the

eventual split even more inevitable. King Herod, who was guilty of much moral depravity, was also a product of inappropriate additions to the Jewish community. See Tosafot Bava Bathra 3b, s.v. *kol de-amar*, and *Encyclopaedia Judaica*, s.v. Herod I.

31. These are the standards for child conversion of the Rabbinical Council of America, the largest Orthodox rabbinic organization in the United States.

32. Cf. the studies by Dr. Alvin Schiff done under the auspices of the New York Board of Jewish Education.

33. Ketubot 11a. For discussion of this entire issue, see Rabbi M. Schachter, "Various Aspects of Adoption," in *Halachah and Contemporary Society*, ed. A. Cohen (New York, 1984), pp. 31–53; see also Rabbi M. Feinstein, *Iggerot Mosheh*, Yoreh De'ah 1:162

34. In addition to the Christians, the Karaites are another group that followed this pattern; see J. D. Eisenstein, *Otzar Yisrael*, s.v. *kara'im* for sources and history.

Chapter 25
Citizenship and the Jew

W e Jews have spent much of our history as a subject
population in one country or another.[1] Though the
experiences have varied, one issue was always a concern. The government of the state represents a source of
authority, sometimes benevolent, sometimes hostile, sometimes worse. Judaism, Torah, the commandments, and
Halakhah also represent an authority center. How one bal-
ances the demands of both sources of authority, particularly
when they compete with or contradict one another, is a subject
that engaged many Jewish thinkers. In like fashion it confronts
us here as we take up the question of balancing the Jew's obligations as a citizen against his loyalty to his God. It is a very
sensitive issue, given how often in history we have been
accused of dual loyalty, meaning insincere and even traitorous
lack of commitment to the country in which we live.[2]

In our sources the question is first approached comprehen-
sively in Babylonia in the third century.[3] There we find the
famous formula of Mar Samuel (2nd–3rd century C.E.), who
headed the well-known academy at Nehardea: *dina de-
malkhuta dina* ("The law of the land is the law").[4] Samuel's
guiding principle in this area became Judaism's touchstone as
we struggled with the conflicting authority centers and their
demands in diaspora life.

At first glance this formulation would seem to abrogate Jewish law in any situation where it conflicts with secular law. If this had been so, Judaism would never have survived, as it did, the long centuries of exile. In fact, this understanding of the principle is not correct. For example the Mishnah, while generally accepting contracts declared legally binding in a secular court, specifically rejects divorce documents that come from a non-Jewish source.[5] Control of personal-status issues, such as marriage and divorce, was not ceded by the Jewish community to the secular government.[6]

This helped create a serious problem in our own day. The issue was first joined when Reform Judaism decided to accept secular divorce as part of its understanding of *dina de-malkhuta dina*.[7] The scenario of a woman marrying, obtaining a divorce in a secular court, and then remarrying is a frightening tableau from a traditional perspective. Due to the lack of a proper halakhic divorce, her second marriage would be an act of adultery, and any children produced by it would be illegitimate (*mamzerim*).[8] Halakhically, illegitimate children cannot marry within the community. Nonetheless, the Reform movement's decision to accept civil divorce made it a virtual certainty that such children would be born in significant numbers.

Rabbi Moses Feinstein (1895–1996), our most important contemporary American decisor of halakhic questions, took up this problem out of concern for the innocent offspring of the second marriage.[9] Realizing that marriages performed within the Reform movement rarely, if ever, conformed to Halakhah, Rabbi Feinstein suggested analyzing the first marriage for halakhic problems. If any legal shortcomings were found, they could be used to mitigate the first marriage and, therefore, its consequences for the children of the second relationship. In this way the *mamzerut* problem would be avoided.

This decision has been used by some in the non-Orthodox world to attack Orthodoxy as intolerant on the grounds that it rejects Reform marriages. The truth is that Rabbi Feinstein's decision was a compassionate attempt to maintain the halakhic legitimacy of the children of the second marriage, so that, as a community, we do not find ourselves in a situation where Orthodox and Reform Jews are unable to marry one another.[10]

In any case, Reform acceptance of secular divorce was a departure from talmudic practice. Samuel's dictum that the law of the land is law was not intended to include this aspect of life.

Further analysis of the sources that speak of *dina de-malkhuta dina* shows that the scope of the authority of the secular government is limited to financial and perhaps some civil matters,[11] and does not reach into the area of ritual or religious observance.[12] Different theories as to why this rule holds sway as it does can be found among our sages. The theories define different purviews and different limits as to what is and is not incorporated under the rubric of *dina de-malkhuta dina*.

We will cite two of the leading approaches in our literature. Rabbenu Nissim of Gerona, also known as Nissim ben Reuben Gerondi (1310–1375), a Spanish talmudist regarded by many as the most important political thinker in Jewish tradition, sees the power of a king or a secular government as emanating from his or its ownership of the land.[13] As such, the government can compel compliance with any law concerned with property as a condition of allowing us to live on the land.[14]

On the other hand, Rabbi Samuel ben Meir, also known as Rashbam (ca. 1080–ca. 1174), a grandson of Rashi, sees the rationale for the authority of *dina de-malkhuta dina* in what we would today call social contract theory. Says Rashbam, "All taxes and imposts and customary acts of the law of kings which they normally enact in their kingdoms are law because all members of the kingdom accept these laws upon themselves willingly."[15]

The idea of government deriving its legitimacy from the consent of the governed sounds very modern and Western. Its origin is usually credited to Thomas Hobbes and John Locke, who lived in the seventeenth and eighteenth centuries. How interesting to find it much earlier in the words of a talmudic commentator who was in his prime in the twelfth century. Apparently, Jews had so much experience with government, its power and its excesses, that we were thinking about these things much earlier than others.

Nonetheless, and somewhat surprisingly, Rashbam's theory allows the government far greater latitude in its exercise of authority than does the opinion of Rabbenu Nissim. Limiting control exclusively to areas related to property gives significantly less leeway than granting authority in areas that fall under the rubric of "consent of the governed." The governed can agree to many things that are not issues of property.

Take the example of crossing against a red light as an illustration. Is jaywalking a violation of *dina de-malkhuta dina*? Certainly the governed can agree to limit their walking to certain acceptable circumstances, such as a green but not a red light. According to Rashbam, this would fit the criterion, and crossing against a red light would violate *dina de-malkhuta dina*. However, traffic laws are not usually considered property laws. They are matters of public safety and traffic management. For Rabbenu Nissim, there might well be halakhic concerns about personal safety[16] and about the *hillul hashem* ("desecration of God's name") that comes from a Jew's violating the law,[17] but this would not seem to be a violation of *dina de-malkhuta dina*.

The limitations placed on the scope of *dina de-malkhuta dina* can readily be understood. It is only by retaining some element of control over the legal structure and ritual performance in one's life that a sense of national and religious identity can survive in a minority population. This importance of retaining identity through legal autonomy is reflected in the comments of Rabbi Moses Maimonides, also known as Rambam (1138–1204), perhaps our foremost post-talmudic sage, about the treatment of resident alien populations in a Jewish state: "If a Jew and a resident alien have a civil court case, we advantage the resident alien by always using *his* legal system (and not Halakhah) to determine who prevails."[18]

This, says Maimonides, is part of our duty to sustain (*le-hahayoto*) such an individual.[19] We do so by allowing him to retain his legal structure in the face of a majority culture whose laws are different. In this way the resident alien can preserve his identity, his cultural norms, and his way of life.

Beyond *dina de-malkhuta dina* and its legal ramifications, a general sense that it is necessary to be a good citizen also prevails.[20] For example, the government is allowed to draft citizens for military service, and Jews are expected to do their part.[21] So, too, citizenship obligations like voting and jury duty are activities that we should willingly participate in, both out of gratitude for what our country has done for us[22] and because it sanctifies God's name when Jews act in an upstanding and appropriate manner.[23]

For the record, Jews have served with distinction and valor in the military services of every country that has allowed them to serve. In fact, it is said that Jews have served loyally on both sides of every major conflict between non-Jewish nations from the fall of the Roman Empire until the Second World War. Only the Nazi monstrosity brought all Jews together on the same side of the hostilities.

Conscientious objection also exists as a value in Jewish law.[24] Immoral and illegal orders can and must be opposed to the extent possible. The Bible tells the story of the schism between David and Saul. Before news of the split became public, David, who was seeking to escape from Saul, got some help from Nob, the city of priests. Not knowing that Saul was pursuing him, the city and its leaders helped David, who they thought was Saul's trusted lieutenant. When King Saul immorally ordered the destruction of Nob in retribution, two of his officers refused to comply.[25] Interestingly, the Talmud records an opinion that this was not enough; the officers should have taken action or at least protested to prevent Saul's terrible order from being carried out by someone else who was willing to obey his command.[26]

Similarly though less dramatically, the Talmud allows one to avoid paying taxes, even by lying to the tax collector, if the taxes are illegal. Payment of legal taxes is a requirement of *dina de-malkhuta dina*, but immoral and illegal taxation requires opposition, not compliance.[27] Some have inappropriately tried to use this source to rationalize cheating the United States government. There is simply no license in this or any other rabbinic teaching that would allow such immoral conduct.

One final halakhic point. Even within the citizenship framework, internal Jewish problems are to be dealt with internally if at all possible. This is most evident in the requirement that Jews not sue one another in a secular court.[28] Instead a bet din (rabbinic court) is to decide all such issues. Only if one party refuses to attend a bet din or abide by its decision may the rabbinic court give a litigant permission to sue in a secular forum.

Today, batei din constitute themselves under the American legal system as binding arbitration panels. If both litigants agree in writing, before the trial, to accept the Rabbis' decision as binding, final recourse can be had to the secular authorities to enforce a judgment made by the rabbinic court. In this way we can solve our own problems within our own community and not end up washing our dirty linen in public.

Finally, on the charge of dual or divided loyalty, one important point should be made. It is not difficult for a child to love both mother and father. So, too, one has the capacity to love two countries for what they are and for what they each have provided to us.

This book goes to press as my congregant and friend, Joseph Lieberman, having completed his historic candidacy for vice president of the United States, has begun to pursue the Democratic nomination for President in 2004. His campaign represents the pinnacle of the observant Jew functioning in the capacity of the ultimate "good" citizen.[29]

1. The literature on the subject of this chapter includes: H. Schachter, "Dina De'malchusa dina: Secular Law as a Religious Obligation," *Journal of Halachah and Contemporary Society* 1:1 (1981), pp. 103–132; S. Schaffer, "Dina Demalkhuta Dina," *Jewish Law Association Studies* 1 (1985), pp. 121–124; Leo Landman, "Dina D'malkhuta Dina: Solely a Diaspora Concept," *Tradition* 15:3 (1975), pp. 89–96; Aaron Rakeffet-Rothkoff, "Dina D'malkhuta Dina: The Law of the Land in Halakhic Perspective," *Tradition* 31:2 (1972), pp. 5–23.

2. The first antisemitic canard in recorded history was Pharaoh's allegation that in time of war the Jews would join with Egypt's enemies (Exodus 1:10). In substance it parallels Haman's charge, made much later in biblical history, that the Jews, scattered throughout Persia, did not keep the king's laws and thus implicitly represented a potential fifth column (Esther 3:8). A similar theme can be found in the accusation by the enemies of the Jews returning to rebuild the Second Temple that they were building a "rebellious city" (Ezra 4:12–16) and in many postbiblical libelous attacks.

3. Earlier brief statements exist; see Jeremiah 29:7, Mishnah Avot 3:2, and the discussion below.

4. The phrase appears in the Babylonian Talmud, Nedarim 28a, Gittin 10b, Baba Kamma 113a (three times) and 113b, Baba Bathra 54b and 55a. It does not appear in the Jerusalem Talmud. For further discussion, see H. Schachter, op. cit.

5. Mishnah Gittin 1:5.

6. This issue came to the fore at the founding of the State of Israel. In an effort to placate the observant minority in the nascent state, David Ben-Gurion, the first Prime Minister of Israel, offered them one area of law that would be under their control. They chose the area of personal status: conversion, marriage, and divorce. Many of the conflicts surrounding the question of "Who is a Jew?" that have erupted in Israel in recent years center around this area. From a traditional perspective, the area of personal status must be controlled in order to protect the appropriate boundaries of Jewish identity. For those who are not in control, this state of affairs comes across as highly unfair. Hence the conflict of the last few years. See the discussion of conversion and who is a Jew in Chapter 24.

7. Cf. CCAR Responsa, *American Reform Responsa* 5, 90 (1980), pp. 84–86

8. Yevamot 49a. See generally *Encyclopaedia Judaica*, s.v. Mamzer.

9. *Iggerot Mosheh*, Even ha-Ezer 1:76.

10. Rabbi Moshe Tendler (Rabbi Feinstein's son-in-law), personal communication.

11. See *Encyclopedia Talmudit*, s.v. *dina de-malkhuta dina,* and J. D. Eisenstein, *Otzar Yisrael*, s.v. *dina de-malkhuta dina,* for two different formulations of this limitation.

12. In addition to the issue of *get* (religious divorce), concern is raised in the Talmud regarding secular law interfering with the biblical requirement of primogeniture (Bava Bathra 54b).

13. Commentary to Nedarim 28a and see the talmudic discussion of taxes on land as opposed to taxes on the person (Baba Bathra 54b).

14. Not everyone reads Rabbenu Nissim this way.

15. Commentary to Baba Bathra 54b, s.v. *dina de-malkhuta dina.*

16. Deuteronomy 4:15 is understood as requiring concern for personal safety. See the discussion of tobacco, alcohol, and drugs in Chapter 27.

17. See Eisenstein, *Otzar Yisrael*, s.v. *hillul hashem*; also *Encyclopedia Talmudit*, s.v. *hillul hashem*, subsection 6, *bifnei nakhrim.*

18. Maimonides, *Misnneh Torah*, Hilkhot Melakhim 10:11–12.

19. This is based on Leviticus 25:35. See Rashi on Pesahim 21b, s.v. *ger atah.*

20. As we began our first exile in Babylonia, the prophet Jeremiah urged us "to seek the peace of the city to which I have exiled you, and pray on its behalf to God, for in its peace you will have peace" (Jeremiah 29:7). Seeking the peace of the city or country in which we live would seem to require us to

be good, responsible citizens. Rabbi Moses Feinstein, *Iggerot Mosheh*, Hoshen Mishpat 2:29, speaks in eloquent terms of the debt we owe to the United States in particular.

21. The powers of the king are enumerated in two biblical passage, Deuteronomy 17:14–20 and I Samuel 8:11–17. The draft is mentioned in the latter source, vv. 11–12. Meiri (1249–1316) on Nedarim 28a and the Vilna Gaon (1720–1797) on Hoshen Mishpat 369:4 say that these powers are granted to gentile as well as Jewish kings.

22. See above, n. 20.

23. This is the inverse of the idea that inappropriate behavior creates a *hillul hashem*; see discussion and sources above.

24. Two articles on this subject are M. Greenberg, "Rabbinic Reflections on Defying Illegal Orders: Amasa, Abner and Joab," and Maurice Lamm, "After the War: Another Look at Pacifism and Selective Conscientious Objection," both in *Contemporary Jewish Ethics*, ed. M. Kellner (New York, 1978).

25. I Samuel 22.

26. Sanhedrin 20a.

27. Nedarim 27b–28a.

28. For the rationale, see Rashi on Exodus 21:1, citing Gittin 88b. See also Joseph Caro, *Shulhan Arukh*, Hoshen Mishpat 26:1–2.

29. See Joseph Lieberman, *In Praise of Public Life* (New York, 2000).

Chapter 26
Evolution and Life on Other Planets

Recently, the Kansas State Board of Education passed a resolution eliminating the teaching of evolution as a requirement in state-accredited schools.[1] This may allow the teaching of creationism in that state's school system, and it led to my receiving an interesting phone call. The activities director at a nonsectarian private school in my neighborhood asked if I would come to debate evolution vs. creation. I told her that I would be glad to, but first she would have to tell me which side of the question she wanted me to argue.

The response stunned her into silence. Finally, she managed to stammer her surprise that an Orthodox Rabbi could possibly be comfortable with either position.

While it is true that some important Jewish thinkers take a creationist approach—"it all began in six days of twenty-four hours"[2]—many do not. In fact, many possible resolutions of the apparent conflict between the Bible and Charles Darwin's theory can be found. It should be noted that the Association of Orthodox Jewish Scientists published a book some years back called *Challenge* on the interface of science and Judaism. Fully a third of what is a rather thick volume deals with Jewish responses to scientific theories on the age of the earth and evolution. These responses range from total

rejection of evolutionary theory to virtually total acceptance.[3] For us, then, the issue is not anywhere near as important as it is for some in the Christian community.[4] This is an
example of our general historical reluctance to invest religious authority in scientific theories.[5] Given the negative
experiences of faith groups that have given ecclesiastical
weight to scientific hypotheses, this seems to be a very wise
way of doing business.[6]

One can find a possible reconciliation between Torah and
evolution in the word used by the Bible to describe the six
periods of creation. While the word *yom* which is used to
describe these six epochs can mean "day," it also appears in
the Bible with the meanings "year"[7] and "period of time."[8] If
the last definition is accepted as the meaning in the account of
creation, many of the problems disappear or at least diminish
significantly.

One can also point out that the Torah is not interested in
presenting contemporary scientific truth. Information of this
kind would have been unintelligible to the people who first
received the Torah and would be far too technical for most of
us today.

In any case, biological and geological truth is not the goal of
the Torah. Especially in the first few chapters of Genesis, as
prelude to the appearance of the Jewish people and the giving
of the Torah, what would seem to be most in order, and precisely what we are given, is an explanation of why human
nature leads to the need for that revelation and the emergence
of that people. Discussions of the evolution of different types
of DNA have no place here.

Presenting this introduction in stories that are superficially
easy to understand but on continuing study present no end to
profundity draws people to the biblical text. These stories are
similar, though with a demonstrably higher moral tone, to
tales told in much of the ancient Near East in biblical times.[9]

This, too, would help readers who first received the Torah to understand its message and importance for their lives.

As the failure of humans to live up to their noble role as the most significant of God's creations is retold,[10] as the abject moral collapse of humankind leading to the flood and the restart of creation is understood,[11] as the hubris and technological cruelty of the Tower of Babel civilization is recalled,[12] the need for the structure and morality of God's revealed Torah becomes obvious. This is far more important for Torah purposes than a list of one-celled plants and animals that eventually evolved into more complex structures.[13] Even the ages and names of the dinosaurs, intriguing as some people find them, wouldn't come close to eclipsing these truths of the human condition as worthy study for the Bible.

In summation, then, for those who accept evolutionary theory, a home can be found in Torah ideology.[14] As long as one understands that evolution, if it occurred, occurred with God's guidance and according to His plan, Judaism can feel comfortable with it. In fact, some would say, finding that the universe has developed according to natural law that reveals God's wisdom is more to the glory of God than finding Him needing to be involved in every individual act of creation.[15] This position was widely held by medieval theologians.[16] It is strange that a number of significant modern scientists seem to think that the discovery of natural law is, somehow, a blow against the existence of God. For many religious thinkers, precisely the opposite is true.

Since evolution is no great issue for an Orthodox Jew, it is somewhat intriguing to watch the battle on this subject unfold. While Christian orthodoxies preclude acceptance of evolution, scientific orthodoxy seems to be, at times, just as limited.

Evolution is not a theory without problems.[17] For example, the amount of time that some scientists theorize was needed to allow for the present development of the species existing on earth is far longer than the age of the earth as determined by astronomy. So, too, there is no fossil record or living remnant of intermediary species, the so-called missing links, such as between apes and humans. Sadly, raising such questions is often impermissible in a scientific or academic setting. Continuing to raise them will usually evoke dismissive name-calling, delegitimitizing, or worse. Science can create its own orthodoxies.

For traditional Jews, happily, on this issue the chips can fall where they may. If creationism is true, we will embrace those who have taken such a position. If evolution is true, many ways exist to bring it into the fold. If a third theory emerges, I am sure we can deal with that as well.

Finally, evolutionary theory suggests that similar processes occur on other planets, perhaps even leading to sentient life. While this might present theological problems for other faith systems concerning whether these alien life-forms have a soul and need salvation, Judaism has no requirement that everyone be Jewish, and thus their possible presence would seem to be no great problem.[18] Certainly, the basic morality encompassed in the seven Noahide laws must exist for such beings to survive. As such, they would have all they would need to achieve life in the World-to-Come. Further, some rabbinic sources speak of God creating many worlds.[19] The question of the existence today of life on such worlds is for astronomers and other scientists to tell us. If the answer turns out to be yes, we will face many challenges, but for Judaism they will almost certainly not be theological.

1. A marvelous resource on the subjects covered in this chapter is Aryeh Carmel and Cyril Domb, eds., *Challenge: Torah Views on Science and Its Problems* (New York, 1978). The book includes a section more than 150 pages

long (pp. 124–287) that presents many primary sources and more than ten approaches to the question of evolution from a Torah perspective, though with great diversity of response to the problem. It also contains an article by Rabbi Dr. Norman Lamm entitled "The Religious Implications of Extraterrestrial Life" (pp. 354–398).

2. Cf. Rabbi Menahem Mendel Schneersohn, "A Letter on Science and Judaism," in *Challenge*, pp. 142–149.

3. Cf. Reuben Gross, "On Creation and Evolution," in *Challenge*, pp. 236–239.

4. The book, play, and movie *Inherit the Wind* about the so-called Scopes Monkey Trial gives one a clear sense of the issues and emotions involved. See Jerome Lawrence and Robert Lee, *Inherit the Wind* (London, 1961). See also Nicholas Aksionczyk, *A Second Look at Fundamentalism, the Scopes Trial and "Inherit the Wind"* (El Cajon, Calif., 1999), for an example of how passions, at least on the creationist side, remain hot to this day.

5. See the debates on celestial and solar dynamics between the sages of Israel and the sages of other nations, Pesahim 94b. It is clear from the Talmud (despite some suggestions to the contrary) that when it comes to science the sages of Israel are not presumptively right, and that the facts of nature determine what is correct. This is true here because we are dealing with a matter of science and not of Halakhah. If Halakhah were the subject, rabbinic authority would, of necessity, be decisive. For further discussion of this idea, see Abraham ben Maimonides, *Ein Ya'akov*, introduction.

6. For the Catholic experience with this issue, see George Haven Putnam, *The Censorship of the Church of Rome* (New York, 1967).

7. Cf. Exodus 13:10, at least according to the opinion of Rabbi Akiva, Menahot 36b.

8. The prophecies of the end of days that speak of *ba-yom ha-hu* are, in many cases, not events of a single day's duration but contextually must mean "in that era"; see Isaiah 11:10–11.

9. See James Pritchard, *The Ancient Near East: An Anthology of Texts and Pictures* (Princeton, 1971). See especially the Creation Epic, pp. 31–39, and the Epic of Gilgamesh, pp. 40–74. Some scholars see the similarities between this material and the biblical stories as challenging the latter's authenticity. In my view they support just the opposite conclusion. Any good teacher of morals will use contemporary cultural material to make a point. The familiarity is of great assistance to the pedagogy. For example, a Rabbi may cite a modern

novel or television program to help his message get through. The material in Genesis was familiar to the people of the ancient Near East. Presenting these well-known stories in such an ethically superior way would maximize the impact of their moral lessons. The truly remarkable element is the consistent and unrelenting morality of the Bible as compared to other ancient Near Eastern texts. The presence of this moral tone, so unlike the writings of other ancient societies, provides a strong support for the idea that a divine hand authored the Bible.

10. Genesis 3–4.

11. Genesis 6–9.

12. Genesis 11:1–9.

13. For further discussion of these issues, see Rabbi Dr. J. H. Hertz, "Additional Notes to Genesis," in his *The Pentateuch and Haftorahs* (London, 1961), pp. 193–198.

14. This is discussed by Reuben Gross (see above, n. 3) and in several other articles in *Challenge*.

15. See Chapter 17.

16. See Dan Cohn–Sherbok, *Divine Intervention and Miracles in Jewish Theology* (Lewiston, N.Y., 1996).

17. There is a great deal of literature on this subject. In addition to the material in *Challenge*, especially Morris Goldman, "Critical Review of Evolution," see Ronald Numbers, *Creation–Evolution Debates* (New York, 1995) and Baruch Sterman, "Judaism and Darwinian Evolution," *Tradition* 29:1 (Fall 1994), pp. 48–75.

18. See Chapter 8.

19. Genesis Rabbah 3:9; see also Avodah Zarah 3b.

Chapter 27
Tobacco, Drugs, and Alcohol

Intuitively, we would expect traditional Judaism to oppose the misuse of all destructive chemical substances.[1] And certainly it does, but there are nuances, history, and underlying philosophies that are worth discussing at greater length.[2]

Nonetheless, generally speaking, Jewish law requires us to protect our lives and our health. We are told by the Torah, "you shall be extremely careful about your souls."[3] This is understood to mean both avoidance of dangerous situations and active pursuit of healthy activities.[4] Certainly, shunning harmful drugs falls under this category. As we discuss in Chapters 5 and 23, every human life is infinitely valuable and irreplaceable. We must treat our own life in that way.

Taking the three troublesome substances one at a time, we begin with tobacco. Our present understanding of its dangers would prohibit us from taking up smoking and would require anyone who does so to stop if at all possible.[5] However, this was not always the case.

Beginning in the late nineteenth century, many rabbinic authorities permitted smoking on holidays (Yom Tov).[6] Though most aspects of work are prohibited on these days, preparation of food through cooking is biblically allowed.[7] Derivatively, any use of fire is also permitted as long as the use serves a need[8] and has a generally positive effect on those who use it in this way.[9] When the responsa on the subject of smoking on Yom Tov were written, the permissive decisions were based on the belief that smoking was healthy.[10] Specifically, it was thought to aid such things as digestion and concentration while studying. Obviously these are desirable outcomes, valuable to all and satisfying of appropriate needs. For these reasons, smoking became a permissible activity on holidays.[11]

It is remarkable how far we have come in our scientific understanding of the effects of tobacco. The change in our knowledge changes the halakhic outcome. Once tobacco was understood to be at all unhealthy, smoking on Yom Tov became prohibited.[12] As the dangers of tar and nicotine have become even clearer, it should be prohibited on weekdays as well.[13] So, too, one must be concerned about the effects that one's second-hand smoke is having on others.[14] I am obviously precluded from harming anyone else in pursuit of my own pleasure.

As suggested in the last paragraph there was an intermediate stage when the full danger of smoking was not known. During this period, some argued that smoking was simply a statistical danger that would harm some, but not all, smokers.[15] Since people were not generally concerned about this danger in regard to tobacco,[16] it was still an activity one could choose to participate in, just as people drive cars despite the fact that some will be harmed by doing so..

However, even at that stage smoking would still have violated the requirement to ingest only items that promote bodily health.[17] Maimonides, who was a physician as well as one of our greatest Torah scholars, put it this way, "A healthy body is essential to the pursuit of the knowledge of God."[18] As indicated even then, smoking on Yom Tov would have been prohibited.

Today, any lenient position would seem to have lost its claim to halakhic validity. We know that cigarette smoking has immediate and long-term negative effects on the body of everyone who smokes. Moreover, people no longer see it as an activity to engage in without fear.

This history of changing halakhic conclusions is in no way a challenge to the eternal nature of Jewish law. Scientific conclusions are not the subject of halakhic decision-making. Rather, they comprise the body of information necessary to make such conclusions. If the information is incorrect or changes, the halakhic conclusion will change, but the halakhic principle remains the same.

Specifically, unhealthy or dangerous substances are prohibited,[19] and when fire is involved in such cases, that use of fire is prohibited on Yom Tov.[20] This principle remained true throughout the eighteenth, nineteenth, and twentieth centuries, and is still true in the twenty-first. In fact, it was and will always be true. However, contemporary science must provide a correct understanding of what falls in the categories of "healthy" and "dangerous", and it must accurately explain the nature of the danger. If scientific understanding changes, the halakhic conclusion will change with it. The reason for the change lies in science's changing understanding, not in Halakhah. Similarly, if science were to change its mind and decide that smoking was, in fact, healthy (as unlikely as that now seems), we would return to the halakhic conclusions of the late nineteenth century.

Alcohol is somewhat different. First, in moderation alcohol may in fact have healthy effects. Second, wine is a requirement or at least a desideratum in many ritual situations, such as for Kiddush (the sanctification prayer) that begins two of the Sabbath meals.[21] This use of wine raises and sanctifies this ubiquitous beverage and the sense of joy it creates to the point where it is used in a holy setting rather then simply as a hedonistic experience.

In any case, overindulgence is prohibited. Many rabbinic statements condemn drunkenness,[22] and one cannot fulfill such basic commandments as prayer when one is mentally impaired due to alcohol consumption.[23]

Even on the holiday of Purim, when drinking wine is part of the tradition, the Talmud tells a cautionary tale of a murder and miraculous resurrection or perhaps of an imagined murder,[24] evoked under the influence of alcohol.[25] This should stand as a warning to avoid excess even on the most celebratory of all our holidays.

At times, people raise the question of why alcohol may be acceptable in some situations but marijuana is not. This question has become less frequent as the negative mental and physical effects of marijuana and its bridging effect, which leads many users to other drugs, have become more obvious. Nonetheless some comments should be made on this subject.

First, marijuana is illegal, whereas alcohol is not. Even if one disagrees with this public policy, respect for the law is an important Jewish value. By the same token, being a good citizen may be a halakhic requirement, and avoiding profanation of God's name by being identified as a Jew who violates the law is certainly an obligation.[26]

One other critical difference between marijuana and alcohol must be highlighted. Drugs come with a drug culture that is not at all the same as the culture surrounding alcohol. The drug culture sees the altered mental state that one achieves under the influence of narcotics as a desirable outcome. New insights, better perspectives, clearer and more heightened awareness of reality are claimed to be the product of drug use, at least in some circles.

No such claims are made about alcohol. One way to sense the difference is to compare someone who smokes marijuana before attending a party or other social gathering because, so they claim, they can only truly be themselves in this way, with someone who uses liquor in the same fashion. When said about drugs this is often considered to be "cool." However, if alcohol is the substance being used and someone were to admit to needing a drink for the same reason, everyone would understand that this person had a serious problem.

The drug culture is profoundly at odds with Jewish thought. The idea that human beings need to ingest a substance that alters their nature in order to achieve a new pinnacle of perception flies in the face of the idea that God made the human being to be the best thing in the created universe.[27] In fact, any ideology that diminishes the status of human beings borders on idolatry, as it allows other elements to intervene between man and God.[28] Drugs should certainly not be allowed to do this.

Finally, as to the claim that drugs provide valuable enhanced perceptions, the best response is a famous story, now told in many versions, that actually originated with Supreme Court Justice Oliver Wendell Holmes. According to the original version, Holmes once underwent surgery. In those days, the anesthetic was morphine, a powerful narcotic.

After surgery, while still under the influence of the drug, Holmes awoke. In his diary he writes that as he opened his eyes, "the fundamental secret of the universe, the key to all existence and meaning was revealed to me."

Holmes realized two things. First, that he was about to fall asleep again, and second, that he would likely forget this most profound of all truths. With his strength significantly diminished by surgery and morphine, Holmes managed to pull himself up to the nightstand by his bed. There, having left a pen and pad before surgery, he managed to scrawl his unparalleled truth on the paper before collapsing into a deep sleep.

Many hours later, no longer under the influence, he awoke, and sure enough he had forgotten his truth. But he did remember that he had written it down. Excitedly he took his pad, and there, in barely legible handwriting, were the immortal words, "This room smells of turpentine."

I encountered something similar while in college. I happened to be in an apartment in a less affluent neighborhood in

Brooklyn, New York, with someone who unfortunately was "under the influence." This fellow spent several minutes staring at some underwear flapping on the clothesline that was visible outside the window while commenting on how exquisitely beautiful it was.

When turpentine is the universal fundamental truth and underwear on a clothesline exquisitely beautiful, we do not have enhancement of the mind. We have gross distortion. No matter how good it might feel, this distortion of the intellect deforms one of humankind's fundamental and defining characteristics.[29] There is no possibility that Judaism could countenance this denigration of our basic humanity.

When it comes to harder drugs than marijuana, all that has been said so far applies. In addition, the greater health risk, and the danger of addiction (which can occur, at least as a psychological dependency, even with marijuana), simply puts these things completely outside the pale as far as Judaism is concerned.

1. Judaism sees itself as a religion of life; cf. Deuteronomy 30:19, and note the prohibition limiting the contact of the kohanim (priests) with the dead. The kohanim are biblically to be at the center of Jewish religious life, and they are to emphasize the final word of that phrase in their spiritual functioning.

2. For further information on Judaism and drugs, see Leo Landman, ed., *Judaism and Drugs* (New York: Commission on Synagogue Relations, 1973). On Judaism and alcohol, see David Novak, "Alcohol and Drug Abuse in the Perspective of Jewish Tradition," *Judaism* 33:2 (1984), pp. 221–232. On Judaism and smoking, see Moses Aberbach, "Smoking in Halakhah," *Tradition* 10:3 (1969), pp. 49–60; Fred Rosner, "Cigarette Smoking in Jewish Law," *Journal of Halachah and Contemporary Society* 4 (1982), pp. 33–45; idem, "Smoking and Jewish Law: An Update," *Le'ela* 37 (1994), pp. 13–16.

3. Deuteronomy 4:15. Though the context is a prohibition against engaging in idol worship, the verse has been generalized into a requirement to be care-

ful regarding one's life and health. The first usage of the verse in this way appears in Berakhot 32b as an issue raised by a non-Jew to a Jew. For the contemporary usage of the term, see Rabbi Solomon Ganzfried, *Kitzur Shulhan Arukh* 32:1.

4. For general discussion, see Shmuel Boylan, "Heshash Sakanah le-Or Halakhah," *Or ha-Mizrah* 32:1 (Tishrei 5744 [1984]), p. 112.

5. Moses Feinstein, *Iggerot Mosheh*, Yoreh De'ah 2:49.

6. For sources and discussion, see *Biur Halakhah* 511, s.v. *ein osin mugmar*. For additional sources and contemporary debate on the issue, see Eliezer Waldenberg, *Responsa Tzitz Eliezer* 17:21; Feinstein, *Iggerot Mosheh*, Orah Hayyim 5:34; Jeffrey Woolf, Reuven Bulka, Daniel Landes, and Saul Berman, "Proposal on Smoking," The Orthodox Roundtable, New York.

7. Maimonides, *Mishneh Torah*, Hilkhot Yom Tov 1:4.

8. Ketubot 7a, Tosafot Betzah 12a, s.v. *hakhi garis rashi*.

9. Ketubot, loc. cit.

10. Cf. Jacob Joshua ben Zevi Falk, *Penei Yehoshua* to Shabbat 39b.

11. There has always been some opposition; see the sources quoted in n. 6 above.

12. Some halakhic authorities remain hesitant to say so. See Waldenberg, *Tzitz Eliezer* 17:21.

13. See Boylan, "Heshash Sakanah le-Or Halakhah."

14. Feinstein, *Iggerot Mosheh*, Hoshen Mishpat 2:18 and the Orthodox Roundtable proposal cited in n. 6 above.

15. See *Iggerot Mosheh*, Yoreh De'ah 2:49, and J. David Bleich, "Survey of Recent Halakhic Periodical Literature: Smoking," *Tradition* 16:4 (Summer 1977), pp. 121–123.

16. Based on the principle *shomer petayim hashem* ("God protects the simple"), Shabbat 129b et passim.

17. Maimonides, Hilkhot De'ot 3:2.

18. Ibid., 3:3.

19. See the sources cited in n. 3 and 4 above.

20. Ketubot 7a.

21. *Shulhan Arukh*, Orah Hayyim 271.

22. Midrash Tanhuma, Noah 14, and see the story mentioned in the next paragraph of the main text.

23. Berakhot 31b.

24. Cf. Isaiah ben Abraham ha-Levi Horowitz, *Shenei Luhot ha-Berit*, Sefer Shemot, Derush ve-Atah Tetzaveh 2.

25. Megillah 7b.

26. See Chapter 25.

27. See Chapter 5.

28. Cf. Jeremiah 2:27.

29. Cf. Maimonides, *Guide for the Perplexed* 1:1.

Chapter 28
Abortion

Few issues in modern Western society are as divisive as the issue of abortion.[1] Heated debates, large rallies, even tragic violence and murder are all part of the pro-choice/pro-life contretemps.[2] With the passage of time, the issue has come to symbolize many things other than abortion for secular society. These include feminism, women's roles, the source of morality, sexual freedom, and the meaning of personal responsibility.

For Judaism, none of these concerns are central to the abortion discussion.

Two factors help make this statement a reality. First, the language of pro-choice/pro-life is a language of rights, and the question of the proper application of rights is a basic pursuit of Western society and its legal and cultural institutions.[3] For Judaism, however, the language of rights is rarely central, is often a poor fit, and can even be inappropriate if one is seeking to understand Judaism in its own terms. "Right to choose," "right to life," and "right to one's body" are the slogans of the abortion debate, and they are, at the least, uncomfortable concepts for Judaism. Substituting "responsible choices," "responsible to one's life," and "responsible for one's body" would bring to bear a language much more familiar and comfortable to Jewish tradition. Responsibility is the touchstone of Judaism, not rights.[4]

Second, from our earliest discussion of the subject, Judaism has never taken what one might describe as either a pro-choice or a pro-life position. Our sources simply do not allow us to do so. As a telling example, virtually all the authorities who discuss this issue from a Jewish perspective begin with the following passage from Tractate Ohalot in the Mishnah:

> If a woman is in hard travail, one cuts up the child in her womb and brings it forth member by member, because her life comes before that of [the child]. But if the greater part has proceeded forth, one may not touch it, for one may not set aside one person's life for that of another.[5]

This Mishnah is obviously not pro-life, at least in the radical iteration of that position, as Halakhah here allows and even requires an abortion when a mother's life, and perhaps her health, is in danger.

This "requirement" to have an abortion played a small role in recent American legislative history. The United States Supreme Court in 1990, in a case known as Employment Division v. Smith, removed many constitutional protections from people practicing their religion. An attempt was made to restore those protections through a bill known as the Religious Freedom Restoration Act, or RFRA. Some Christians were concerned that people might use this act to claim that they had a right to an abortion under American law, on the grounds that their religion mandated abortion in certain circumstances. When the question of which religious groups might have a tradition requiring an abortion was thoroughly researched, only one was found—traditional Jews.

Returning to the mishnah quoted above, it is also clearly not pro-choice. It does not allow abortions under any and all circumstances, only when the mother is in distress. While the question of how much distress is enough is a critical consideration that will occupy much of the rest of our discussion, clearly inconvenience or unhappiness with the gender of the fetus would be insufficient grounds for such a procedure.

Our medieval commentators and codifiers appear to have been of two minds in understanding the law of abortion and the mishnah we are discussing.

An important position on this subject was taken by Rabbi Moses Maimonides, also known as Rambam (1138–1204), perhaps our most important post-talmudic sage.[6] Although some authorities, such as Rabbi Jair Hayyim ben Samson Bacharach (1638–1702) and Rabbi Yehiel Yaakov Weinberg (1885–1966), challenge the usual understanding of Maimonides' view,[7] he is generally held to believe that a woman in difficult labor is, in effect, being pursued by the fetus. Just as one may injure and even kill, if no other option is available, someone chasing another individual and trying to kill him,[8] so, too, the fetus, by endangering the mother's life, becomes a functional pursuer who may be terminated as a last resort.[9]

Rambam's formulation of the fetus as pursuer seems to grant the fetus significant status,[10] perhaps even full human status.[11] A non-fetal pursuer is a human being. The only reason he can be terminated is because he is engaged in actions that are a direct threat to the pursued and no other means of protection is available. Maimonides seems to be equating "human being as pursuer" with "fetus as pursuer."[12] As such, a fetus commands a presumption that it must be protected. Overcoming this presumption is a heavy burden that presumably can only be met either by a direct threat to the life of the mother or perhaps by something almost as serious.

Supporting this view is Maimonides' acceptance and codification of the position (debated in the Talmud)[13] that abortion is a capital crime for a gentile,[14] and Tosafot's assumption in the same context that gentile abortion is murder.[15] As such, abortion should occur, by Maimonides' formulation, only under very restricted circumstances.[16]

Others, among them Rabbi Solomon ben Isaac, generally known as Rashi (1040–1105), Judaism's foremost commentator on the Bible and Talmud, take a very different view. For them, abortion is performed for a mother in difficulty because a fetus is not a full-fledged human life until it emerges from its mother.[17] Since the mother's human status is obviously complete and intact, she will come first whenever her significant interests and those of the fetus are at cross-purposes.[18]

Adding support to this approach are a number of talmudic sources and one biblical passage.[19] In the latter, those who cause the accidental death of a fetus by miscarriage pay money to the fetus's father.[20] Were the fetus a full human being, and its death, therefore, negligent homicide, monetary compensation would not be the expected punishment.[21] Negligent homicide, by biblical law, requires the perpetrator to leave his home and undergo a period of exile in one of forty-eight designated refuge cities.[22] Monetary compensation is prohibited in such a case.[23] This would seem to indicate that causing a miscarriage is not negligent homicide, and, therefore, that the fetus is not fully a human being.[24]

As an example of the talmudic material supporting this position, one source allows aborting a fetus carried by a woman guilty of a capital crime prior to her execution to ease her concern that after the execution she will spontaneously miscarry and be disgraced in this way.[25] Not only do we not wait for a woman so convicted to give birth (we are required to do so only if labor has commenced),[26] but we allow an abortion to ease her mental distress over what might occur after she is dead.

This talmudic course of action would seem to grant no more than minimal status to the fetus. As a result, this source specifically, and this approach generally, would permit abortion in a far broader range of situations than reliance on Maimonides' formulation would lead us to accept.[27]

Mentioning labor brings up the question of stages in pregnancy and their effect on the abortion question. Emergence of the fetus is mentioned in the mishnah cited above is an important turning point. This stage in the pregnancy process is described in some sources as "the emergence of the head of the fetus"[28] (which makes partial-birth abortion prohibited by Jewish law according to all authorities),[29] and in others as "emergence of most of the fetus from the mother."[30] As we have seen, the beginning of labor is also an important transition for our discussion.[31] Furthermore, some more modern commentators understand the subservient nature of fetal life to maternal life as reflecting the dependence of the fetus on the mother.[32] Therefore, when the fetus reaches the point of independent viability, this may represent a change in its status.[33]

So, too, the very beginning of pregnancy may be different. Many sources teach that a fetus is merely fluid through day forty after conception.[34] Please note that the count is from actual conception, not from the date of the last menstrual period, as contemporary doctors calculate it. The halakhic count subtracts about two weeks from the number, thus putting this transition point at what contemporary doctors would call the end of the second month of pregnancy. Many authorities are more lenient about allowing abortion during these first forty days or two months than they would be subsequent to this moment in the development of the fetus.[35]

A contemporary discussion that incorporates and illustrates many of the elements just detailed is the debate between Rabbi Eliezer Waldenberg and Rabbi Moses Feinstein on aborting a fetus that tested positive for Tay-Sachs disease. Tay-Sachs is a Jewish genetic disease afflicting primarily people of Eastern European ancestry. If both parents carry the Tay-Sachs gene, they can produce (statistically in one out of four cases) a baby that has two Tay-Sachs genes in its genetic makeup. Tragically, that baby will contract the disease and will die, probably by age three or four, though certainly not much later.[36]

Bearing such a child and watching it wither and pass away is, to say the least, emotionally difficult for the parents. But is that sufficient to allow abortion? Rabbi Waldenberg permits such an abortion until the seventh month of pregnancy.[37] Rabbi Feinstein, evoking Maimonides' conceptualization and Tosafot's equation of abortion as murder, does not.[38]

It is here that the extent of the range of opinions on abortion can be seen. Neither Rabbi Waldenberg nor Rabbi Feinstein would prohibit abortion if the mother's life was in danger. Neither would permit abortion if the baby was healthy and the couple merely wanted to delay having children for a few years.[39] Where the debate is joined is on the relative value of fetal life vs. parental emotional distress. On this question Rabbi Feinstein seems to follow Maimonides' view, while Rabbi Waldenberg appears to be a disciple of Rashi.

The breadth of the debate may lead us to choice in one very unfortunate circumstance, but that choice may be very humane. Imagine a woman who is pregnant but who also, unfortunately, has cancer. If she takes chemotherapy for the cancer, the fetus will die, but this may be her only chance to survive. If she doesn't take chemotherapy, she may well die but the baby will have a chance. Analyzing the situation halakhically, Rambam would seem to forbid the use of chemotherapy. The fetus is not the pursuer, the cancer is. There should be no license to kill an innocent bystander to save the mother.

Rashi, on the other hand, who sees the fetus as subservient to the mother, should require chemotherapy. As stated above, the mother's survival interests come before those of the fetus.

At least one contemporary responsum allows the mother's choice in such a case to be the determining factor.[40] Her determination that she wants to take the chemotherapy can find support in Rashi's position, thus allowing her to save her own life, or we can support her decision not to take the medicine from Rambam's words and allow her child to provide a legacy for her. As long as the options are presented with full disclosure of all necessary and relevant information, her choice can be respected and accepted.

Finally, this author is saddened that so many Jewish groups have aligned themselves with either the pro-choice movement (and this is by far the largest group) or (more rarely) the pro-life movement. As we have seen, Judaism accepts neither position. It would seem to be far more authentic and appropriate to stand for—what we stand for. Particularly as most polls show that the majority of Americans do not want unrestricted abortions, but do want safe abortion available under serious circumstances, there seems to be a responsive audience for what we have to say. We do not need the polls to validate our position, but they do tell us that we can serve a valuable societal role in supporting the popular morality on this sensitive issue simply by being true to our tradition.

1. Some articles on this subject from a Torah perspective are Aaron Lichtenstein, "Abortion: A Halakhic Perspective," *Tradition* 25:4 (1991), pp. 3–12; J. David Bleich, "Abortion and Jewish Law," in *New Perspectives on Human Abortion*, ed. T. Hilgers (Baltimore, 1981), pp. 405–419; idem, "Abortion in Halakhic Literature," *Tradition* 10:2 (1968), pp. 72–120; Fred Rosner, "The Jewish Attitude Toward Abortion," ibid., pp. 48–71.
2. See Eva R. Rubin, *The Abortion Controversy: A Documentary History* (Westport, Conn., 1994).
3. In the United States, the language of the Declaration of Independence and the Constitution makes the pursuit and protection of rights the center of the American enterprise.

4. The Torah presents us with 613 commandments or responsibilities. We never speak of the number of rights presented to us.

5. Mishnah Ohalot 7:6.

6. Maimonides, *Mishneh Torah*, Hilkhot Rotze'ah u-Shemirat ha-Nefesh 1:9.

7. See Bacharach, *Responsa Havvot Ya'ir* 31; Weinberg, *Responsa Seridei Aish* 3:127, particularly in light of Maimonides' use of the term *rodef* ("pursuer") in *Mishneh Torah*, Hilkhot Nizkei Mamon 14:15.

8. Sanhedrin 57a, 72a ff.

9. *Seridei Aish*, loc. cit.

10. See ibid., citing Rabbi Ezekiel ben Judah Landau (1713–1793), *Responsa Noda Beyehudah*, Mahadurah Tinyanah, Hoshen Mishpat 59.

11. See *Seridei Esh*, loc. cit., citing Rabbi Hayyim Ozer Grodzinsky (1863–1940), *Responsa Ahiezer* 3:72:3.

12. See Rabbi Joseph ben Moses Babad (1800–1874/75), *Minhat Hinnukh* 296.

13. Sanhedrin 57b. See Rabbi Eliezer Judah Waldenberg (b. 1917), *Responsa Tzitz Eliezer* 9:51:3.

14. *Mishneh Torah*, Hilkhot Melakhim u-Milhamoteihem 9:4.

15. Sanhedrin 59a, s.v. lekah, see Rabbi Moses Feinstein (1895–1986), *Responsa Iggerot Moshe*, Hoshen Mishpat 2:69.

16. See Feinstein, op. cit., and *Responsa Noda bi-Yehudah*, cited in n. 10.

17. Sanhedrin 72b, s.v. *yatzah rosho*. See also *Minhat Hinnukh*, loc. cit., and the commentary of Hazon Ish to Maimonides, Hilkhot Rotze'ah u-Shemirat ha-Nefesh 1:9.

18. See Joseph ben Moses di Trani (1568–1639), *Responsa Maharit* 1:99. Rabbi Feinstein, loc. cit., denies the authenticity of this responsum, but others accept it (see *Tzitz Eliezer* 7:48). See also *Responsa Tzitz Eliezer* 9:51, citing *Responsa Torat Hesed* and *Responsa Yaavetz* 1:43.

19. Along with the source from Tractate Arakhin cited below, see Shabbat 151b, Sanhedrin 80a–b, 84b, Gittin 23b, Nazir 51a.

20. Exodus 21:22.

21. Numbers 35:31 specifically prohibits such payments.

22. Exodus 21:13, Numbers 35, Joshua 20. Maimonides, Hilkhot Rotze'ah u-Shemirat ha-Nefesh 8:9, based on Numbers 35:6–7.

23. Numbers 35:32.

24. *Responsa Maharit*, loc. cit., and *Tzitz Eliezer* 9:51:3.

25. Arakhin 7a–b.

26. For different understandings of exactly what this means, compare Rashi's

comment to the Mishnah with the comment by Tosafot, s.v. *yashvah al ha-mashber*.

27. See the general discussion in the responsa from *Seridei Esh* and *Tzitz Eliezer* cited here.

28. Sanhedrin 72b; Tosefta, Yevamot 9:9.

29. See Matthew Berke, "Jews Choosing Life," *First Things* 90 (February, 1999), pp. 34–36, and *Responsa Tzitz Eliezer* 9:51:3.

30. This is the reading of the mishnah from Ohalot cited above; see also Jerusalem Talmud, Shabbat 77a (14d). Interestingly, Jerusalem Talmud, Sanhedrin 44a–b (26c) reads, "if the head and most of the body emerged."

31. The passage from Tractate Arakhin cited above mentions this point in time as significant.

32. Rabbi Israel ben Gedaliah Lipschutz (Germany, 1782–1860), *Tiferet Yisrael*, Boaz to Ohalot 7:6.

33. This appears to be the source of *Tzitz Eliezer's* limiting permission for abortion in the Tay-Sachs case to no later than the seventh month. See the comments of Rabbenu Nissim of Gerona, also known as Nissim ben Reuben Gerondi and as Ran (1310–1375?), and of Rabbenu Asher ben Jehiel, also known as Asheri and as Rosh (1250–1327), to Yoma 82b; they pave the way for this position in their discussion of circumstances where a fetus *in utero* can become a "child with a door locked in front of it."

34. Yevamot 69b, Niddah 30a.

35. See *Responsa Havot Ya'ir*, loc. cit.; *Tzitz Eliezer* 7:48; *Seridei Esh*, loc. cit.

36. From the National Institute of Neurological Disorders and Stroke, NINDS Tay-Sachs Information Page.

37. *Responsa Tzitz Eliezer* 13:102.

38. *Igrot Mosheh*, loc. cit.; "Testing to Determine the Health of a Fetus and the Prohibition of Abortion for Tay-Sachs Disease," *Halachah Urefuah* 1 (Chicago, 1980), pp. 304–306.

39. Even the most lenient scholar would see abortion as a serious violation if performed when halakhically unjustified; see Responsa Tzitz Eliezer 7:48.

40. *Responsa Tzitz Eliezer* 9: 51:3, and see also *Responsa Seridei Esh*, loc. cit.

Chapter 29
Women

W e tread gently into what is arguably the most emotionally charged area discussed in this book. The
issue of women and their place in Judaism is one that
causes great divides and evokes the most raw of emotions
throughout the Jewish world.[1]

For most Jews, the role of women is the primary difference
between the Orthodox and non-Orthodox communities.
People often tell me that they cannot consider Orthodoxy as an
option because of the perceived second-class status of women
in our synagogues. Admittedly, from outside it is easy to
arrive at this judgment of the status of females in our institution. Thankfully, from the inside a much more complex picture
emerges.

Let us begin by debunking a few misconceptions. It is often
said that rabbinic Judaism, a creation of men, advantages men
and creates an element of servitude or worse for women.
Nonetheless, few topics occupied the attention of the Rabbis more
than protecting a woman's place in the family and society.[2]

Perhaps the prime example of this is the ketubah,[3] a document with a history extending back in time for over twenty-
one hundred years.[4] This Jewish marriage contract traditionally burdens the husband, and the husband only, with ten areas
of financial and other marital responsibilities that are in effect
during the marriage as well as in the event that the marriage is
terminated by his death or by divorce.[5] Designed to rectify

women's weaker status, particularly economically, and to prevent husbands from simply abandoning or easily divorcing their wives,[6] the document remains a requirement that must be executed before a couple can live together in marriage.[7]

One provision of the ketubah is very instructive. Under the terms of the document (to which reference would be made only in the event of extreme conflict),[8] a husband must provide food, clothing, and shelter for his wife. To prevent ill feeling, she must turn her financial assets over to her husband.[9] This relationship is reversible. Under some circumstances, he is freed from his obligation in this area, and she can keep her assets. The decision as to which arrangement will apply, meaning whether or not the husband will be responsible for the wife's food, clothing, and shelter, and whether or not she will keep her assets, is solely and entirely up to one person: the wife.[10] Hardly an arrangement of enslavement—at least for the woman.

Second, certain incorrect stereotypes must be erased. Judaism requires members of only one gender to marry[11] and members of only one gender to have children.[12] In both cases it is the man who carries the responsibility and not the woman, although contemporary intuition would doubtless assume the opposite. Moreover, financial responsibility for the children's needs—which are defined quite generously in the Talmud and in subsequent halakhic writings—falls entirely on the father.[13] Nonetheless, the children are not necessarily sent to live in his home should there be a divorce.

On this latter question Jewish courts are duty bound to follow the best interests of the child in determining where a child should live.[14] However, if all things are essentially equal, the following formula prevails: Children below age six go to the mother. Over age six, boys go to the father and girls to the mother, as same-sex role modeling is considered to be critically important.[15]

In sum, then, virtually all the obligations that go toward creating and sustaining a family fall on men. The only exception is that a divorced woman must continue to nurse a child with whom she has bonded out of concern for the well-being of the child. Absent such bonding, even nursing the child is not a requirement.[16]

Our own society is tragic witness to how easy it is for men to commit paternity and leave. The large number of single-parent homes almost always headed by women, particularly in less affluent communities, is tragic testimony to this biological reality. Judaism attempted to rectify the many social ills caused by this situation by placing heavy burdens for the creation of a family structure and particularly for the maintenance of children on men. Should a man refuse to live up to his financial obligations, remedies as dramatic as public shaming[17] and auctioning off his seat in the synagogue to provide for his children[18] have been applied through the ages. This is hardly a male-dominated structure.

Obviously, a family cannot begin without the female participant. Jewish thought assumed that most women would want to fill this role.[19] This assumption is borne out today by the rage of many women in their forties and fifties who never married because feminism promised that fulfillment could be found more completely in other ways. Having now passed the age of childbearing, the loss of this important part of being a woman has gone by without career success or anything else serving as adequate compensation.

As we have seen Jewish law was designed to provide protection for women, who were in the weaker position in so many ways in the arena of marriage and family. The law served its part and nature was allowed to do the rest.

We can move from here to a general discussion of women's role in the traditional community. No amount of apologetics can make a woman and a man congruent in Jewish tradition. They are simply not the same.[20] Equal, yes; absolutely equivalent, no. Thankfully, secular society has moved away from the claim that once was quite ubiquitous of an absolute parallel between the genders to some realization that gender differences exist and must be accommodated.

I would argue that traditional Judaism tries to do just that for both men and women. We have seen such an attempt in the economic structure it creates for marriage. A similar rationale may lie behind the prohibition against women serving as witnesses (but not against their offering evidence) in court cases.[21] Formal witnesses not only testify in Jewish courts, but in capital cases they may be called upon to cast the first stone at the guilty party.[22] The callousness one needs to develop in order to perform this function is not something Judaism wanted to see occur in its women and mothers.

The synagogue is probably the place where the women's issue is most frequently joined. The mehitzah (the physical barrier separating men and women),[23] the fact that women do not count in the prayer quorum or minyan,[24] the absence of women from any performance role in the synagogue[25]—all these are concerns to many women, both traditional and non-traditional. In actuality, there are three separate issues here, and they need to be treated individually.

The primary activity of the synagogue is prayer. Its architecture should, therefore, work to promote that activity. We are asked during prayer to create a truly heartfelt connection with an invisible, incorporeal being. This is hard enough to accomplish in the best of situations. Sitting next to someone with whom one has the strongest of human relationships, one's husband or one's wife, makes the task all the more difficult.

Further, proper prayer is all about creating the right mood. Part of this mood is seeing oneself as standing alone before God and feeling a sense of awe at His presence. Again, this is much harder to accomplish when standing together with one's spouse, who is the source of one's strength. The spouse's presence simply creates an emotional contradiction with the mood that is most necessary.[26]

In addition, one of the greatest enemies of proper prayer is using the synagogue for socializing during services.[27] Difficult as it is to combat socializing in single-gender settings it is even more problematic in a mixed setting. This is particularly true when singles are present. In such a circumstance, questions of who is sitting next to whom become much more important and add another level of complication to the prayer process.

The presence of a separation between men and women grants a synagogue the proper *kedushat beit ha-kenesset* ("sanctity of a house of worship").[28] Kedushah implies both specialness[29] and restriction.[30] A sense of both elements is necessary to create the delicate and ephemeral mood that can lead to a real connection with God. We strive for such a connection in prayer and so rarely achieve it that we must structure our synagogues to help us in this pursuit.

Turning to the question of minyan and involvement in the services, we must recognize a critical paradigm shift between Western understanding of the nature of society and the way traditional Judaism looks at the same thing. For contemporary Western culture, society is all about rights.[31] As such, not being counted in a minyan and not being able to lead services are seen as violations of a woman's rights and thus of her status in society.

Traditional Judaism's perspective, on the other hand, is that responsibilities are the critical elements of societal structure,[32] and that men and women have differing obligations.[33] Again, I would contend that this is because of Judaism's attempt to respond to the differences between the genders. In this context the important distinction is that women are exempt from affirmative commandments the performance of which is limited to a particular time frame. For example, women need not eat in a sukkah on the holiday of Tabernacles because this affirmative requirement applies only to the few days of the holiday and to no other time during the year.[34]

There are different opinions as to why women have been exempted in this way. Some suggest that women have an internal sense of the sanctity of time associated with their monthly menstruation and the laws surrounding it that make these other laws redundant.[35]

Others suggest that, although not mandated, women have traditionally focused much of their time on family and particularly on bearing and raising children. The demands of these activities can easily conflict with tasks that must occur in a limited time frame. For this reason, given the centrality in Judaism of family, which we view as our most important religious institution, the potential conflict is resolved before it begins by exempting women from these time-constrained obligations.[36]

Among the acts that are obligatory for men but not for women is the requirement to take part in public prayer. Women certainly can and do attend services if they choose, but, and here is the key, as they are not obligated to do so, they cannot count in the quorum required for this activity.[37] In short, the minyan is simply a community of at least ten who are obligated to be part of such a community of prayer.

This is not discriminatory against women per se. Male children below age thirteen are also not obligated and, therefore, cannot be part of a minyan.[38] Even an adult male may find himself in such a situation. Between the death and burial of a close relative, a Jew is in the category of *onen*.[39] During this period one's affirmative obligations are removed. One's only responsibility is to arrange for and ensure proper burial of the dead. It often happens that an *onen* will seek the comfort of the synagogue. Certainly he is welcome. Nonetheless he cannot be part of the minyan because he is not obligated to be there.[40]

For this reason, too, women cannot lead a minyan in prayer. Having no obligation to be part of the service, they cannot perform the role of prayer leader, whose task it is to help fulfill the obligations of the other participants in the service.[41] Only someone who himself has that obligation can fulfill it for others.

Part of the problem here is the somewhat increased importance placed on the synagogue in diaspora communities. Following the model of the church, the synagogue has become, for the diaspora Jew, very much the center of religious life. On the other hand, in Israel the model is more reflective of what originally existed. The synagogue is a place to pray, to fulfill one's obligation, and then to go home. Classes, social activities, communal organizational functions, far more often than not, occur in entirely different settings.

Because of the larger role of the synagogue in the diaspora, the exclusion of women from many positions in its structure becomes more troubling. If one looks at the issue with Israeli eyes, a very different perspective may emerge.

For these and perhaps other reasons, some traditional women have experimented with women's prayer services.[42] While these groups do not and cannot constitute a minyan, which precludes their reciting a number of significant prayers, they do provide opportunities for women to pray together, to lead a service, and often to read from the Torah and to receive various honors in that context.

While there is no halakhic objection to women gathering in prayer, these groups and many aspects of their practices are extremely controversial. Some claim that there are clear halakhic violations involved. Others see a need to oppose these institutions out of concern that they will lead to halakhic violations, such as demands for egalitarian services. Still others defend the groups as halakhically legitimate and as a genuine spiritual experience for the participants.

The issue is unlikely to be resolved any time soon. One critical test for these groups, at least as far as the last two opinions are concerned, will be their staying power. Will women be able to sustain their interest and commitment to these groups for decades or perhaps generations? Will they do so in ways that remain halakhically defensible, or will the feared violation of legal standards occur? The test of time will ultimately be very important to the final acceptance or rejection of these groups.

A four-thousand-year tradition embraces innovation only very slowly, and with constant reference to and concern that its basic principles are not being violated. This is entirely appropriate for the stability, continuity, and fealty to God's law that are the hallmark of traditional Judaism. One need only explore the history of the hasidic movement, which was first rejected by the rabbinic establishment as dangerous and then ultimately accepted as legitimate, to see an example of the process described here.[43] It will be interesting to see whether these groups can successfully walk the same path.

Another test, it seems to me, will be whether these groups can come to be seen as true searchers for increased spirituality and not, as some claim, simply manifestations of secular feminism or a desire to do what men do. Those who support these groups will be helped if they can find ways to show that the former is true.

A further, and happily less controversial development has been the training of "poskot": women knowledgeable, particularly in the area of family purity law, who can respond halakhically, but with caring and personal empathy, to other women's questions in this area.

Beyond the borders of Orthodox acceptability are traditional egalitarian services and a very few others that allow women to be called to the Torah and, perhaps, also to lead some limited parts of the service. Though no halakhically persuasive argument has been advanced to support such services, the fact that some have tried to justify what is being done from our sources, however unsuccessfully, coupled with the desire of these groups to, at least initially, maintain the traditional liturgy, means that the challenge of the role of women in the synagogue is not over. In fact, even among those who take no part in any of the controversial activities described here, the question of the proper role of women is often the subject of discussion and debate.

One area where all can agree that women are disadvantaged is on the issue of divorce. Biblically, a man can divorce his wife without warning and against her will.[44] Recognizing the problem of wives being abandoned in this way, the Rabbis spent much effort to rectify the inequities.[45] With the ketubah as one important step, the Rabbis eventually banned divorce without the woman's consent except in very special circumstances.[46]

Today, the opposite problem exists. It is not that husbands divorce wives too quickly, but that they may refuse to grant a religious divorce even when the marriage is long over. In the past this was never a problem. If the court ordered a divorce and the man refused, he could be beaten until he gave the divorce or died.[47] In either case the woman would be free. So, too, in contemporary Israel, a recalcitrant husband can be jailed, lose his driver's license, and face other serious sanctions.[48] Unfortunately, enforcement in the diaspora is more of a problem.

Recently, a series of prenuptial agreements have been proposed, and one has been adopted by the Rabbinical Council of America (R.C.A.).[49] The aim of such a document is to create financial penalties for the recalcitrant husband without violating the very strict rules concerning what types of coercion may be used to produce a get (religious divorce).[50] Ultimately the get must have at least the veneer of having been done voluntarily, which means that prenuptial agreements must be worded very carefully. An added complication is the need for the marriage commitment and particularly the ketubah obligations to be absolute when they are entered into. Imposing conditions for divorce at the time of the marriage can violate the absolute nature of those institutions. This too would be unacceptable.

Even the prenuptial agreement accepted by the RCA has its detractors and critics, and it will likely face secular legal challenges. If in time it wins wide acceptance and is universally required before a marriage is performed, the problem of recalcitrant husbands may well diminish and even disappear. If it is ultimately rejected, other solutions will be devised. Rabbis and the community are bound by Jewish law to prevent the problem of agunah (a woman bound by force of law to a marriage that, as a living reality, no longer exists), in any way possible.[51]

We come finally to traditional Jewish statements about women. While it is true that one can find extremely negative comments about women, particularly in our midrashic literature, one can also find extremely positive statements.[52] It is very interesting in this regard that the Bible personifies wisdom, one of our most prized values, as a beautiful woman.[53] In many other cultures, such a woman could only be a temptress and the personification of sin. Further, our midrashic tradition, while it is far broader than our legal sources, is also far less authoritative.[54] As we have seen, concern for women's circumstances and well-being is a hallmark of Halakhah, the more authoritative tradition.

One particular negative comment deserves analysis because it has become part of our liturgy. Each morning men praise God for not having created them as women, while women praise God for having created them according to His will.[55]

Though often seen as offensive, and though these blessings are usually explained by the greater number of commandments that men must perform as opposed to women,[56] the truth may be very different. Several elements must be introduced to reach that truth.

First, the blessing "who has not created me a woman" is part of a series of three blessings, the other two being "who has not created me a slave" and "who has not created me a gen-

tile." Second, these blessings are in the negative, which is highly unusual if not unprecedented in our liturgy. Third, the
blessing "who has created me according to His will" is twelve
hundred years younger than the three negative blessings. The
three appear initially in the Talmud, in a discussion between
two scholars of the second century C.E.[57] "Who has created me
according to His will" does not emerge until the fourteenth
century in the work of Abudraham, a scholar and authority of
our liturgy.

Fourth and most important is this passage from Paul
describing his vision of the changes that had come to the world
as a result of what he saw as the arrival of the Messiah. For
Paul the world was now a place where: "There is no such thing
as Jew and Greek, slave and freeman, male and female."[58]

Some have, therefore, suggested that the three negative
blessings were originally a polemic against the early Judeo-
Christians and their beliefs and a challenge to these fundamental Pauline ideas. Paul saw the "Kingdom of Heaven" as having
come and wanted Christians to implement his understanding
of what that meant in their lives. Among other elements of this
kingdom were what we would call his negative attitudes to
women and sexuality. Paul may well have been suggesting that
the early Christian believers ought to live in celibate unisex
communities that would downplay and denigrate the uniqueness of women. In response, the Rabbis instituted a negative
blessing attacking this belief and affirming that men and
women remained different, thereby validating and supporting
women's roles. Far from denigrating women, this blessing was
designed to enhance and support them.

Some twelve hundred years later, when these issues had
long passed from the scene as part of the central debate
between Judaism and Christianity, a need arose for a blessing
that could be recited by women.[59] To this end Abudraham provided a blessing praising God's will.[60]

The other two negative blessings can be analyzed in much the same way, though that is beyond our focus here.[61] However, the understanding that comes from thorough analysis and scholarly research, showing that "who has not created me a woman" was intended not to denigrate but to protect women, should serve as a note of caution and bring us back to where we began. It is all too easy to assume simplistic and stereotypical attitudes concerning women on the part of Orthodoxy. A little fairness and some effort will usually uncover a very different reality.

1. There are many books and articles on this subject. I will suggest three that either encompass the range of opinions on the subject or are themselves even-handed in their treatment of it. Menahem Brayer, *The Jewish Woman in Rabbinic Literature*, 2 vols. (Hoboken, N.J., 1986); Elyakim G. Elinson, *Ha-Ishah ve-ha-Mitzvot* (Jerusalem, 1975); Joel Wolowelsky, *Women, Jewish Law and Modernity* (Hoboken, N.J., 1997).

2. One-sixth of the Talmud and one-quarter of the *Shulhan Arukh* are devoted to women and the law.

3. For general discussion, see J. D. Eisenstein, *Otzar Yisrael*, s.v. *ketubah*.

4. Tosefta Ketubot 12:1 credits the institution to Shimon ben Shetah, one of the heads of the Sanhedrin in the first century B.C.E. The parallel source in Ketubot 82b speaks of him as amending the functioning of the ketubah, which indicates that it was an even older institution. Interestingly, the Elephantine papyri, from a Persian-Jewish colony in Egypt several hundred years before Shimon ben Shetah, contain documents that appear to be proto-ketubot.

5. Eisenstein, *Otzar Yisrael*, loc. cit.

6. Tosefta, loc. cit.

7. See *Sefer ha-Hinnukh* 570.

8. The standard *tena'im*, for example, state that the couple agrees to share equal control over their assets.

9. Both provisions are mentioned in Mishnah Ketubot 46b, and the reasons are discussed in the Talmud, Ketubot 47b. See also Maimonides 12:4.

10. The issue is debated in Talmud Ketubot 58b, decided on Ketubot 58b, and codified in Maimonides, loc. cit. and *Shulhan Arukh*, Even ha-Ezer 69:4.

11. *Shulhan Arukh,* Even ha-Ezer 1:1 as a derivative of the requirement to procreate. However, even when procreation is not possible, a man is required to be married. Yevamot 61b.

12. Mishnah Yevamot 65b.

13. Kiddushin 29a, 30b.

14. The expression *bet din avihen shel yetomin* ("the court is the father of the orphans") appears in the Talmud, Gittin 37a and Bava Kama 37a, in a different context. Its use in our context can be found quite frequently in post-talmudic literature; see *Responsa Rashba* 38.

15. Cf. *Shulhan Arukh,* Even ha-Ezer, 82:7. See also *Responsa Rosh* 82:2.

16. Maimonides, Hilkhot Ishut 21:16.

17. See Ketubot 49b.

18. An action approved by Rabbi Moses Sofer in the nineteenth century. *Responsa Hatam Sofer* 4, Even ha-Ezer 2:157.

19. Cf. Yevamot 118b.

20. Stated most dramatically in the opinion of Ulla, recorded on Shabbat 62a, that "women are an independent people."

21. Maimonides, Hilkhot Edut 9:1–2; Meir ben Baruch of Rothenburg, *Responsa Maharam* 920.

22. Cf. Deuteronomy 17:7.

23. For history and discussion, see Baruch Litvin, *The Sanctity of the Synagogue* (New York, 1987).

24. *Shulhan Arukh,* Orah Hayyim, 55:1.

25. This is based on a number of sources: Mishnah Rosh Hashanah 3:8, Tosefta Rosh Hashanah: 2:4. The basic premise is that the person who leads the services fulfills the obligation of those in attendance. This necessitates that the leader and the other worshipers be under the same obligation. Since women are not required to engage in thrice-daily prayer, whereas men are, women cannot lead services because they cannot fulfill thereby the obligations of the men in attendance. Torah honors fall in a different category, Megilah 23a.

26. See Norman Lamm, "Separate Pews in the Synagogue," *Tradition* 1:2 (1959). For further discussion, see above, Chapter 14.

27. See Sukkah 51b for the origin of the separation, and Moses Feinstein (1895–1986), *Iggerot Mosheh,* Orah Hayyim 3:23, for the definition of *kalut rosh* (the concern that the separation is designed to prevent) as socializing.

28. See Litvin, *Sanctity of the Synagogue*.

29. See Seforno to Leviticus 19:2.

30. See Ramban ad loc.

31. The Constitution, the Bill of Rights, and Western society's common conversation are all about rights.

32. We speak of the Torah and its 613 commandments and our common discussion focuses on the question of what we are required to do according to Halakhah.

33. Women are exempt from affirmative commandments that are associated with time, at least as a first approximation, though there are a significant number of exceptions to the rule. See Berakhot 20b, Kiddushin 33b–35a. On the other hand, there are some commandments that are specifically emphasized for women, such as the laws associated with the menstrual cycle, the lighting of Shabbat and holiday candles, and the removal of part of the dough (originally as a gift to the priests) when baking bread. See Shabbat 31b, et passim.

34. Mishnah Sukkah 2:8.

35. Moshe Meiselman, *Jewish Woman in Jewish Law* (New York, 1978), chap. 8.

36. See S. Berman, "The Status of Women in Halakhic Judaism," *Tradition* 14:2 (Fall 1973), pp. 5–28.

37. Cf. Rachel Biale, *Women and Jewish Law* (New York, 1995), pp. 17–24.

38. See sources cited in nn. 24– 25 and 35–37.

39. Cf. Aaron Levine, *Sefer Zichron Meir al Avelut* (Toronto, 1985), chap. 13.

40. For sources and some discussion, see Eliezer Waldenberg, *Responsa Tzitz Eliezer* 5, Ramat Rachel, chap. 47.

41. Mishnah Rosh Hashanah 3:8.

42. Much has been written, pro and con, on the subject. A brief list follows: Avi Weiss, *Women at Prayer: A Halakhic Analysis of Women's Prayer Groups* (New York, 1990); the title article in Hershel Schachter, *Be-Ikvei Hatzon* (Jerusalem, 1997), pp. 21–36; Dov Frimer and Aryeh Frimer, "Women's Prayer Services: Theory and Practice," *Tradition* 32:2 (Spring 1998), pp. 5–118; and the articles in subsequent issues of this journal on the same subject.

43. See generally *Encyclopaedia Judaica*, s.v. Hasidism.

44. David W. Amram, *The Jewish Law of Divorce* (New York, 1968), chap. 2.

45. Ibid., chaps. 3–6.

46. Ibid., chap. 4.

47. The most famous formulation of this principle appears in Maimonides, Hilkhut Gerushin 2:20. Rambam provides a rationale to explain why acting under compulsion can still yield a get that meets the criteria of being executed through free will. Argues Maimonides, "he [really] wants to fulfill all the commandments. . . . It is only his [evil] inclination that is compelling him [to refuse to give a get]."

48. A recent State Department warning reminded divorced Jewish men who had refused to give a get to avoid travel in Israel precisely because the state will use all available sanctions, including confiscation of passport and imprisonment, even against tourists who are citizens of other countries, to help free women who cannot get their husbands to give a get when the marriage is over.

49. For full discussion, see Kenneth Auman, and Basil Herring, *The Prenuptial Agreement: Halakhic, Legal and Pastoral Considerations* (Northvale, N.J., 1995).

50. See ibid., introduction by Norman Lamm; *Responsa Rosh* 51:2.

51. *Mishum agunah heikilu* ("they [the Rabbis] were lenient for the sake of preventing a woman from being tied [to a husband without a real marriage]") is a principle found throughout Jewish legal literature. An early statement is Jacob ben Asher, *Tur*, Hoshen Mishpat 35. For discussion of the breadth of this leniency, see Waldenberg, *Tzitz Eliezer* 7:41; I. Herzog *Responsa Heikhal Yitzhak*, Even ha-Ezer 2:45; Y. Adas, *Responsa Hiddot Yaakov*, Even ha-Ezer 4.

52. Many books and articles cite these sources, including the ones listed above in n. 1. For a sampling of both types of comments, see B. Cohen, *Everyman's Talmud* (New York, 1949), pp. 159–161.

53. A frequent theme in the Book of Proverbs, esp. chap. 8.

54. Cf. *Encyclopedia Talmudit*, s.v. *halakhah*, subsection *aggadot, midrashot vezohar*.

55. Philip Birnbaum, *The Daily Prayer Book* (New York, 1949), p. 17.

56. Cf. Joseph Caro, *Bet Yosef*, Orah Hayyim 46:4.

57. Tosefta Berakhot 6:23 presents R. Judah as the originator, while Menahot 43b credits R. Meir with that role.

58. Galatians 3:28.

59. Birnbaum, *Daily Prayer Book*, loc. cit.

60. David b. Joseph Abudarham, *Abudarham ha-Shalem* (Jerusalem, 1963), p. 42.

61. For general discussion, see Bernhard S. Jacobson, *The Weekday Siddur* (Tel Aviv, 1973), pp. 41–44; idem, *Meditations on the Siddur* (Tel Aviv, 1966), pp. 99–101; see also Ismar Elbogen, *Jewish Liturgy: A Comprehensive History* (New York, 1993), p. 78.

Chapter 30

Sex

J
udaism has always lived in a world where the attitudes toward sex and sexuality of the dominant cultures were dramatically out of sync with its own approach.[1] Given the sensitive nature of the subject, with its powerful pull on the human personality, it is often a struggle for Jews to maintain our standards and our morality.

The pagan world in which Judaism was born was a world of fertility cults that featured ritual prostitution[2] and orgiastic behavior.[3] So, too, the Roman world was known for its libertine practices.[4] This free approach, in modern guise, has come to dominate popular culture since the so-called sexual revolution of the 1960s.

At the opposite end of the spectrum, the doctrinal belief in some expressions of Christianity that sees sex as the transmission point of original sin casts sexuality as something negative or dirty.[5]

Neither position is representative of Jewish tradition. Many of our sources attest to Judaism's positive attitude to sexuality.[6] For example, there is an obligation and expectation that a husband will provide sexual relations for his wife.[7] It is particularly desirable that Friday night, the evening of our holiest day, the Sabbath, be such a time.[8] The slower pace, the longer meal, the lack of electronic distractions, such as phone and TV, the end of the work week, all mean that husband and wife have a chance to connect personally and emotionally as a prelude to connecting physically. In any case, favoring sex as a Sabbath activity must mean that Judaism sees it as having a significant positive side.

So, too, the Talmud validates and values the place of spontaneous passion in the husband-wife relationship. Based on a series of verses, the Talmud offers proof that a child conceived as a result of a wife's arousing her husband's desire at a time when they would normally not have been intimate, will be a particularly blessed child.[9]

This positive attitude toward sexuality does not come without significant restrictions. As with all basic drives, such as those for food or for the acquisition of material goods, Jewish law places limits around that which is permissible. In this way a balance can be struck that allows for a healthy outlet of desire and basic need while preventing destructive excess. In addition, through proper sexual morality, our most important religious institution, the family, can be protected, strengthened, and preserved.

The first area of restriction embodies one of Judaism's most basic institutions, *taharat ha-mishpahah* (family purity).[10] From the moment that a woman begins to menstruate until seven days after she stops, marital relations are prohibited, as are many other activities that evoke intimacy. At the end of that time, the wife goes to a ritual bath called a mikvah, which at its root is built around a source of natural water, such as rainwater. After a complete immersion in the mikvah pool, marital relations can and should resume.[11] Though sex in Judaism is not only for purposes of procreation[12] (marital relations with, for example, sterile or post-menopausal women are permitted and even required),[13] having children is not only desirable, but also represents the fulfillment of a mitzvah.[14] In the average woman's monthly cycle, the time for mikvah will come at the height of her fertility, so that the possibility of pregnancy is at its greatest.[15]

Prior to a women's immersion she is in a state of *tumah*, while subsequently we speak of her as having achieved *taharah*.[16] No adequate English translation exists for these concepts. Terms such as impurity vs. purity or cleanliness vs. uncleanliness are far more pejorative in meaning than the original concept. *Tumah* appears in many places and is always associated with death. One who contacts a dead body becomes *tamei* to the highest degree.[17] (It is important to note that *tumah* of this kind does not create any restrictions on marital relations. Different types of *tumah* have different consequences.) Nonetheless if one is involved in, for example, preparing the dead for burial, one has accomplished the greatest kindness (*chesed shel emet*) conceivable because it is a kindness which cannot be repaid.[18] Obviously *tumah* cannot be an intrinsically bad thing if one who does the greatest kindness imaginable contracts *tumah*.

Why is the law of *taharat ha-mishpahah* necessary? Taking the talmudic rationale[19] and putting it in statistical terms, it has been said that in most American marriages, if the couple were to put a penny in a jar every time they had relations during the first two years of marriage and then removed five cents from the jar every time they had relations thereafter, they would never empty the jar.[20] Frequency often declines dramatically with time.

This would be highly unusual in a marriage that follows the laws of family purity. The period of restriction rebuilds desire. There is also an obligation that husbands have to provide marital relations for their wives, particularly on the night of mikvah so that intimacy remains relatively constant.[21] As a result, marriages are generally healthier and better able to survive when *taharat ha-mishpahah* is observed. The lower divorce rates in the traditional community than in the general population may be an indication of the positive effect of this institution.

As indicated there is a particular burden on husbands to make mikvah night special for their wives.[22] I know of someone who passed up a dinner that might have been very important to his career to be with his wife on a night that she went to mikvah. This display of love and personal commitment cemented their relationship and moved it to a new and even closer level. In addition, it spurred the couple to involve themselves in greater exploration of their religious heritage and, thereby, to become more observant and committed to their faith.

Implicit in what has been said thus far is that premarital sex is prohibited.[23] Since unmarried women do not immerse in a mikvah,[24] relations would be prohibited on that very serious basis alone.[25] In addition, intimacy outside of marriage is itself a violation.[26]

Though the level of severity of this latter violation is not equivalent to a violation of other sexual laws, such as adultery with a married woman,[27] still it is a serious concern. Reflecting this concern and the rabbinic understanding that "no watchman is sufficient when it comes to sexual immorality,"[28] Jewish tradition regulates intergender interaction in very significant ways.[29] Any affectionate physical contact is prohibited, and being alone in a situation that might allow for intimacy is proscribed.[30]

While radically counter-cultural and heavily restrictive by modern standards, living by these rules allows one to avoid many societal ills, ranging from teenage pregnancy to sexual harassment. Further, it limits one's most intimate sharing of oneself to the context of a lifetime commitment. Finally, it encourages developing one's most important relationship, the relationship, hopefully, of a lifetime, on the basis of more significant things than simple physical attraction. Physical attraction is certainly important,[31] but relationships are built much more securely on shared values and compatible personalities.

As indicated, adultery is outside the pale.[32] So too, not surprisingly, is incest.[33] Since biblical law permitted polygamy,[34] adultery is defined, from a biblical perspective, by the marital status of the woman and only the woman. If she is married, it is adultery regardless of the man's marital status.[35] So too, if she is not married, it is not adultery no matter who he is.[36] Remember that in biblical times, the possibility of marrying a second woman remained open to the man if the woman in question was unmarried.[37] Hence, the man's action cannot be considered adultery. Today, we no longer permit polygamy and haven't done so for a thousand years in Ashkenazic countries.[38] However, as a technical matter the biblical definition remains. Nonetheless, a husband who violates the marital structure is treated quite severely in Jewish legal writings.[39]

One other important point must be discussed here, and that is illegitimacy. A child becomes illegitimate in Jewish law if he or she is the product of a relationship that is incestuous or adulterous (on the part of the mother) and in no other circumstance.[40] A father's indiscretion does not create a *mamzer* (an illegitimate offspring) who cannot marry within the community. Again, the mother's status determines the outcome.

We come now to the sensitive issue of homosexuality.[41] Although all Orthodox thinkers agree as to the prohibitive conclusions reached by Jewish law concerning behavior of this type, differences exist in explaining the rationale for the prohibition and the implications to draw from it. My own approach to the subject, published some fifteen years ago, remains essentially unchanged. I present it here, but the reader should be aware that others disagree and that, at least some of their views may be found by consulting the articles listed in the footnotes to this chapter.

For traditional Judaism, "homosexual" is an adjective, not a noun. It describes an activity, not a person.[42] Jewish law knows of no individual called a homosexual.[43] It knows only of an activity described as homosexuality. In this way Jewish law opposes the behavior without attacking the person. After all, almost everyone engages in some activity that is wrong—at least sometimes.

This approach avoids making sexual activity and desire the defining element of any human being. It reminds us that we consist of far more than our activity in the bedroom or our sexual desires. Frankly, it is hard to understand why any activity or desire should define an individual in the same way that gender, skin color, or religion does, especially as someone may go through long periods of abstinence and diminished desire and therefore may engage in no sexual activity. This would suggest that the person had changed his societal designation. There is no real parallel to this in the realm of color, gender, or religion. Even conversion, the closest parallel, is vastly different in that it requires a conscious change of belief system and behavior.[44]

Thinking about homosexuality in this way requires a paradigm shift that affects the way we see other people. Once we stop seeing their identity as dependent on their sexual activity or desire, it becomes much easier to talk objectively about the subject.

Judaism prohibits homosexual activity and never sees homosexuality as an acceptable alternative lifestyle.[45] Many reasons suggest themselves. The Bible describes physical intimacy as a man cleaving to his wife and their becoming one flesh.[46] Further, the requirement that a man father children and the concern that they be raised within a family that includes a mother and a father is an issue here as well.[47] So too the general concern for family as our most important religious institution also plays a part in Jewish opposition to this activity.[48] On a more spiritual plane, perhaps the primary goal of our existence is to develop our capacity to appreciate and relate to the ultimate "other"—God.[49] If our most intimate human relations focus on one who is the same as we are, we will have squandered what may be our best opportunity to learn to appreciate the "other" on a physical plane.

Male homosexuality involves a biblical prohibition of the most stringent variety. Female homosexuality, while prohibited, does not rise to this level.[50] One of the biblical sources cited above offers a possible explanation.[51] The physical oneness of man and woman described in the Bible can be replicated in some fashion by men but not by women. Perhaps the reason for the difference lies here. Nonetheless we must recognize that sexuality touches the most basic and elemental parts of the human being. While the Torah and halakhah's prohibitions against homosexuality are clear and unwavering, dealing with people who are attracted to this type of activity must be done with great compassion and sensitivity.

Finally, we take up the issue of modesty.[52] We most often think of applying this value when it comes to the way we dress.[53] In this regard, two points should be made. First, modesty is a value that applies to men as well as to women.[54] Concern in choosing one's clothing applies to both genders.

Second, three standards of appearance must be met in determining what constitutes immodest dress. One, there are certain absolute standards of modesty, certain parts of the body that must not be displayed in any situation and in all societies.[55] One's genitals would certainly be covered by this standard.[56] Two, societal custom can create an imperative to conform and not be immodest in violation of the culture's contemporary practices.[57] I cannot resist making the observation that it is difficult to find an example of such a concern in our "let it all hang out" society. However, one can certainly think of examples from other times and other cultures.[58] Third, dress that is significantly inappropriate for a particular situation can also be problematic if it draws immodest attention.[59]

Modesty also goes beyond dress. It is a far more significant and broader concern than simply which outfit to put on in the morning, for it reflects an entire state of mind that affects thought, speech, dress, behavior, and attitude.[60] When implemented properly, it brings with it a nobility and a dignity in the one who practices it. It also protects us from the coarser interactions that society, particularly this society, imposes upon us.

Today, modesty is, unfortunately, given little importance by our culture. Five minutes of watching almost any prime-time TV show will prove this claim. Nonetheless, those who strive for modesty as a guiding value in their lives will find that they are living in an atmosphere made up of the better things that life has to offer. After all, when the prophet Micah asks the eternal question, "What does the Lord your God require of you?" one-third of the answer is, "Walk modestly with your God."[61]

1. The many books on this subject, both ancient and modern, are of very mixed quality and must be consulted with care. A good starting point is the discussion in Menahem Brayer, *The Jewish Woman*, 2 vols. (Hoboken, N.J., 1986).

2. The biblical term *kedeshah*, etymologically related to *kadosh* ("holy"), designated a ritual prostitute. See Genesis 38:21–22, Deuteronomy 23:18.

3. Brayer, *Jewish Woman*, vol. 1, p. 176.

4. Cf. Shabbat 33b.

5. Cf. David Feldman, *Marital Relations, Birth Control, and Abortion in Jewish Law* (New York, 1968), pp. 83–90.

6. Ibid., chaps. 4–5. For some ancient sources, see Abraham David of Posquières, *Ba'alei ha-Nefesh le-Rabad* (Bene-Berak, 1989), and Seymour J. Cohen, trans., *The Holy Letter: A Study in Medieval Jewish Sexual Morality* (New York, 1993).

7. Feldman, *Marital Relations*, chap. 4.

8. Brayer, *Jewish Woman*, vol. 1, p. 134.

9. Eruvin 100b.

10. Many books discuss this topic. One that I particularly like is Tehilla Abramov, *The Secret of Jewish Femininity: Insights into the Practice of Taharat HaMishpachah* (Spring Valley, N.Y., 1988). For a discussion of philosophy and rationale, see Norman Lamm, *A Hedge of Roses* (New York, 1987).

11. The contemporary propensity to ignore this requirement is simply wrong: see *Shulhan Arukh*, Orah Hayyim 240:1 and Even ha-Ezer 76:4; Moses Feinstein, *Iggerot Mosheh*, Even ha-Ezer 3:28; Jacob Emden, *She'ilat Ya'avetz* 2:10.

12. See Feldman, *Marital Relations*, chaps. 4–5.

13. Eruvin 47a; Rema, Even ha-Ezer 23:5.

14. There are actually four imperatives involved in procreation. See the talmudic discussion in Yevamot 61a–62b, 65b. These include Genesis 1:28 or 35:11, Isaiah 45:18, Ecclesiastes 11:6, and the mystical idea that all the souls that will ever exist were created at the beginning of time and must be brought into this world before the Messiah can come. Thus, every birth is a step toward the coming of the Messiah. (See chap. 22.)

15. For most women, the onset of menstruation occurs fourteen days after ovulation. Since mikvah immersion usually occurs twelve days after menstruation begins, marital relations, for most women, resume within a day or two of ovulation, at the optimum time for procreation.

16. See Lamm, *Hedge of Roses*, for further discussion.

17. Numbers 19, esp. vv. 11–20, and cf. Rashi, Eruvin 104b, s.v. *lo*.

18. The origin of the term appears to lie in Genesis 47:29 (see Rashi ad loc.), and perhaps 24:49. Its earliest appearance as employed here appears to be Genesis Rabbah 96:5.

19. Niddah 31b.

20. I thank my friend Saul Singer, a former actuary, for the statistical analysis.

21. See above, nn. 7, 11.

22. See above, n. 11.

23. Yevamot 59b, 61a–b; Maimonides, *Mishneh Torah*, Hilkhot Ishut 1:4, Hilkhot Issurei Bi'ah 18:2, Hilkhot Na'arah Betulah 2:17, and *Sefer ha-Mitzvot* 355; *Shulhan Arukh*, Even ha-Ezer 6:8; see also Rabbenu Jonah, *Sha'arei Teshuvah* 3:95; Isaac ben Sheshet Perfet, *Responsa Rivash* 425. For discussion of the history of halakhic treatment of the issue, see Brayer, *The Jewish Woman*, vol. 1, pp. 141–150.

24. Rivash, ad loc.

25. Leviticus 18:19, *Mishnah Berurah* 75:17.

26. See above, n. 13.

27. Rivash, ad loc.

28. Ketubot 13b et passim.

29. See Brayer, *The Jewish Woman*, vol. 1, pp. 141–150.

30. Ibid. and n. 13.

31. Kiddushin 41a.

32. Hagigah 9b, Sotah 4b, Rambam to Sanhedrin 15:13.

33. Leviticus 18:7–30; Maimonides, Hilkhot Issurei Bi'ah 1:10.

34. Jacob had four wives (Genesis 35:23–26); see also Deuteronomy 21:15.

35. See the sources cited in nn. 13 and 32.

36. Ibid.

37. Exodus 22:15.

38. *Shulhan Arukh*, Even ha-Ezer 1:10.

39. Rema, Even ha-Ezer 154:1; David W. Amram, *The Jewish Law of Divorce According to the Bible and Talmud* (New York, 1975), p. 76; Meshullam Rath, *Responsa Kol Mevaser* 1:50.

40. J. D. Eisenstein, *Otzar Yisrael*, s.v. *mamzer*.

41. For additional discussion, see my "Homosexuality and Judaism," *Journal of Halachah and Contemporary Society* 11 (1986), pp. 70–87. For a different approach, see Norman Lamm, "Judaism and the Modern Attitude to Homosexuality," *Encyclopaedia Judaica Yearbook*, 1974, pp. 194–205.

42. The relevant verses, Leviticus 18:22 and 20:13, speak only about the activity.

43. There is no term for "homosexual" in halakhic literature.

44. See above, Chapter 24.

45. See above n. 41; Sanhedrin 54a; Maimonides, Issurei Bi'ah 1:4 and Sanhedrin 15:10; *Shulhan Arukh*, Even ha-Ezer 24:1.

46. Genesis 2:24.

47. See the discussion of procreation above and Mishnah Yevamot 65b.

48. For sources praising married life, see A. Cohen, *Everyman's Talmud* (New York, 1949), pp. 162 ff.

49. See Martin Buber, *I and Thou* (New York, 1970).

50. Yevamot 76a; Maimonides, Issurei Biah 21:8; *Shulhan Arukh*, Even ha-Ezer 20:2.

51. See above, n. 46.

52. Eisenstein, *Otzar Yisrael*, s.v. *zeniut*.

53. E. Elinson, *Haznei'a Lekhet* (Jerusalem, 1987), chaps. 4–5.

54. Ibid. and *Arukh ha-Shulhan*, Orah Hayyim 74:1–3, 75:1.

55. Elinson, *Haznei'a Lekhet*, p. 140.

56. Berakhot 24a.

57. See Elinson, *Haznei'a Lekhet*, pp. 153 and 178 ff. for examples.

58. The example of the veil in those societies that require it comes to mind. See Maimonides, Hilkhot Ishut 24:12.

59. This would seem to derive from Psalms 45:14. See *Responsa Seridei Esh* 1:78, for a similar understanding of this verse.

60. Cf. Midrash Tanhuma, Ki Tissa 16.

61. Micah 6:8.

Chapter 31
The Holocaust

The thirty chapters that make up the body of this book speak to issues that raise fundamental theological and ethical challenges. Answers can be found to these questions in our sacred and religious literature. This addendum, on the other hand, deals with a single, overarching historic event: the Holocaust[1]. Contemporary Orthodox Jews live by the principles described to this point. But we also live with the reality of that singular monstrosity and the fact that we are still within, at most, a very few generations of its dark abyss. As such, its full impact, meaning and the lessons to be learned from this paroxysm of death and horror can not yet be completely understood despite the fact that, because of our proximity to it in time, this is when the impact will be felt most acutely.

Before discussing some of the lessons that I do see as having emerged thus far from the Holocaust, we will take a moment to discuss why it is such a uniquely horrific event . . . why, in fact, in the all too lengthy history of man's inhumanity to man, the Holocaust truly occupies a special and unique position of infamy.

There are, sadly, many, many examples of one group of people attempting genocide against another group. However, only rarely has racial and ethnic murder come with as complete and thorough a philosophical justification for the idea of ridding the planet of those in the despised group as was presented by the Nazis in their war against the Jews.

Further—and quite significantly—virtually always when one group attacks another in genocidal fashion, the victims either have the "out" of capitulation—meaning accepting the philosophy or religious beliefs of the oppressor, or of subjugation through self-abasement and self degradation before the aggressor no matter how distasteful those options are. In simpler terms, one can almost always convert to the attacker's religion or philosophy, or grovel and demean oneself, perhaps even accepting servitude or second-class citizenship to mollify the enemy. No such options existed in dealing with the Nazis. Acceptance of the Nazi ideology by a Jew (if one could conceive of such an absurd circumstance) would simply mean that the Jew had come to accept his or her own murder as justifiable. Aryan ideology did not allow for the "inferior" and "subhuman" Jew to repair his or her claimed fundamental shortcomings through ideological or philosophical conversion. The Jew simply needed to be destroyed.

For this reason, people who were fully Christian in belief and behavior but who had one Jewish grandparent were slated for extermination by the Nazis. So too a person who had one Jewish great-grandparent and another Jew somewhere else in his or her genealogy would not pass muster for the Nazis. Diluting Jewish blood to a ratio of anything less than seven-to-one was not enough for the murderers to stay their hand[2].

One final point in this regard: the hatred of the Jews on the part of the Nazis was so powerful and so all-consuming that as Germany began to lose the Second World War, as it became clear that the apparatus of death was taking manpower and materiel away from the war-effort, and that stopping the activity of the death camps might help Nazi Germany win the war or at least survive, the Nazis—without remorse or hesitation—continued their murderous campaign to rid the world of the Jewish people, even against their own immediate and obvious self-interest.

This constellation of factors does not, to my knowledge, appear on any other bloodstained page of the record of human cruelty. The Holocaust is, therefore, horribly unique and uniquely horrible.

Add to this the staggering numbers: six million dead, including one million children[3]. One third of the Jewish people gone in just five years. And along with the human cost, the unrelenting destruction of Jewish institutions; synagogues, schools, and similar organizations and Jewish artifacts, particularly books, cemeteries and sacred religious objects.

To give some sense of the magnitude of the number "six million", it represents 2,000 World Trade Center tragedies. In other words, over the course of the five years of the active genocide of the Nazis[4], the Jews experienced more than one World Trade Center tragedy per day. To give another statistical parallel, "six million" is one hundred twenty times the number of lost lives suffered by the United States military during the entire Viet Nam war. Viet Nam was a national trauma for America. What word do we then use to accurately describe the effect of the Holocaust on the Jewish people?

What sense can we make of the Holocaust, and what meaning or lessons can we draw from it? Part of whatever answer we may come to, however inadequate, can be found in the chapter on *Theodicy [chapter 6]*. The Holocaust may be history's most extreme example, but it is part of the ongoing challenge posed by the presence of evil in this world as against the Almighty's benevolence.

However, if the Holocaust is truly a unique event in history, it must come with unique meaning, at least if we believe that God's hand directs the course of human history. Frankly, even if the event were not unique in all the way's described above, its sheer magnitude alone requires that it must have a particular and individual meaning.

A classic approach to putting some historical perspective on the Holocaust is to associate it with the founding of the State of Israel. While it is true that three years after the Holocaust, the all-too-momentary pangs of conscience and remorse suffered by the world community may have helped the United Nations make its historic decision creating the Jewish State, and while it is true that, as indicated in the chapter on Israel [chapter 9], these events redefined the purpose of the State, suggesting that it might serve as a redoubt and refuge against a possible future coming to power of someone like the Nazis, nonetheless, to my mind, any suggestion that the birth of the State somehow compensates for the Holocaust is a moral abomination. The immensity of the horror does not find compensation in even the glorious return to Zion.

For many years I thought that the most important message of the Holocaust was its challenge to the conceits of modern society. Germany under the Nazis was the epitome of the embodied concept of the modern nation state: affluent, well run, powerful. The notion that the modern state would always bring vast improvement to the quality of life of its citizens came crashing down in WWII Germany.

During much of the twentieth century, science and technology were presented as the cures to mankind's ills. In its day no nation was as technologically sophisticated as Nazi Germany, yet it used that sophistication to destroy rather than to build.

Sometimes people see culture and education as the way for modern human beings to create the best of all possible worlds. Few, if any countries could match pre-World War II Germany in these areas. Yet from all the culture and education this monstrosity was born.

For these reasons, the Holocaust seemed to me, first and foremost, to challenge the arrogance of contemporary mankind and its excessive pride in its own accomplishments.

All of those things that modern society saw as its great achievements, as the source of hope for a better tomorrow, were all shown to have a dark, dark, underside. It is a painful reminder that claiming that it is the power of the human being alone that brings good to the world is false[5]. God, morality, and a clear sense of right and wrong are critical, as well. It is only if these elements are in place that we can assure that human progress and accomplishment will be a true blessing. This lesson, therefore, appeared to me to be an important part of the message of the Holocaust.

It also seemed to me that Jews were meant to relearn, in the most painful of ways, our age-old belief in the preciousness of every Jewish soul. In the aftermath of the loss of so many of our people, any Jew even remotely sensitive to the magnitude of the event must come to understand this ideal. To that end, the recent appearance and growth of large numbers of outreach organizations that try to bring Jews back to their heritage seemed to be an appropriate response to this challenge. So, too, the tendency of rabbinic scholars to search our sources with remarkable diligence in order to permit as many methods of infertility management as could legitimately be supported by Jewish legal literature (discussed in chapter 22), seemed to me to receive additional impetus from this terrible chapter in our history. Trying to hold on to what we have left and to replace what had been lost however inadequately, became an obvious desideratum. Further, the concern for Jewish continuity that one finds in almost all Jewish organizations today is fueled directly by memories of what once was that is now gone.

Finally, those who do not limit their heartfelt disagreement with the beliefs and behaviors of other Jews to respectful debate and challenge, but instead go beyond that line and through word and deed do and say things that serve to alienate rather than heal seem to me to have missed this point. Telling people that you believe that they are in error, even that they are profoundly and historically wrong, may allow room for them to reconsider their positions. Calling them names, treating them as if they are less than fully human makes the disrespectful behavior the issue, and allows those being challenged to avoid confronting the issues that have been raised. Further, it chases people away from Judaism rather than allowing them to maintain and hopefully strengthen their connection.[6]

These two important moral challenges served for many years as partial responses to the question of how we are to live after the Holocaust—at least for me. Again, they were and are not sufficient to provide anything near a complete answer, but I found some solace in them.

Recently I have come to find them less satisfying. In part this is because they have had their day and their impact. We no longer see technology, the state, and/or culture as the answer to all problems. We all see their uses and benefits, but we also see their flaws and limitations.

So, too, the "preciousness of every Jewish life" idea has had its positive impact, and we can also sadly point to those who have failed to get the message. Perhaps that may yet change, but if that happens, the changes are likely to be incremental, rather than dramatic. As such much of the impact of these ideas may have essentially run its course. Yet the question of coming to grips with the Holocaust remains. At least to me, any of the answers discussed so far have not sufficiently diminished the challenge of making sense of this cataclysmic event.

Recently I have begun to think along different lines, and my thoughts are both profoundly disturbing and at least somewhat hopeful. Part of that hope comes from the fact that in the approach we are about to discuss the entire world and not just the Jews are involved in a very real way in the issue. This gives the Holocaust a more overarching and universal meaning that includes several important practical and pragmatic implications. An approach that incorporates these elements would seem to be more appropriate to an event of this magnitude than any suggestion that is only theoretical or more limited in scope.

It has long intrigued me that the Holocaust and the invention and use of nuclear weapons occurred in the same war. In fact, post-9/11, I have come to believe that Auschwitz and Hiroshima are even more closely linked than they were before.

If the Holocaust taught us anything, it is that no human cruelty is unthinkable. Therefore refusing to combat an evil that threatens unspeakable horror is morally unacceptable. The motto "never again"[7] must mean at least that. Particularly as Auschwitz, the symbol of that cruelty was juxtaposed with Hiroshima, the dawn of the era of weapons of mass destruction; the horrifying reality of what we could face in our lifetimes cannot be avoided. It is this recognition that murder on a mass scale is not inconceivable, that it is a frightening possible part of contemporary reality, and that it must be opposed at all costs that is one very significant message of the Holocaust.

So, too, we cannot avoid other critical conclusions that will bring us full circle in this volume and allow us to end by evoking the theme with which we began in our introduction.

1- Any ideology such as that of the Nazis or contemporary terrorists, that promotes and even glorifies mass murder of innocents must be combated as vigorously as possible on every level: militarily, economically, and perhaps most importantly, ideologically. It is only by presenting a better and more ennobling vision of existence and by winning people to that vision that we can finally do away with the threat that we face.

2- The sanctity and infinite worth of life as the core value of contemporary society must be preached, taught and reiterated. It is only someone who sees moral difficulty in killing any single individual—no matter how much that action may be deserved or justified—who can be expected to see mass murder as inconceivable.

3-These first two points can only be accomplished if we allow ourselves to base our own lives and the underlying philosophy of our society on appropriate objective values.

Hiroshima and Auschwitz were two separate events in a larger conflict. The overarching angst of contemporary society is the possibility that Auschwitz and Hiroshima might occur again, but this time in the same place and time. It is only by learning the lessons of the Holocaust, that include understanding the potential dangers of technology along with its benefits and the infinite preciousness of every human soul, that we can keep the two places as signal events of the past and prevent them from being reprised in our world. It is a daunting task. But the thin blue line of values, the search for transcendence and appropriate meaning in life, and the spark of God in all of us are the best and perhaps only long-term weapons that we have to bring to bear in this struggle. Along the way, living in pursuit of these ideals and bringing them into our own lives makes our existence just that much more meaningful and significant all the time.

1. The literature on this subject is immense and ever expanding. Two authors that I recommend are, Lucy Dawidowicz for historical research, as in her "The War against the Jews, 1933–1945", Toronto, 1986 and for philosophical analysis Emil Fackenheim who has several volumes on the subject.

2. According to the First Decree of the Reich citizenship law of November 14, 1935, individuals who were one-eighth Jewish or less were considered Germans. This meant that having one Jewish great-grandparent was officially acceptable. However any greater "taint" of Jewish blood was not.

3. Others suffered at the hands of the Nazis as well and their tragedies must be recognized, appreciated and remembered. However the systemic, all-consuming genocide described here that was directed at the Jews was not employed in any similar way by the Germans against any other group.

4. There are a number of stages that involved different types of atrocities over the course of the Holocaust. The period that saw the consistent "extermination" of as many Jews as possible lasted from 1941–1944/45. In the very last part of the period starvation and disease become the source of much of the death in the Concentration camps and on the long "death" marches that the remnant were forced to undergo as the Germans retreated across Europe.

5. Deuteronomy 8:17.

6. See A. Karelitz, Sefer Hazon Ish, Yoreh De'ah 2:16.

7. This slogan has come to be associated with post-holocaust Jewry's response to the Holocaust.

Sources

Chapter 1 *God*

שמות רבה (וילנא) פרשה ג

ו ויאמר אלהים אל משה, אמר רבי אבא בר ממל אמר ליה הקב"ה למשה שמי אתה
מבקש לידע, לפי מעשי אני נקרא פעמים שאני נקרא באל שדי, בצבאות, באלהים,
בה', כשאני דן את הבריות אני נקרא אלהים, וכשאני עושה מלחמה ברשעים אני
נקרא צבאות, וכשאני תולה על חטאיו של אדם אני נקרא אל שדי, וכשאני מרחם
על עולמי אני נקרא ה', שאין ה' אלא מדת רחמים שנאמר (שמות לד) ה' ה' אל
רחום וחנון, הוי אהיה אשר אהיה אני נקרא לפי מעשי, ר' יצחק אומר א"ל הקב"ה
למשה אמור להם אני שהייתי ואני הוא עכשיו ואני הוא לעתיד לבא, לכך כתיב
אהיה שלשה פעמים,

Midrash Rabbah - Exodus III:6

6. AND GOD SAID UNTO MOSES (III, 14). R. Abba b.
Mammel said: God said to Moses: ' You want to know My
name. Well, I am called according to My work; sometimes I
am called "Almighty God", "Lord of Hosts", "God", "Lord".
When I am judging created beings, I am called " God",' and
when I am waging war against the wicked, I am called "Lord
of Hosts". When I suspend judgment for a man's sins, I am
called "El Shadday " (Almighty God), and when I am merciful
towards My world, I am called "Ado-nai", for "Ado-nai"

301

refers to the Attribute of Mercy, as it is said: The Lord, the Lord (Ado-nai, Ado-nai), God, merciful and gracious (ib. XXXIV, 6). Hence I AM THAT I AM in virtue of My deeds.' R. Isaac said: God said to Moses: ' Tell them that I am now what I always was and always will be'; for this reason is the word "eheyeh" written three times.

Chapter 2 *Bible*

תלמוד בבלי מסכת מגילה דף יד עמוד א

תנו רבנן: ארבעים ושמונה נביאים ושבע נביאות נתנבאו להם לישראל, ולא פחתו ולא הותירו על מה שכתוב בתורה, חוץ ממקרא מגילה. מאי דרוש? אמר רבי חייא בר אבין אמר רבי יהושע בן קרחה: ומה מעבדות לחירות אמרינן שירה – ממיתה לחיים לא כל שכן... ותו ליכא? והכתיב +שמואל א' א'+ ויהי איש אחד מן הרמתים צופים – אחד ממאתים צופים שנתנבאו להם לישראל! – מיהוה טובא הוו. כדתניא: הרבה נביאים עמדו להם לישראל, כפלים כיוצאי מצרים, אלא, נבואה שהוצרכה לדורות – נכתבה, ושלא הוצרכה – לא נכתבה.

Talmud - Mas. Megilah 14a

Our Rabbis taught: 'Forty-eight prophets and seven prophetesses prophesied to Israel, and they neither took away from nor added aught to what is written in the Torah save only the reading of the Megillah'. How did they derive it [from the Torah]? — R. Hiyya b. Abin said in the name of R. Joshua b. Korha: If for being delivered from slavery to freedom we chant a hymn of praise, should we not do so all the more for being delivered from death to life? ...Were there no more prophets than these [forty-eight]? — Is it not written, There was a man from Ramathaim-Zophim, [which we interpret], one of two hundred prophets [zophim] who prophesied to Israel? — There were actually very many, as it has been taught, 'Many prophets arose for Israel, double the number of [the Israelites] who came out of Egypt', only the prophecy that contained a lesson for future generations was written down, and that which did not contain such a lesson was not written.

Chapter 3 *Halakhah*

תלמוד בבלי מסכת בבא מציעא דף נט עמוד ב

יצאתה בת קול ואמרה: מה לכם אצל רבי אליעזר שהלכה כמותו בכל מקום! עמד רבי יהושע על רגליו ואמר: לא בשמים היא. – מאי +דברים ל'+ לא בשמים היא? – אמר רבי ירמיה: שכבר נתנה תורה מהר סיני, אין אנו משגיחין בבת קול, שכבר כתבת בהר סיני בתורה +שמות כ"ג+ אחרי רבים להטת. – אשכחיה רבי נתן לאליהו, אמר ליה: מאי עביד קודשא בריך הוא בההיא שעתא? – אמר ליה: קא חייך ואמר נצחוני בני, נצחוני בני.

Babylonian Talmud – Baba Meziah 59b

A voice went out and said, "Why are you arguing against Rabbi Eliezer when the halakhah is according to him in every instance?" Rabbi Yehoshua stood up and said, "It is not in heaven." What does "not in heaven" [a quote from Deuteronomy 30] mean? Rabbi Yirimiyah said, "Since the Torah was given on Mount Sinai we do not follow a voice from heaven, for You have already written at Mount Sinai in Your Torah that the law is according to the majority [Exodus 23]."

Rabbi Nathan found Eliyahu [Elijah the Prophet] and asked him, "How did the Holy One respond at that time?" He said to him, "He chuckled and said, 'My sons have triumphed over me, My sons have triumphed over me.'"

Chapter 4 *Prophecy*

ירמיהו פרק א

(ד) ויהי דבר יקוק אלי לאמר:
(ה) בטרם אצורך בבטן ידעתיך ובטרם תצא מרחם הקדשתיך נביא לגוים נתתיך:
(ו) ואמר אהה אדני יקוק הנה לא ידעתי דבר כי נער אנכי: פ
(ז) ויאמר יקוק אלי אל תאמר נער אנכי כי על כל אשר אשלחך תלך ואת כל אשר אצוך תדבר:
(ח) אל תירא מפניהם כי אתך אני להצלך נאם יקוק:

Tanach - Jeremiah Chapter 1

4. Then the word of the Lord came to me, saying,
5. (K) Before I formed you in the belly I knew you; and before you came forth out of the womb I sanctified you, and I ordained you a prophet to the nations.
6. Then said I, Ah, Lord God! behold, I cannot speak; for I am a child.
7. But the Lord said to me, Say not, I am a child; for you shall go to all to whom I shall send you, and whatever I command you you shall speak.
8. Be not afraid of their faces; for I am with you to save you, said the Lord.

במדבר פרק יב

(ו) ויאמר שמעו נא דברי אם יהיה נביאכם ידוד במראה אליו אתודע בחלום אדבר
בו:
(ז) לא כן עבדי משה בכל ביתי נאמן הוא:
(ח) פה אל פה אדבר בו ומראה ולא בחידת ותמנת ידוד יביט ומדוע לא יראתם
לדבר בעבדי במשה:

Tanach - Numbers Chapter 12

6. And he said, Hear now my words; If there is a prophet among you, I the Lord will make myself known to him in a vision, and will speak to him in a dream.
7. Not so with my servant Moses, for he is the trusted one in all my house.
8. With him I speak mouth to mouth, manifestly, and not in ridddles; and he perceives the form of the Lord. Why then were you not afraid to speak against my servant Moses?

Chapter 5 *Humankind's Place*

משנה מסכת אבות פרק ג

משנה יד
הוא)רבי עקיבא(היה אומר חביב אדם שנברא בצלם חבה יתירה נודעת לו שנברא
בצלם שנאמר (בראשית ט) בצלם אלהים עשה את האדם

Mishna - Mas. Avoth Chapter 3

Mishnah. He [also] used to say: beloved is man in that he was created in the image [of God]. [It is a mark of] superabundant love [that] it was made known to him that he had been created in the image [of God], as it is said: for in the image of God made he man.

משנה סנהדרין ד:ה (כתב יד קויפמן)

לפיכך נברא אדם יחידי, ללמדך שכל המאבד נפש אחת – מעלה עליו הכתוב כאילו איבד עולם מלא, וכל המקיים נפש אחת – מעלה עליו הכתוב כאילו קיים עולם מלא...
כל אחד ואחד חייב לומר: בשבילי נברא העולם

Mishnah Mas. Sanhedrin 4:5 (mss. Kaufmann)

For this reason was man created alone, to teach thee that whosoever destroys a single soul of Israel, scripture imputes [guilt] to him as though he had destroyed a complete world; and whosoever preserves a single soul of Israel, scripture ascribes [merit] to him as though he had preserved a complete world...
Every single person is obliged to say: the world was created for my sake.

Chapter 6 *Theodicy*

תלמוד בבלי מסכת ברכות דף ה עמוד א

אמר רבא ואיתימא רב חסדא: אם רואה אדם שיסורין באין עליו – יפשפש במעשיו, שנאמר +איכה ג'+ נחפשה דרכינו ונחקורה ונשובה עד ה'; פשפש ולא מצא – יתלה בבטול תורה, שנאמר: +תהלים צ"ד+ אשרי הגבר אשר תיסרנו יה ומתורתך תלמדנו. ואם תלה ולא מצא – בידוע שיסורין של אהבה הם, שנאמר: +משלי ג'+ כי את אשר יאהב ה' יוכיח. אמר רבא אמר רב סחורה אמר רב הונא: כל שהקדוש ברוך הוא חפץ בו – מדכאו ביסורין, שנאמר: +ישעיהו נ"ג+ וה' חפץ

דכאו החלי; יכול אפילו לא קבלם מאהבה – תלמוד לומר +ישעיהו נ״ג+ אם תשים
אשם נפשו, מה אשם לדעת – אף יסורין לדעת. ואם קבלם מה שכרו – +ישעיהו
נ״ג+ יראה זרע יאריך ימים; ולא עוד אלא שתלמודו מתקיים בידו, שנאמר:
+ישעיהו נ״ג+ וחפץ ה' בידו יצלח.

Talmud - Mas. Berachoth 5a

Raba (some say, R. Hisda) says: If a man sees that
painful sufferings visit him, let him examine his conduct. For
it is said: Let us search and try our ways, and return unto the
Lord. If he examines and does not find an answer, let him
attribute it to the neglect of the study of the Torah. For it is
said: Happy is the man whom You chasten, O Lord, and
teach out of Your law. If he did attribute it [thus], and still did
not find [this to be an adequate answer], let him be sure that
these are chastenings of love. For it is said: For whom the
Lord loves He corrects.

תלמוד בבלי מסכת ברכות דף ה עמוד ב

רבי חייא בר אבא חלש, על לגביה רבי יוחנן. אמר ליה: חביבין עליך יסורין? אמר
ליה: לא הן ולא שכרן. אמר ליה: הב לי ידך! יהב ליה ידיה ואוקמיה. רבי יוחנן
חלש, על לגביה רבי חנינא. אמר ליה: חביבין עליך יסורין? אמר ליה: לא הן ולא
שכרן. אמר ליה: הב לי ידך! יהב ליה ידיה ואוקמיה. אמאי? לוקים רבי יוחנן
לנפשיה! – אמרי: אין חבוש מתיר עצמו מבית האסורים. – רבי אלעזר חלש, על
לגביה רבי יוחנן. חזא דהוה קא גני בבית אפל, גלייה לדרעיה ונפל נהורא. חזייה
דהוה קא בכי רבי אלעזר. אמר ליה: אמאי קא בכית? אי משום תורה דלא אפשת –
שנינו: אחד המרבה ואחד הממעיט ובלבד שיכוין לבו לשמים! ואי משום מזוני –
לא כל אדם זוכה לשתי שלחנות! ואי משום בני – דין גרמא דעשיראה ביר. אמר
ליה: להאי שופרא דבלי בעפרא קא בכינא. אמר ליה: על דא ודאי קא בכית, ובכו
תרוייהו. אדהכי והכי, אמר ליה: חביבין עליך יסורין? אמר ליה: לא הן ולא שכרן.
אמר ליה: הב לי ידך, יהב ליה ידיה ואוקמיה.

Talmud - Mas. Berachoth 5b

R. Hiyya b. Abba fell ill and R. Johanan went in to visit him. He said to him: Are your sufferings welcome to you? He replied: Neither they nor their reward. He said to him: Give me your hand. He gave him his hand and he raised him.

R. Johanan once fell ill and R. Hanina went in to visit him. He said to him: Are your sufferings welcome to you? He replied: Neither they nor their reward. He said to him: Give me your hand. He gave him his hand and he raised him. Why could not R. Johanan raise himself? — They replied: The prisoner cannot free himself from jail.

R. Eleazar fell ill and R. Johanan went in to visit him. He noticed that he was lying in a dark room, and he bared his arm and light radiated from it. Thereupon he noticed that R. Eleazar was weeping, and he said to him: Why do you weep? Is it because you did not study enough Torah? Surely we learnt: The one who sacrifices much and the one who sacrifices little have the same merit, provided that the heart is directed to heaven. Is it perhaps lack of sustenance? Not everybody has the privilege to enjoy two tables. Is it perhaps because of [the lack of] children? This is the bone of my tenth son! — He replied to him: I am weeping on account of this beauty that is going to rot in the earth. He said to him: On that account you surely have a reason to weep; and they both wept. In the meanwhile he said to him: Are your sufferings welcome to you? — He replied: Neither they nor their reward. He said to him: Give me your hand, and he gave him his hand and he raised him.

Chapter 7 *Teshuvah*

אמר ריש לקיש: גדולה תשובה, שזדונות נעשות לו כשגגות, שנאמר +הושע יד+
שובה ישראל עד ה' אלהיך כי כשלת בעונך. הא עון מזיד הוא, וקא קרי ליה
מכשול. איני? והאמר ריש לקיש: גדולה תשובה שזדונות נעשות לו כזכיות,
שנאמר +יחזקאל לג+ ובשוב רשע מרשעתו ועשה משפט וצדקה עליהם (חיה)
+מסורת הש"ס: [הוא]+ יחיה! – לא קשיא; כאן – מאהבה, כאן – מיראה.

Talmud - Mas. Yoma 86b

Resh Lakish said: Great is repentance, for because of it
premeditated sins are accounted as errors, as it is said:
Return, O Israel, unto the Lord, your God,' for you have
stumbled in your sin. 'Iniquity' is premeditated, and yet he
calls it 'stumbling' But that is not so! For Resh Lakish said
that repentance is so great that premeditated sins are
accounted as though they were merits, as it is said: And when
the wicked turneth from his wickedness, and doeth that
which is lawful and right, he shall live thereby! That is no
contradiction: One refers to a case [of repentance] derived
from love, the other to one due to fear

רבי מאיר אומר: גדולה תשובה, שבשביל יחיד שעשה תשובה מוחלין לכל העולם
כולו, שנאמר +הושע יד+ ארפא משובתם אהבם נדבה כי שב אפי ממנו. מהם לא
נאמר, אלא ממנו.

Babylonian Talmud – Mas. Yoma 86b

Rabbi Meir says: Repentance is so great that for the sake of one person who repented the entire world is forgiven, as it says in Hoshea [14:5] "I will heal their backsliding, I will love them voluntarily, for my anger is turned away from him" "From them" is not said [which would match the plural phrasing at the beginning of the verse] but "from him"

Chapter 8 *Gentiles*

שמות רבה (וילנא) פרשה יט

אמר איוב (איוב לא) בחוץ לא ילין גר, שאין הקב"ה פוסל לבריה אלא לכל הוא מקבל, השערים נפתחים בכל שעה וכל מי שהוא מבקש ליכנס יכנס,

Midrash Sh'mot Rabba 19:4

Iyov [Job] said: "The stranger will not lie outside; I shall open my doors to the traveler" [31:32]. G-d does not disqualify any creature, but accepts all. The gates are open at all times, and whoever wants to enter may enter.

Chapter 9 *Israel*

תלמוד בבלי מסכת כתובות דף קי עמוד ב

מתני'. הכל מעלין לארץ ישראל ואין הכל מוציאין, הכל מעלין לירושלים ואין הכל מוציאין, אחד האנשים ואחד הנשים.

Talmud - Mas. Kethuboth 110b

Mishnah. [a man] may compel all [his household] to go up
[with him] to the land of Israel., but none may be compelled
to leave it. All [one's household] may be compelled to go up
to Jerusalem, but none may be compelled to leave it. [This
applies to] both men and women.

תלמוד בבלי מסכת כתובות דף קן עמוד ב

ת"ר: לעולם ידור אדם בא"י אפי' בעיר שרובה עובדי כוכבים, ואל ידור בחו"ל
ואפילו בעיר שרובה ישראל, שכל הדר בארץ ישראל – דומה כמי שיש לו אלוה,
וכל הדר בחוצה לארץ – דומה כמי שאין לו אלוה, שנא': +ויקרא כ"ה+ לתת לכם
את ארץ כנען להיות לכם לאלהים, וכל שאינו דר בארץ אין לו אלוה? אלא לומר
לך: כל הדר בחו"ל – כאילו עובד עבודת כוכבים; וכן בדוד הוא אומר: +שמואל
א' כ"ו+ כי גרשוני היום מהסתפח בנחלת ה' לאמר לך עבוד אלהים אחרים, וכי מי
אמר לו לדוד לך עבוד אלהים אחרים? אלא לומר לך: כל הדר בחו"ל – כאילו עובד
עבודת כוכבים.

Talmud - Mas. Kethuboth 110b

Our Rabbis taught: One should always live in the
Land of Israel, even in a town most of whose inhabitants are
idolaters, but let no one live outside the Land, even in a town
most of whose inhabitants are Israelites; for whoever lives in
the Land of Israel may be considered to have a God, but
whoever lives outside the Land may be regarded as one who
has no God. For it is said in Scripture, To give you the Land
of Canaan, to be your God. Has he, then, who does not live in
the Land, no God? But [this is what the text intended] to tell
you, that whoever lives outside the Land may be regarded as
one who worships idols. Similarly it was said in Scripture in
[the story of] David, For they have driven me out this day
that I should not cleave to the inheritance of the Lord, saying:

Go, serve other gods. Now, whoever said to David, 'Serve other gods'? But [the text intended] to tell you that whoever lives outside the Land may be regarded as one who worships idols.

Chapter 10 *Messiah*

תלמוד בבלי מסכת סנהדרין דף צח עמוד א

ואמר רבי אבא: אין לך קץ מגולה מזה, שנאמר +יחזקאל ל"ו+ ואתם הרי ישראל ענפכם תתנו ופריכם תשאו לעמי ישראל וגו'. ...אמר עולא: אין ירושלים נפדית אלא בצדקה, שנאמר +ישעיהו א'+ ציון במשפט תפדה ושביה בצדקה. ... אמר רבי יוחנן: אם ראית דור שמתמעט והולך – חכה לו, שנאמר +שמואל ב' כ"ב+ ואת עם עני תושיע וגו'. אמר רבי יוחנן: אם ראית דור שצרות רבות באות עליו כנהר – חכה לו, שנאמר +ישעיהו נ"ט+ כי יבא כנהר צר (ורוח) [רוח] ה' נססה בו, וסמיך ליה ובא לציון גואל. ואמר רבי יוחנן: אין בן דוד בא אלא בדור שכולו זכאי, או כולו חייב. בדור שכולו זכאי – דכתיב +ישעיהו ס'+ ועמך כלם צדיקים לעולם יירשו ארץ, בדור שכולו חייב – דכתיב +ישעיהו נ"ט+ וירא כי אין איש וישתומם כי אין מפגיע, וכתיב +ישעיהו מ"ח+ למעני אעשה.

אמר רבי אלכסנדרי: רבי יהושע בן לוי רמי, כתיב +ישעיהו ס'+ בעתה, וכתיב, אחישנה! זכו – אחישנה, לא זכו – בעתה. אמר רבי אלכסנדרי: רבי יהושע בן לוי רמי, כתיב +דניאל ז'+ וארו עם ענני שמיא כבר אנש אתה, וכתיב +זכריה ט'+ עני ורכב על חמור! – זכו – עם ענני שמיא, לא זכו – עני ורוכב על חמור.

Talmud - Mas. Sanhedrin 98a

R. Abba also said: There can be no more manifest [sign of] redemption than this: viz., what is said, But you, O mountains of Israel, you shall shoot forth your branches, and yield your fruit to my people of Israel, for they are at hand to come…

'Ulla said: Jerusalem shall be redeemed only by righteousness, as it is written, Zion shall be redeemed with judgment, and her converts with righteousness.

R. Johanan said: When you see a generation ever dwindling, hope for him [the Messiah], as it is written, And the afflicted people you will save. R. Johanan said: When you see a generation overwhelmed by many troubles as by a river, await him, as it is written, when the enemy shall come in like a flood, the Spirit of the Lord shall lift up a standard against him; which is followed by, And the Redeemer shall come to Zion.

R. Johanan also said: The son of David will come only in a generation that is either altogether righteous or altogether wicked. 'in a generation that is altogether righteous,' — as it is written, Thy people also shall be all righteous: they shall inherit the land for ever. 'Or altogether wicked,' — as it is written, And he saw that there was no man, and wondered that there was no intercessor; and it is [elsewhere] written, For mine own sake, even for mine own sake, will I do it.

R. Alexandri said: R. Joshua b. Levi pointed out a contradiction. it is written, in its time [will the Messiah come], whilst it is also written, I [the Lord] will hasten it! — if they are worthy, I will hasten it: if not, [he will come] at the due time. R. Alexandri said: R. Joshua opposed two verses: it is written, And behold, one like the son of man came with the clouds of heaven while [elsewhere] it is written, [behold, your king comes unto you . . .] lowly, and riding upon an ass! — if they are meritorious, [he will come] with the clouds of heaven; if not, lowly and riding upon an ass.

Chapter 11 *Dogmas*

משנה מסכת סנהדרין פרק י

ואלו שאין להם חלק לעולם הבא האומר אין תחיית המתים מן התורה ואין תורה
מן השמים ואפיקורס רבי עקיבא אומר אף הקורא בספרים החיצונים והלוחש על
המכה ואומר (שמות ט"ו) כל המחלה אשר שמתי במצרים לא אשים עליך כי אני
ה' רפאך אבא שאול אומר אף ההוגה את השם באותיותיו:

Mishnah Sanhedrin 10:1

But the following have no portion in the World to Come: he
who maintains that resurrection is not a biblical doctrine, the
torah was not divinely revealed, and an epikoros. R. Akiba
added: one who reads uncanonical books. Also one who
whispers [a charm] over a wound and says, I will bring none
of these diseases upon you, which I brought upon the
Egyptians: for I am the Lord that heals you.' Abba Saul says:
also one who pronounces the divine name as it is spelled.

Chapter 12 *Shabbat and Kashrut*

תלמוד בבלי מסכת שבת דף קיח עמוד ב

אמר רב יהודה אמר רב: כל המענג את השבת נותנין לו משאלות לבו, שנאמר
+תהלים לז+ והתענג על ה' ויתן לך משאלות לבך. עונג זה איני יודע מהו, כשהוא
אומר וקראת לשבת ענג, הוי אומר: זה ענג שבת. – במה מענגו? – רב יהודה
בריה דרב שמואל בר שילת משמיה דרב אמר: בתבשיל של תרדין, ודגים גדולים,
וראשי שומין. רב חייא בר אשי אמר רב: אפילו דבר מועט, ולכבוד שבת עשאו –

הרי זה עונג. מאי היא? – אמר רב פפא: כסא דהרסנא...אמר רב יהודה אמר רב:
אלמלי שמרו ישראל שבת ראשונה לא שלטה בהן אומה ולשון, שנאמר +שמות
טז+ ויהי ביום השביעי יצאו מן העם ללקט וכתיב בתריה ויבא עמלק. אמר רבי
יוחנן משום רבי שמעון בן יוחי: אלמלי משמרין ישראל שתי שבתות כהלכתן –
מיד נגאלים.... אמר רבי יוסי: יהא חלקי מאוכלי שלש סעודות בשבת.

Talmud - Mas. Shabbath 118b

Rab Judah said in Rab's name: He who delights in the
Sabbath is granted his heart's desires, for it is said, Delight
yourself also in the Lord; And he shall give you the desires of
your heart. Now, I do not know what this 'delight' refers to;
but when it is said, and you shall call the Sabbath a delight,
you must say that it refers to the delight of the Sabbath.

Wherewith does one show his delight therein? — Rab
Judah son of R. Samuel b. Shilath said in Rab's name: With a
dish of beets, large fish, and heads of garlic. R. Hiyya b. Ashi
said in Rab's name: Even a trifle, if it is prepared in honor of
the Sabbath, is delight. What is it [the trifle]? Said R. Papa: A
pie of fish-hash....

Rab Judah said in Rab's name: Had Israel kept the first
Sabbath, no nation or tongue would have enjoyed dominion
over them, for it is said, And it came to pass on the seventh
day, that there went out some of the people to gather; which
is followed by, Then came Amalek. R. Johanan said in the
name of R. Simeon b. Yohai: If Israel were to keep two
Sabbaths according to the laws thereof, they would be
redeemed immediately, ...

R. Jose said: May my portion be among those who eat
three meals on the Sabbath

Chapter 13 *The Experience of Prayer*

סדור תפלה - סדר השכמת הבוקר

מודה אני לפניך מלך חי וקים. שהחזרת בי נשמתי בחמלה. רבה אמונתך

The Daily Prayer Book

The first words a Jew says each morning are:
I thank You, living and eternal King, for You have restored my soul to me with compassion; Your constancy is beyond measure.

Chapter 14 *Prayer—Additional Thoughts*

תלמוד בבלי מסכת ברכות דף לא עמוד א

תנו רבנן: המתפלל צריך שיכוין את לבו לשמים. אבא שאול אומר, סימן לדבר: +תהלים י'+ תכין לבם תקשיב אזנך. תניא, אמר רבי יהודה: כך היה מנהגו של רבי עקיבא, כשהיה מתפלל עם הצבור – היה מקצר ועולה, מפני טורח צבור, וכשהיה מתפלל בינו לבין עצמו – אדם מניחו בזוית זו ומוצאו בזוית אחרת, וכל כך למה – מפני כריעות והשתחויות.

Talmud - Mas. Berachoth 31a

Our Rabbis taught: When a man prays, he should direct his heart to heaven. Abba Saul says: A reminder of this is the text, "If their heart is directed, You will cause Your ear to pay attention". It has been taught: Such was the custom of

R. Akiba; when he prayed with the congregation, he used to cut it short and finish in order not to inconvenience the congregation, but when he prayed by himself, a man would leave him in one corner and find him later in another, on account of his many genuflections and prostrations.

Chapter 15 *Tzedakah*

תלמוד בבלי מסכת כתובות דף סז עמוד ב

ת"ר: יתום שבא לישא, שוכרין לו בית ומציעין לו מטה וכל כלי תשמישו, ואחר
כך משיאין לו אשה, שנאמר: +דברים ט"ו+ די מחסורו אשר יחסר לו, די מחסורו
– זה הבית, אשר יחסר – זה מטה ושלחן, לו – זו אשה, וכן הוא אומר: +בראשית
ב'+ אעשה לו עזר כנגדו. תנו רבנן: די מחסורו – אתה מצווה עליו לפרנסו, ואי
אתה מצווה עליו לעשרו; אשר יחסר לו – אפילו סוס לרכוב עליו ועבד לרוץ
לפניו. אמרו עליו על הלל הזקן, שלקח לעני בן טובים אחד סוס לרכוב עליו ועבד
לרוץ לפניו; פעם אחת לא מצא עבד לרוץ לפניו, ורץ לפניו שלשה מילין

Talmud - Mas. Kethuboth 67b

Our Rabbis taught: If an orphan applied for assistance to marry, a house must be rented for him, a bed must be prepared for him and [he must also be supplied with] all [household] objects [required for] his use, and then he is given a wife in marriage, for it is said in Scripture, Sufficient for his need in that which he is lacking: 'sufficient for his need', refers to the house; 'in that which he is lacking', refers to a bed and a table; 'he' refers to a wife, for so it is said in Scripture, I will make him a help meet unto him.

Our Rabbis taught: 'Sufficient for his need' [implies] you are commanded to maintain him, but you are not commanded to make him rich; 'in that which he is lacking' [includes] even a horse to ride upon and a slave to run before him. It was related about Hillel the Elder that he bought for a certain poor man who was of a good family a horse to ride upon and a slave to run before him. On one occasion he could not find a slave to run before him, so he himself ran before him for three miles.

תלמוד בבלי מסכת סוכה דף מט עמוד ב

תנו רבנן: בשלשה דברים גדולה גמילות חסדים יותר מן הצדקה, צדקה – בממונו, גמילות חסדים – בין בגופו בין בממונו. צדקה – לעניים, גמילות חסדים – בין לעניים בין לעשירים. צדקה – לחיים, גמילות חסדים – בין לחיים בין למתים.

Talmud - Mas. Sukkah 49b

Our Rabbis taught, In three respects is Gemiluth Hasadim superior to charity: charity can be done only with one's money, but Gemiluth Hasadim can be done with one's person and one's money. Charity can be given only to the poor, Gemiluth Hasadim both to the rich and the poor. Charity can be given only to the living. Gemiluth Hasadim can be done both to the living and to the dead.

Chapter 16 *Mysticism*

עמוס פרק ח

(יא) הנה ימים באים נאם אדני יקוק והשלחתי רעב בארץ לא רעב ללחם ולא צמא למים כי אם לשמע את דברי יקוק:

(יב) ונעו מים עד ים ומצפון ועד מזרח ישוטטו לבקש את דבר יקוק ולא ימצאו:

(יג) ביום ההוא תתעלפנה הבתולת היפות והבחורים בצמא:

(יד) הנשבעים באשמת שמרון ואמרו חי אלהיך דן וחי דרך באר שבע ונפלו ולא
יקומו עוד: ס

Tanach - Twelve Prophets - Amos Chapter 8

11. Behold, the days come, says the Lord God, when I will send a famine in the land, not a famine of bread, nor a thirst for water, but of hearing the words of the Lord;

12. And they shall wander from sea to sea, and from north to east, they shall run to and fro to seek the word of the Lord, and shall not find it.

13. In that day all the pretty young women and young men shall faint for thirst.

14. Those who swear by the sin of Samaria, and say, As your god, O Dan, lives, and, As the road to Beersheba lives, they shall fall, and never rise up again.

Chapter 17 *Miracles*

תלמוד בבלי מסכת ברכות דף נד עמוד א

ההוא גברא דהוה קא אזיל בעבר ימינא, נפל עליה אריא, אתעביד ליה ניסא
ואיתצל מיניה; אתא לקמיה דרבא, ואמר ליה: כל אימת דמטית להתם – בריך ברוך
שעשה לי נס במקום הזה! ומר בריה דרבינא הוה קאזיל בפקתא דערבות וצחא
למיא, אתעביד ליה ניסא איברי ליה עינא דמיא ואישתי. ותו, זמנא חדא הוה קאזיל
ברסתקא דמחוזא ונפל עליה גמלא פריצא, איתפרקא ליה אשיתא, על לגויה; כי
מטא לערבות, בריך: ברוך שעשה לי נס בערבות ובגמל, כי מטא לרסתקא
דמחוזא, בריך: ברוך שעשה לי נס בגמל ובערבות! – אמרי: אניסא דרבים כולי
עלמא מיחייבי לברוכי, אניסא דיחיד – איהו חייב לברוכי.

Talmud - Mas. Berachoth 54a

There is the case of the man who was once traveling through Eber Yemina when a lion attacked him, but he was miraculously saved, and when he came before Raba he said to him, Whenever you pass that place say, Blessed be He who made a miracle for me in this place! There was the case, too, of Mar the son of Rabina who was once going through the valley of 'Araboth and was suffering from thirst and a well of water was miraculously created for him and he drank, and another time he was going through the manor of Mahoza when a wild camel attacked him and at that moment the wall of a house near him fell in and he escaped inside; and whenever thereafter he came to 'Araboth he used to say, Blessed be He who made miracles for me in 'Araboth and with the camel, and when he passed through the manor of Mahoza he used to say, Blessed be He who made miracles for me with the camel and in 'Araboth?-The answer [is that] for a miracle done to a large group of people it is the duty of everyone to say a blessing, for a miracle done to an individual he alone is required to say a blessing.

Chapter 18 *Afterlife*

תלמוד בבלי מסכת שבת דף לא עמוד א

אמר רבא: בשעה שמכניסין אדם לדין אומרים לו: נשאת ונתת באמונה, קבעת
עתים לתורה, עסקת בפריה ורביה, צפית לישועה, פלפלת בחכמה, הבנת דבר
מתוך דבר

Talmud - Mas. Shabbath 31a

Raba said, When man is led in for Judgment he is asked, Did you deal faithfully [i.e., with integrity], did you fix times for learning, did you engage in procreation, did you hope for salvation, did you engage in the dialectics of wisdom, did you understand one thing from another?

Chapter 19 *Astrology*

תלמוד בבלי מסכת פסחים דף קי״ג עמוד ב

אמר רבה בר בר חנה אמר רבי שמואל בר מרתא אמר רב משום רבי יוסי איש
הוצל: מניין שאין שואלין בכלדיים – שנאמר +דברים יח+ תמים תהיה עם ה׳
אלהיך

Talmud - Mas. Pesachim 113b

Rabbah b. Bar Hanah said in the name of R. Samuel b. Martha in Rab's name on the authority of R. Jose of Huzal: How do we know that you must not consult astrologers? Because it is said: You shall be whole-hearted with the Lord your God.

Chapter 20 *Authority versus Autonomy*

משנה מסכת אבות פרק ו משנה ב

והלוחות מעשה אלהים המה והמכתב מכתב אלהים הוא חרות על הלוחות אל
תקרא חרות אלא חירות שאין לך בן חורין אלא מי שעוסק בתלמוד תורה וכל מי
שעוסק בתורה תדיר הרי זה מתעלה

Mishna - Mas. Avoth Chapter 6:2

 And the tablets were the work of God, and the writing was
the writing of God, carved upon the tablets. Read not haruth
[which means 'carved'] but heruth [which means 'freedom'].
For there is no free man, but he that occupies himself with the
study of the Torah; and whoever regularly occupies himself
with the study of the Torah, is exalted.

Chapter 21 *Ethics*

תלמוד בבלי מסכת בבא מציעא דף פג עמוד א

רבה בר בר חנן תברו ליה הנהו שקולאי חביתא דחמרא. שקל לגלימייהו, אתו
אמרו לרב. אמר ליה: הב להו גלימייהו. – אמר ליה: דינא הכי? – אמר ליה: אין,
+משלי ב׳+ למען תלך בדרך טובים. יהיב להו גלימייהו. אמרו ליה: עניי אנן,
וטרחינן כולה יומא, וכפינן, ולית לן מידי. אמר ליה: זיל הב אגרייהו. – אמר ליה:
דינא הכי? – אמר ליה: אין, +משלי ב׳+ וארחות צדיקים תשמר.

Babylonian Talmud: Baba Metzia 83a

Some porters broke a barrel of wine that belonged to Rabbah, son of Rav Huna. He seized their garments. They went and complained to Rav. He ordered, "Return the garments." "Is that the law," he asked. He answered, "yes [quoting the first half of Proverbs 2:20] "That you may walk in the ways of good people"." Their garments having been returned, they said, "We are poor men, have worked all day, and are in need; are we to get nothing?" He ordered, "Go and pay them" [although the porters were responsible for their negligence in breaking the barrel]. "Is that the law?" he asked. He said, "Yes [quoting this second half of the same verse], "and keep the path of the righteous" [do more than the halakhah requires]."

Chapter 22 *Beginning of Life Ethics*

תלמוד בבלי מסכת יבמות דף סג עמוד ב

אמר רבי אסי: אין בן דוד בא עד שיכלו כל הנשמות שבגוף, שנאמר: +ישעיהו נ״ז+ כי רוח מלפני יעטוף ונשמות אני עשיתי. תניא, רבי אליעזר אומר: כל מי שאין עוסק בפריה ורביה – כאילו שופך דמים, שנאמר: +בראשית ט׳+ שופך דם האדם באדם דמו ישפך, וכתיב בתריה: ואתם פרו ורבו. רבי יעקב אומר: כאילו ממעט הדמות, שנאמר: +בראשית ט׳+ כי בצלם אלהים עשה את האדם, וכתיב בתריה: ואתם פרו וגו׳. בן עזאי אומר: כאילו שופך דמים וממעט הדמות, שנאמר: ואתם פרו ורבו. אמרו לו לבן עזאי: יש נאה דורש ונאה מקיים, נאה מקיים ואין נאה דורש, ואתה נאה דורש ואין נאה מקיים! אמר להן בן עזאי: ומה אעשה, שנפשי חשקה בתורה, אפשר לעולם שיתקיים על ידי אחרים.

Talmud - Mas. Yevamoth 63b

R. Assi stated: The son of David will not come before all the souls in Guf (the region inhabited by the unborn souls.) are disposed of; since it is said, For the spirit that wraps itself [in the human being] is from Me, and the souls I have made.

It was taught: R. Eliezer stated, He who does not engage in propagation of the race is as though he sheds blood; for it is said, "Whoever sheds man's blood, by man shall his blood be shed", and this is immediately followed by the text, "And you, be fruitful and multiply". R. Jacob said: It is as though he has diminished the Divine Image; since it is said, "For in the image of God made He man", and this is immediately followed by, "And you, be fruitful etc". Ben 'Azzai said: It is as though he sheds blood and diminishes the Divine Image; since it is said, "And you, be fruitful and mutltiply".

They said to Ben 'Azzai: Some preach well and act well, others act well but do not preach well; you, however, preach well but do not act well! Ben 'Azzai replied: But what shall I do, seeing that my soul is in love with the Torah; the world can be carried on by others.

Chapter 23 *End of Life Ethics*

ילקוט שמעוני תורה פרשת עקב רמז תתעא

מעשה באשה אחת שהזקינה הרבה ובאת לפני רבי יוסי בן חלפתא אמרה ליה רבי
הזקנתי יותר מדאי ומעכשיו חיים של נוול הם שאיני טועמת לא מאכל ולא משקה
ואני מבקשת להפטר מן העולם, א"ל מה מצוה את למודה לעשות בכל יום, א"ל
למודה אני אפילו יש לי דבר חביב אני מנחת אותו ומשכמת לבית הכנסת בכל
יום, א"ל מנעי עצמך מבית הכנסת שלשה ימים זה אחר זה, הלכה ועשתה כן וביום
השלישי חלתה ומתה,

Yalkut Shimoni Torah Parshat Akeiv # 871

An incident occurred with a woman who had become very
old, who came before Rabbi Jose B. Halafta. She said to him,
"My Rabbi, I have become too old and from here on, it is a life
of degradation for I cannot taste either food or drink and I
wish to be freed from this world." He said to her, "What
good deed are you in the habit of doing each day?" She said
to him, "My habit is that even if I am involved with
something that I like very much, I leave it alone and I go early
to synagogue each day." He said to her, "Keep yourself away
from the synagogue for three straight days. She went and did
so, and on the third day she became ill and died.

Chapter 24 *Conversion, Who is a Jew?*

תלמוד בבלי מסכת יבמות דף מז עמוד א

תנו רבנן: גר שבא להתגייר בזמן הזה, אומרים לו: מה ראית שבאת להתגייר? אי
אתה יודע שישראל בזמן הזה דוויים, דחופים, סחופים ומטורפין, ויסורין באין
עליהם? אם אומר: יודע אני ואיני כדאי, מקבלין אותו מיד. ומודיעין אותו מקצת
מצות קלות ומקצת מצות חמורות, ומודיעין אותו עון לקט שכחה ופאה ומעשר
עני. ומודיעין אותו ענשן של מצות, אומרים לו: הוי יודע, שעד שלא באת למדה
זו, אכלת חלב אי אתה ענוש כרת, חללת שבת אי אתה ענוש סקילה, ועכשיו,
אכלת חלב ענוש כרת, חללת שבת ענוש סקילה. וכשם שמודיעין אותו ענשן של
מצות, כך מודיעין אותו מתן שכרן,

Babylonian Talmud: Y'vamot 47a

Our Rabbis learned: when a person now comes to convert, we
say to him, "What did you see that you have come to
convert? Don't you know that Israel is now scattered, pushed
around, tossed about, preyed on, and sufferings confront
them?" If he says, "I know, and I am not worthy," we accept
him immediately and tell him a few of the "light"
commandments and a few of the "heavy" commandments.
We tell him the offense of gleanings [the poor man's share of
the crop], the corner [the portion of the harvest at the edge of
the corner of the field that had to be left for the poor], the
tithe for the poor [mitzvot given in Leviticus 10:9.
Deuteronomy 24:19 and 26:12], and we inform him of the
punishment. We say to him, "Do you know that until you
reached this point if you ate the forbidden fat of an animal
you were not subject to punishment, and now if you eat the
fat or violate the Sabbath you are subject to punishment?"

Just as we inform him of the punishment for [violating]
commandments, we tell him about the reward [for observing
them].

Chapter 25 *Citizenship*

ירמיהו פרק כט

(א) ואלה דברי הספר אשר שלח ירמיה הנביא מירושלם אל יתר זקני הגולה ואל
הכהנים ואל הנביאים ואל כל העם אשר הגלה נבוכדנאצר מירושלם בבלה:
(ב) אחרי צאת יכניה המלך והגבירה והסריסים שרי יהודה וירושלם והחרש
והמסגר מירושלם:
(ג) ביד אלעשה בן שפן וגמריה בן חלקיה אשר שלח צדקיה מלך יהודה אל
נבוכדנאצר מלך בבל בבלה לאמר: ס
(ד) כה אמר ידוד צבאות אלהי ישראל לכל הגולה אשר הגליתי מירושלם בבלה:
(ה) בנו בתים ושבו ונטעו גנות ואכלו את פרין:
(ז) ודרשו את שלום העיר אשר הגליתי אתכם שמה והתפללו בעדה אל ידוד כי
בשלומה יהיה לכם שלום:

Tanach - Jeremiah Chapter 29

1. And these are the words of the letter that Jeremiah the
prophet sent from Jerusalem to the remnant of the elders who
were carried away captives, and to the priests, and to the
prophets, and to all the people whom Nebuchadnezzar had
carried away captive from Jerusalem to Babylon;
2. After Jeconiah the king, and the queen mother, and the
eunuchs, the princes of Judah and Jerusalem, and the

craftsmen, and the metal workers had departed from Jerusalem;

3. By the hand of Elasah the son of Shaphan, and Gemariah the son of Hilkiah, whom Zedekiah king of Judah sent to Babylon to Nebuchadnezzar king of Babylon saying,

4. Thus says the Lord of hosts, the God of Israel, to all who are carried away captives, whom I have caused to be carried away from Jerusalem to Babylon;

5. Build houses, and dwell in them; and plant gardens, and eat their fruit;

6. Take wives, and father sons and daughters; and take wives for your sons, and give your daughters to husbands, that they may bear sons and daughters; that you may be increased there, and not diminished.

7. And seek the peace of the city where I have caused you to be carried away captives, and pray to the Lord for it; for in its peace shall you have peace.

Chapter 26 *Evolution*

קהלת רבה (וילנא) פרשה ג ד"ה א [יא] את

א [יא] את הכל עשה יפה בעתו, א"ר תנחומא בעונתו נברא העולם לא היה ראוי
להבראות קודם לכן אלא לשעתו נברא שנא' את הכל עשה יפה בעתו, א"ר אבהו
מכאן שהיה הקב"ה בונה עולמות ומחריבן בורא עולמות ומחריבן עד שברא את
אלו ואמר דין הניין לי יתהון לא הניין לי,

Midrash Rabbah - Ecclesiastes III:13

13. HE HAS MADE EVERY THING BEAUTIFUL IN ITS TIME (III, 11). R. Tanhuma said: In its due time was the

universe created. It did not merit to be created before then, but it was created in its proper time, as it is said, HE HATH MADE EVERY THING BEAUTIFUL IN ITS TIME. R. Abbahu said: From this [we learn] that the Holy One, blessed be He, kept on constructing worlds and destroying them until he constructed the present one and said, ' This pleases Me, the others did not.'

Chapter 27 *Alcohol*

מדרש ילמדנו (מאן) ילקוט תלמוד תורה – בראשית אות מה

ויטע כרם,... בא שטן ונשתתף עמו, הביא כבש והרגו תחת הגפן, אחר כך הביא
ארי והרגו, ואחר כך קוף, ואחר כך חזיר, והשקו מדמיהם. לפיכך קודם שישתה
האדם הוא כרחל שאינה יודעת כלום, שתה חמשה ששה כוסות מתגבר כארי
ואומר אין כמותי בעולם, כיון ששתה עשרה כוסות נעשה כחזיר מתלכלך במי
רגלים ובדבר אחר, נשתכר יותר נעשה כקוף מרקד ומשחק ומוציא נבלות הפה
ואינו יודע מה הוא עושה. וכן עשה נח.

Midrash Yelamdeinu Yalkut Talmud Torah Genesis # 41

"And he (Noah) planted a vineyard... Satan came and joined with him. He brought a sheep and killed it under the vine. Then he brought a lion and killed it. Then a monkey, then a pig (and the vine) drank their blood. Therefore, an individual, before he drinks anything, is like a female sheep, which is naive. When he drinks five or six cups, he acts with courage like a lion and says, "There is none like me in the whole world." Once he drinks ten cups, he becomes like a pig, who wallows in urine and excrement. If he becomes even drunker, he becomes like a monkey who dances and jests and speaks profanity and does not know what he does. And this is what happened to Noah."

Chapter 28 *Abortion*

משנה מסכת אהלות פרק ז משנה ו

האשה שהיא מקשה לילד מחתכין את הולד במעיה ומוציאין אותו אברים אברים מפני שחייה קודמין לחייו יצא רובו אין נוגעין בו שאין דוחין נפש מפני נפש:

Mishnah Ohalot 7:6

If a woman is having difficulty in giving birth, one cuts up the embryo inside her and extracts it limb by limb because her life comes before [the child's] life. If the greater part has emerged, one may not touch it, for one may not push aside one life for another life.

Chapter 29 *Women*

משלי פרק לא

(י) אשת חיל מי ימצא ורחק מפנינים מכרה:
(יא) בטח בה לב בעלה ושלל לא יחסר:
(יב) גמלתהו טוב ולא רע כל ימי חייה:
(יג) דרשה צמר ופשתים ותעש בחפץ כפיה:
(יד) היתה כאניות סוחר ממרחק תביא לחמה:
(טו) ותקם בעוד לילה ותתן טרף לביתה וחק לנערתיה:
(טז) זממה שדה ותקחהו מפרי כפיה נטע נטעה כרם:

(יז) חגרה בעוז מתניה ותאמץ זרעותיה:
(יח) טעמה כי טוב סחרה לא יכבה בלילה נרה:
(יט) ידיה שלחה בכישור וכפיה תמכו פלך:
(כ) כפה פרשה לעני וידיה שלחה לאביון:
(כא) לא תירא לביתה משלג כי כל ביתה לבש שנים:
(כב) מרבדים עשתה לה שש וארגמן לבושה:
(כג) נודע בשערים בעלה בשבתו עם זקני ארץ:
(כד) סדין עשתה ותמכר וחגור נתנה לכנעני:
(כה) עז והדר לבושה ותשחק ליום אחרון:
(כו) פיה פתחה בחכמה ותורת חסד על לשונה:
(כז) צופיה הליכות ביתה ולחם עצלות לא תאכל:
(כח) קמו בניה ויאשרוה בעלה ויהללה:
(כט) רבות בנות עשו חיל ואת עלית על כלנה:
(ל) שקר החן והבל היפי אשה יראת ידוד היא תתהלל:
(לא) תנו לה מפרי ידיה ויהללוה בשערים מעשיה:

Tanach - Proverbs Chapter 31

10. A worthy woman who can find? For her price is far above rubies.

11. The heart of her husband safely trusts in her, and he shall have no lack of gain.

12. She will do him good and not evil all the days of her life.

13. She seeks wool, and flax, and works willingly with her hands.

14. She is like the ships of the merchant; she brings her food from far away.

15. She rises also while it is yet night, and gives food to her household, and a portion to her maidens.

16. She considers a field, and buys it; with the fruit of her hands she plants a vineyard.

17. She girds her loins with strength, and makes her arms strong.

18. She perceives that her merchandise is good; her candle does not go out by night.

19. She puts her hands to the distaff, and her hands hold the spindle.

20. She stretches out her hand to the poor; she reaches forth her hands to the needy.

21. She is not afraid of the snow for her household; for all her household are clothed with scarlet.

22. She makes herself coverlets; her clothing is fine linen and purple.

23. Her husband is known in the gates, when he sits among the elders of the land.

24. She makes linen garments, and sells them; and delivers girdles to the merchant.

25. Strength and dignity are her clothing; and she shall rejoice at the time to come.

26. She opens her mouth with wisdom; and in her tongue is the Torah of loving kindness.

27. (K) She looks well to the ways of her household, and does not eat the bread of idleness.

28. Her children rise up, and call her blessed; her husband also, and he praises her.

29. Many daughters have done virtuously, but you excel them all.

30. Charm is deceitful, and beauty is vain; but a woman who fears the Lord shall be praised.

31. Give her of the fruit of her hands; and let her own deeds praise her in the gates.

Chapter 30 *Sex*

בראשית רבה (וילנא) פרשה ט ד״ה ז רבי נחמן

נחמן בשם רב שמואל אמר הנה טוב מאד זה יצר טוב והנה טוב מאד זה יצר רע,
וכי יצר הרע טוב מאד, אתמהא, אלא שאלולי יצר הרע לא בנה אדם בית ולא נשא
אשה, ולא הוליד ולא נשא ונתן, וכן שלמה אומר (קהלת ד) כי היא קנאת איש
מרעהו.

Midrash Rabbah - Genesis IX:7

Nahman said in R. Samuel's name: BEHOLD, IT WAS VERY
GOOD refers to the Good Desire; AND BEHOLD, IT WAS
VERY GOOD, to the Evil Desire. Can then the Evil Desire be
very good? That would be extraordinary! Without the Evil
Desire, however, no man would build a house, take a wife,
beget children or engage in business; and thus said Solomon:
Again, I considered all labour and excelling in work, that it is
a man's rivalry with his neighbour [that lead's him to this]
(Eccl. IV, 4).

Subject Index